The Objectives of the New International Economic Order

Pergamon Titles of Related Interest

PERGAMON
POLICY
STUDIES

The Objectives of the New International Economic Order

Ervin Laszlo
Robert Baker, Jr.
Elliott Eisenberg
Venkata Raman

Published for UNITAR

Pergamon Press

NEW YORK • TORONTO • OXFORD • SYDNEY • FRANKFURT • PARIS

Pergamon Press Offices:

U.S.A.   Pergamon Press Inc., Maxwell House, Fairview Park,
                         Elmsford, New York 10523, U.S.A.

U.K.   Pergamon Press Ltd., Headington Hill Hall,
                         Oxford OX3 0BW, England

CANADA   Pergamon of Canada, Ltd., 75 The East Mall,
                         Toronto, Ontario M8Z 5W3, Canada

AUSTRALIA   Pergamon Press (Aust) Pty. Ltd., 19a Boundary Street,
                         Rushcutters Bay, N.S.W. 2011, Australia

FRANCE   Pergamon Press SARL, 24 rue des Ecoles,
                         75240 Paris, Cedex 05, France

FEDERAL REPUBLIC   Pergamon Press GmbH, 6242 Kronberg/Taunus,
OF GERMANY   Pferdstrasse 1, West Germany

Library of Congress Cataloging in Publication Data

Laszlo, Ervin, 1932—
The objectives of the new international economic order.

(Pergamon policy studies)
Bibliography: p.
Includes index.
1. International economic relations. I. Title.
HF1411.L364 1978   382.1   78-14766
ISBN 0-08-023697-9

Printed in the United States of America

Contents

25 KEY ISSUES OF THE WORLD ECONOMY IN THE CONTEXT OF THE NIEO

PART I

THE OBJECTIVES OF THE NEW ECONOMIC ORDER CONCERNING 25 KEY ISSUES OF THE WORLD ECONOMY

CHAPTER 1 - AID AND ASSISTANCE ISSUES

CHAPTER 2 - INTERNATIONAL TRADE ISSUES

CHAPTER 3 - INTERNATIONAL FINANCIAL ISSUES

CHAPTER 4 - ISSUES OF INDUSTRIALIZATION, TECHNOLOGY TRANSFER AND BUSINESS PRACTICES

CHAPTER 5 - SOCIAL ISSUES

CHAPTER 6 - POLITICAL AND INSTITUTIONAL ISSUES

PART II

THE POSITION OF SOME STATES AND GROUPS OF STATES ON THE ISSUES

CHAPTER 7 - AID AND ASSISTANCE ISSUES

CHAPTER 8 - INTERNATIONAL TRADE ISSUES

Preface

One of the most significant developments of recent years in the United Nations has been the growth of concern and activity on issues related to social and economic development. An organization primarily committed to political and security issues above all, the United Nations has now evolved into a world system intently devoted to assuring the equitable development of the world's peoples.

This evolution is reflected in the conferences, special sessions, seminars, resolutions, declarations and studies devoted to questions of development. Especially during the course of the Second United Nations Development Decade, the attention of the international community was focused as never before on the problems of development. The Sixth and Seventh Special Sessions of the General Assembly were pathbreaking events, producing historic documents. The idea of a New International Economic Order came to the United Nations through them, and found, if not universal approval on all points, at least a universally serious reception. The Programme of Action on the Establishment of a New International Economic Order (Resolution 3202 (S-VI)) broke ground in the active search for a new system of economic relationships that would provide improved opportunities for the world's millions, indeed billions, who now live on the margins of absolute proverty, and for over one hundred Member States having serious economic difficulties and otherwise somber future prospects.

The need for the New International Economic Order - NIEO for short - is real and urgent. As many as 40 per cent of the world's growing population bear an existence of deprivation, undernourishment or inadequately balanced diet, poor sanitary conditions, substandard housing, insufficient or nonexistent employment opportunities, polluted environment, inadequate or nonexistent health and social services. Yet our planet earth is rich enough to feed not only the present four billion human beings, but twice as much and more. Mankind however does not use the planet's resources rationally and equitably. Precious food-stuff and raw materials are wasted, others left unexploited, and most are imperfectly distributed among the populations. There may not have been any epoch in human history hallmarked by perfect justice and rationality, but, today, the scale of both human errors and accomplishments has grown vast, and the relationship between policies and decisions has grown close. Today, the world community must create a new order extending to all people and all societies, since mismanagement and error, even if unintentional, in one sector or in one country, have great and often grave repercussions in other countries, however far removed. The fate of hundreds of millions and more therefore hangs in the balance.

It is is unlikely that there is any single recipe for transforming the historically haphazard conditions that emerged in the world community into an order that is just, equitable and humane. But even the longest journey starts with the first step, and the first step in creating a more balanced world economy is in correcting the structural imbalances that currently beset it. These are inheritances of times when the majority of humanity was under the domination of a handful of colonial powers, and when the scale of technologies of production and consumption was incomparably smaller. Today, these imbalances threaten human lives and the development of societies. Whereas there is much that still needs to be done on every level, from the village, through the regional to the national, key decisions must now be faced also on the international level. This is the task before the community of the United Nations. Here falls the responsibility for proposing the outlines of a new world economic system, with fairer conditions of trade, fairer distribution of production, fairer access to food and all varieties of manufactures, and fairer opportunities for rewarding and life-sustaining employment. Although these conditions cannot be attained solely by means of international decisions and agreements, they very clearly cannot be attained without them. Thus the international community cannot afford to delegate responsibility elsewhere, but must itself act expeditiously and wisely.

The present volume is a contribution to the works of the United Nations system in assessing the implementation of measures agreed upon in recent years, and, in so doing, deliberating upon measures to be taken in years to come. It is the first of a series of publications to issue from the major international research project undertaken by UNITAR in collaboration with the Center for the Economic and Social Study of the Third World (CESSTW) in Mexico. The project, "Progress toward the Establishment of the New International Economic Order: Obstacles and Opportunities" is under the direction of Professor Ervin Laszlo, a UNITAR Special Fellow. The work now being carried on by him, his staff and their collaborators (including a world-wide research network currently engaged in the production of some sixty studies covering almost all aspects of the NIEO) is dedicated to enhancing the effectiveness of the United Nations in achieving its major objectives in the area of international economic development.

This first volume has a specific purpose, both in the context of the UNITAR-CESSTW project and in that of current United Nations activities in the sphere of the NIEO. It gives a concise summary of the significant work, of often unsuspectedly large volume, that has already been carried out by the United Nations and its various organs, agencies and programmes, in proposing, specifying and developing the basic principles of a new economic order. The accumulated experience and expertise of the past several years, especially those that have elapsed since the Sixth and Seventh Special Session and the adoption of the Charter of Economic Rights and Duties of States in the mid-seventies, are fully requisite for examination and study in the next two years, as the international community prepares for the next Special Sessioon to be held in 1980, on assessing progress in the establishment of the NIEO. The record of this experience and expertisewas scattered among many individuals, the United Nations and other international bodies. There was a great need for it to be brought togehter and systematically catalogued under the heading of specific issues and objectives. This is what has been attempted in this volume.

The systematic overview of the state of the art in negotiations and agreements in the area of the NIEO is completed here through a review of some current national and regional positions on the key issues, as they were expressed in position papers submitted to the Committee of the Whole established under General Assembly Resolution 32/174 in May 1978. This permits all those who are involved with an assessment of the progress necessary for the establishment of the NIEO to form an accurate conception of international decisions, agreements and studies, as well as one of the current positions of some States and groups of States, in the issue areas that make up the subject matter of the NIEO. It is particularly to be hoped that members of the Committee of the Whole, entrusted with the major task of assessing progress and preparing the 1980 Special Session, will find this volume of value in their continuing deliberations.

The international project led by Professor Laszlo at UNITAR places this study at the disposal of the international community in the framework of our ongoing efforts to enhance the effectiveness of the Organization through informative and objective studies on the topics of major interest to the international community.

Davidson Nicol
Executive Director

Introduction

THE OBJECTIVES OF THE NEW INTERNATIONAL
ECONOMIC ORDER IN HISTORICAL
AND GLOBAL PERSPECTIVE

Ervin Laszlo

The New International Economic Order (NIEO) is much discussed but seldom clearly understood. The general concept of the NIEO is often questioned, and the discussion of concrete issues and objectives is replaced by vague debates from different and sometimes contrary points of view. Given these circumstances it is important to place the very concept of the NIEO into its proper historical and global perspective, and to clearly state the specific issues of concern to it. These introductory remarks offer some notes and observations on the NIEO's historical and global context; and the chapters that follow attempt to specify the main objectives of the NIEO on the key issues of the world economy as well as shed some light on the position of some States and groups of States concerning them.

Current Political Relevance

The NIEO is undoubtedly the most intensely debated item before the international community. Judging by the number of major international policy statements, declarations, resolutions, conferences, studies, reports, and the activities of the various United Nations agencies, programmes and organs, it is the number one issue for negotiation and resolution by the world's policy makers. It is outranked in urgency only by actual crisis situations, and it is only challenged for top position on the international agenda by disarmament. Yet even disarmament -- as a host of other issues (most of which appear unrelated at first sight), such as transfer of technology, energy, food production, ocean and space use, etc. -- now come under the general umbrella of the NIEO in their actual treatment and negotiation. (The NIEO aspect of disarmament, for example, is the use of funds liberated by it for development.)

Priority accorded to given issues on the international agenda is reflected in special measures agreed upon by Member States in the United Nations. United Nations World Conferences are one type of priority indictor, Special Sessions of the General Assembly another. All of the United Nations World Conferences had direct relevance to the NIEO whether they dealt with the environment, population, the role of women, food, water, desertification or habitat. However, the most recent ones, namely the 1978 Conference on Technical Cooperation Among Developing Countries (Buenos Aires) and the 1979 Conference on Science and Technology for Development (Vienna) are NIEO Conferences sensu strictu. The need for these events has been raised in debates on the NIEO, and they are taking place explicitly under the NIEO aegis.*

The record of the General Assembly is no less remarkable. Not only did it pass an impressive number of resolutions endorsing and specifying NIEO issues, it decided to devote no less than three Special Sessions to debating them. The famous Sixth and Seventh Special Sessions in 1974 and 1975 respectively, established the concept as a priority item of the international community. Following the disappointing results of the Conferences on International Economic Cooperation (the so-called North-South Conferences) in Paris - at which only a handful of developed and developing countries participated, and none from the socialist bloc - the General Assembly decided to bring the discussions back to the United Nations and devote another Special Session to it in 1980, in connection with the elaboration of the international development strategy for the 1980s. The importance attached to this event is reflected in the creation of a Committee of the Whole charged with its preparation. The Committee began its regular work in May 1978 and is to set it forth until the start of the Special Session in the fall of 1980.†

This is the first time in United Nations history that a committee composed of all Member States is charged to work continuously for such an extended period.

---

* The basic task of the United Nations Conference on Science and Technology for Development," said its Secretary-General J. da Costa, "will be to translate the scientific and technological components of a New International Economic Order into a specific programme of action." (Opening Address to the Second Session of the UNCSTD Preparatory Committee, 23 January 1978)

---

† Statements of national positions on the various NIEO issues in Part II derive from documents submitted and/or verbally presented to the first session of the Committee, 3-13 May, 1978.

The NIEO is not only of current <u>political</u> relevance, it is also of major <u>historical</u> significance. For the first time in recorded history, representatives of almost all the world's nation-states agreed to discuss the creation of a new order among themselves. Previous international discussions involved a smaller share of the world's nations and centered mainly on questions of national security. In dealing with the NIEO, however, the world's decision makers are not merely trying to protect themselves from potential aggressors, but engage in consideration of the ways and means of building a lasting set of relationships conducive to peace through greater equality of economic opportunity, more equity in the sharing of the world's precious natural resources, and higher levels of self-reliance in meeting the basic needs of national and regional populations.

Historical Factors in the Emergence of the NIEO

The historical processes which culminated in the emergence of the call for the NIEO cannot be analyzed here in great detail. A few of the major factors can, however, be identified. The first and most fundamental of these is the international social and political climate that developed after World War II. It encouraged the liquidation of the remaining colonies, and brought to the international scene dozens of newly independent Nation-States. The status of these States was declared to be sovereign and equal to that of all other independent States. Their admittance to United Nations membership, where they participated as partners equal to their former colonial masters, underscored this. However, the newly won political and juridical status of the new countries was not matched by their actual economic conditions. The majority felt that their <u>de jure</u> political colonization ended only to be replaced by a <u>de facto</u> economic colonization.

There is real warrant for this sentiment. To this day, the developing countries account for less than one-fifth of total world trade, and their share has been actually declining. Three-quarters of their exports are destined for the developed market economies, and the exports of many developing countries are nearly fully absorbed by a few industrial countries, often the former colonial power. Four-fifths of all earnings from exports are generated by about a dozen commodities, excluding oil. At the level of production these commodities represent a total value of about $30 billion, whereas after fabrication their value rises to $200 billion. The added value accrues predominantly to the developed industrial countries; the developing countries have a share of less than 7 per cent in world industrial production. The price of individual commodities fluctuates considerably, posing grave threats to the economies of those countries dependent on one or a few exportable items.

Effects of economic colonialism are also felt in the area of financing. In about half of the developing countries a single capital-rich country provides three-fourths of foreign direct investment, and in most of the developing countries foreign investment is controlled by the local subsidiaries of foreign based transnational corporations. Developing countries are also dependent on foreign sources for technology; about 95 per cent of the world's Research and

Development capabilities are concentrated in the developed world, and 94 per cent of the patents are held by developed country individuals and organizations. And even of the remaining 6 per cent of patents, 84 per cent are held by foreigners, often for purposes of preventing the rise of local competition.

The historical process which gave the majority of the world's population sovereign and equal States, but left them at the same time in a position of economic dependence, triggered a second set of factors configuring the context for the emergence of the NIEO. These factors became known as the 'revolution of rising expectations': the urgent and understandable desire of the peoples of the Third World to liberate themselves from their current forms of colonization. Desires for rapid social and economic growth were soon translated by the governments into ambitious plans and programmes of national development. Most of the plans envisaged a quick repetition of the industrial growth processes of the developed world, following a path already long trod by the countries of Latin America. When the unintended side-effects of traditional patterns of industrialization became evident -- uncontrolled growth of cities, relative neglect of rural areas and agriculture, threats to the environment, and the increasing stratification of people in modern and traditional sectors, often with serious damage to social structure and cohesion -- some of the original strategies underwent modification, but hardly ever surrendered the goal of rapid economic growth.

A series of programmes and targets in the early 1960s created a mood of optimistic enthusiasm. Among the major events were the launching of the First United Nations Development Decade in 1961, the creation of UNCTAD in 1964, and such regional agreements as the Alliance for Progress in 1961 and the First Yaunde Convention in 1963. By the late 1960s, however, expectations came to be disappointed and enthusiasm waned. The Development Decade's achievement fell far short of its targets; the Alliance for Progress slipped into the background, and the First Yaunde Convention was replaced by the Second, and by the Arusha Convention (1969), agreements which were soon viewed with reservations. The second and third sessions of UNCTAD, in 1968 and 1972, failed to live up to the expectations engendered by the first.

The Second United Nations Development Decade incorporated a more sober assessment of development prospects, in view of the worsening economic situation of many developing countries relative to the advanced industrial nations. But even these revised expectations were slated for at least partial disappointment. The mid-term review of the Second Development Decade showed mixed results. The greatest gap between targets and achievement came in the area of agricultural production and official development aid. The United Nations' targets for the latter have not been even half achieved in the average of the D.A.C. countries. At the same time service charges on past loans began to put enormous pressures on developing countries' balances of payment, and world poverty showed no signs of diminishing. There was insufficient progress in commodity trade, inadequate access to the markets of developed countries, particularly of agricultural products; tariffs have escalated, especially for semi-processed and processed products, and new restrictions were introduced by developed countries on a number of items, including textiles and leather goods, together with other, non-tariff barriers. The plight of the least developed, island and land-locked developing countries gave rise to additional concern. While some progress was achieved subsequently with respect to the introduction of a generalized system of preferences by the developed countries, and the proposals of the Tokyo Declaration concerning multilateral trade negotiations in the early 1970s, the negative developments weighed heavily in the balance and created widespread dissatisfaction in the developing world.

A third set of factors then came into play. This was the sudden and unexpected rise of Third World economic and political power. The OPEC's 1973 Middle East oil embargo and the subsequent four-fold increase in the price of oil created a world energy crisis. It affected all oil importing nations, developed as well as developing. It also exhibited the dependence of the developed countries on the developing world for several major natural resources, and proved the ability of the Third World to effectively wield economic and political power. The consequences included rises in the price of food, due to the increased cost of chemical fertilizers, and further tensions between producers and consumers of raw materials. But the OPEC-type exercise of Third World economic and political power proved unable to significantly improve the countries of the developing countries as a whole. The OPEC experience could not be replicated in other sectors of the world economy, and the developed countries found themselves beset by economic problems of their own, including inflation, unemployment, and unused industrial capacities. Partly due to the rise in oil prices, economic rates of growth slowed, while balance of payment deficits grew. In the developed market economies, concern with domestic conditions intensified, and the political will to increase levels of aid and assistance to the Third World faltered in direct proportion to the rise of protectionism.

Compounding the economic difficulties of the developed nations were signs of breakdown in the international monetary system which affected all countries, developed as well as developing. Amidst growing tensions between the United States, Japan and the European Community over matters of trade, the Bretton Woods system collapsed and gave rise to a system of floating exchange rates. The value of the U.S. dollar began to erode, creating serious difficulties for those countries which, like most developing countries, held their reserves in dollars. A partial revision of the system through the creation of Special Drawing Rights provided some stabilization, but to this day, neither developed nor developing countries are satisfied with the condition of the world monetary system. All in all, it became evident that some of the fundamental tenants of the post-war international economic system were called into question, and have indeed collapsed.

The NIEO made its appearance as an international political issue in the context of these series of events. The Lusaka Summit of the Non-Aligned Countries of 1970 adopted a major declaration on Non-Alignment and Economic Progress, in sharp contrast to previous Summits where standard political concerns dominated. The Non-Aligned Countries' meeting of Foreign Ministers of 1972 was already prepared by a special economic committee. And their Algiers Summit produced an Action Programme which incorporated the majority of the items found subsequently in the Declaration and Programme of Action on the NIEO at the United Nations Sixth Special Session in 1974. The adoption of the Charter of Economic Rights and Duties of States followed, as well as the resolution of the Seventh Special Session on Development and International Economic Cooperation. Thereafter came a vast series of declarations, resolutions, position papers and studies, all under the aegis of the NIEO. This series includes Resolution 32/174 of the General Assembly, which calls for another special session on the NIEO in 1980.

The NIEO in Context

The confluence of the three sets of factors mentioned above cannot be considered purely fortuitous. The wave of decolonization expressed a long-term historical process of democratization and the rise of universal rights for individuals and societies. It brought about the desire for rapid industrialization by the newly independent countries, and resulted in major frustrations. But as economic interdependence intensifed, as trade and markets expanded, and as energy and raw materials became increasingly crucial to the operation of the developed world's giant economic machinery, the concentration of economic power became modified. It no longer rested with a few powerful Governments but came to be wielded also by fuel and raw material exporting nations, and by transnational corporations.

The historical process which gave birth to a host of independent nation-states placed into sharp relief the inequalities of the previous economic system. It also provided some of the developing countries with significant economic leverage. The NIEO originated with these countries as an attempt to reaffirm their solidarity and wield the new-found leverage for their common good. The good of the developing countries came, however, to be increasingly tied in with the good of the entire world economy. The developing countries, in possession of many of the world's natural resources and, despite their currently low share in world trade and industrial production, offering vast new markets and pools of low-cost labour, became essential partners of the developed countries in the world economic system.* Satisfaction of their demands and expectations is thus crucial to the stability and development of this system. Dependable and sustained growth in the world economy is difficult to conceive without the aggregate demand provided by rising levels of prosperity in the developing world. But the old economic system is unable to bring about such conditions. A new structure of international economic relations is needed, affecting trade, industrialization,

---

*   Developing countries currently absorb about 25 per cent of the exports of the developed market economies. While trade in manufactured products among the industrialized countries declined between 1973 and 1975, exports of these products to the developing countries rose by 16 per cent a year.

transfer of technology, and agricultural productivity. The establishment of the NIEO is not only historically appropriate; it is also universally expedient.*

Contrary Perceptions and Vicious Circles

The emergence of the NIEO as the crucial item of international political-economic negotiation in the mid-1970s was not accidental; it represents the culmination of a series of historical factors which can be ultimately traced to the rise of the formerly colonized people of the Third World, at a time of increasing world trade, energy and materials consumption, and emerging resource constraints. But the rate of implementation of the new international economic order is not pre-ordained by history. Its basic tenets could be implemented in a matter of years, or they could be put off for another decade or more.

The latter is a distinct possibility: the current wave of protectionism in the developed industrial economies threatens the postponement of effective concerted action. It indicates a failure, in some circles to grasp the historical and global relevance of the NIEO as a necessary and universally beneficial next step in the development of world society.

Because the rate of implementation of the NIEO is not determined by fate but is very much dependent on human will and perceptions, it is useful to contrast some current criticisms of the intent and effectiveness of the objectives of the NIEO with the foregoing assessment of its historical and global context.

According to a view frequently heard in some business circles in developed countries, the NIEO constitutes a radical demand by a group of Third World nations to finance their development out of the donations and taxes of people in the industrialized countries. Another view, held by radical intellectuals mainly in the developed but sometimes also in the developing countries, questions whether even the achievement of the NIEO would serve a useful purpose. Since these viewpoints seriously sap the political will needed for the creation of an appropriate and fair international economic system, they merit more detailed consideration.

Even if it were true that the NIEO constitutes a mere reallocation of wealth from the world's rich to the world's poor (an assumption which a closer study of its objectives soon invalidates), such reallocation would not in itself

---

* If, for example, the capital inflows of developing countries were forthcoming to sustain their income growth targets, the rate of income growth in the donor OECD economies would likewise increase. A 1976 UNCTAD study estimates such increases to be 0.7 percentage points per annum for the remainder of the present Development Decade. The same study also estimates a similar growth rate for the U.S. economy specifically, in relation to a 40 per cent annual increase of its exports to non-oil producing developing countries over a six-year period. This increase is roughly equivalent to the increase required in U.S. official development assistance to reach the United Nations target. (UNCTAD TD/B/C.3/134, 15 April 1976)

be contrary to justice and morality. At the present time the world's poor are overwhelmingly, though not exclusively, concentrated in about 115 developing countries (including China) comprising about 70 per cent of the world's population. The developed nations, some 35 in number, comprise about 30 per cent of the population. A transfer of some of the excess wealth of the rich countries to relieve the worst of the deprivation in the many poor ones would be by no means offensive to an informed sense of justice and an enlightened morality.*

However, the NIEO does not constitute a mere shifting of wealth, by charity or otherwise, on the principles of a zero-sum game. Of its objectives, only a handful deal with the provision of aid and assistance. † The rest focus on creating conditions under which the developing countries could grow toward collective self-reliance and take care of their own basic needs. A careful study of the articulation of NIEO principles and objectives is useful in dispelling exaggerated notions of one-sided sacrifices, usually entertained by those who most fear being asked to make them.

The second perception opposed to the NIEO is a more differentiated one. It agrees with the need for rapid development by the poor countries, but casts doubt on the ability of the NIEO to achieve it. It considers that as long as there are hierarchic social structures supported by self-centered and powerful elites in the recipient countries, economic benefits accruing to these countries accrue primarily to the elites and leave the rest of the poplation unaffected. Championed by dedicated humanists, this perception often detracts from the momentum accumulating behind the establishment of the NIEO in favour of some variety of basic needs strategy, including a direct attack on world poverty.

While it is impossible to quarrel with the aim of these aspirations, it is necessary to criticize their strategy. They assume that transformations within nations can occur in the absence of major transformations in the relations between nations. It is more likely, however, that internal structural changes will occur in conjunction with, and under the influence of, international economic restructuring.

Possibilities for achieving peaceful social transformations would increase upon even a preliminary and partial implementation of the NIEO, for structural constraints imposed by the old economic system would be loosened. The present economic system forces the majority of populations and governments into a position of dependence vis-a-vis a few powerful actors. Under conditions of dependence all sectors tend to seek positions affording some measure of security and privilege. These positions are those that correspond to the interests of the dominant economic actors. Since the interest of these actors seldom coincides with the equal and equitable participation of all people in social and economic development, the

---

*   See for example John Rawls, A Theory of Justice. Cambridge, Mass: Harvard University Press, 1971.

---

†   See the 25 Key Economic Issues in the Context of NIEO, below.

alignments of dependence result in conditions where a few prosper and the majority suffer.

In the absence of a restructuring of the international economic system to reduce dependence and provide more options in developing countries, only violent internal revolutions could break the current vicious circle of dependence breeding unjust social structures and these in turn reinforcing dependence. A strategem often attempted by some developed countries, namely using the dependence of Third World countries itself as a means of forcing internal reform - by tying aid and assistance to the donor's concept of human rights and social justice - is strongly resented by the developing countries who claim the full right to set their own goals of socio-economic development. On the other hand a restructuring of international economic relations is politically acceptable and vastly preferable to upheavals provoked by dependence.

But another vicious circle prevents for now the restructuring of international economic relations. This circle begins with the above-mentioned scepticism concerning the effectiveness of restructuring in the absence of internal social and political reforms in the developing countries. Such scepticism prevents the implementation of substantive measures aimed at facilitating international economic restructuring by developed countries, and this in turn conserves and deepens the dependence of developing countries, thereby reinforcing existing inequalities in their internal structures.

This vicious circle has all the attributes of a self-fulfilling prophesy. It is rooted in the democratic political process of developed market economies, as well as in the assessment of historical responsibility for underdevelopment in the socialist countries. In the market economies a broad basis of popular support is required for the implementation of any new policy objective. At the present time there is inadequate popular support in the majority of such countries to permit effective implementation of policies required by the NIEO. The basic aims of the NIEO itself are seldom fully understood, and the benefits accruing to developed countries from an appropriate restructuring of the world economy are usually underestimated.

In the centrally planned economies of Eastern Europe an assessment of historical responsibility hampers effective participation in the restructuring of the world economic system. The problems of the existing system are traced to the exploitation of the Third World by Western imperialist powers and hence the responsibility for correcting the problems are ascribed to them. A division of the world into developed and developing countries is rejected for ignoring essential differences in existing socio-economic systems; assistance is provided mainly for countries that have an affinity with the politics of the socialist world.

Although the vicious circles described here still prevent significant progress in implementation, perceptions of the basic concept of the NIEO are changing. An awareness of the mutuality of interests in the interdependent world economy is arising in the developed market economy countries, and the principle of cooperation between countries having different social and economic systems is affirmed with fresh vigor in the centrally planned economies.*

The Need for Action

The decisive first steps toward the establishment of the NIEO must be taken by the governments of the industrialized countries. A mustering of their political will in taking concrete measures to achieve the NIEO objectives is the first and crucial step in cutting through the self-reinforcing loops of dependence and inequality in the developing world. They must themselves cut through the self-reinforcing loops of scepticism and doubt concerning the warrant and the need for making serious efforts. Policy-makers need to recognize that even as presently formulated, the objectives of the NIEO are not designed simply to assure an increasing flow of wealth to the poor countries' ruling elites, but to cope with the whole gamut of issues relative to development, including international trade, finance, technology, industry, as well as social, institutional and political issues. The implementation of the full set of NIEO objectives would go a long way toward redressing structural imbalances in the world economy, thereby liberating the countries where two-thirds of the human population now lives from structural dependence on foreign economic forces. This would pave the way for positive changes within these countries, and reinforce confidence in the developing world by the people and governments of industrialized countries.

It is essential to realize that an interdependent world economy cannot function efficiently under constraints of major structural imbalances and perceived injustices. A stable economic environment, with reliable processes and policies, and the participation of increasing masses in the process of economic and social development, is in the long term interest of all States. It is only in such an environment that strategic planning for investment, trade, and hence for growth and diversification has reasonable chances of success. It is only in such an environment that the now over 4 and perhaps soon 6 billion members of the human family have reasonable chances of living a life of dignity and self-reliance.

The arguments in favor of creating a new international economic order outweigh the fears and suspicions arguing against it. Establishment of the NIEO is (i) possible in principle in the framework of the current international negotiations, (ii) historically appropriate as a major step toward the creation of a more equitable and sustainable world, and (iii) capable of creating local conditions where the chances of structural reforms required to wipe out poverty and fulfill basic needs become real. The implementation of the NIEO is not the sufficient condition of the creation of a better world. It is, however, very likely its necessary condition.

One further remark must be added. Speaking of "the NIEO" should not be taken to indicate that there is only one new international economic order that is feasible, and that this order is fully grasped by the already defined and

---

*   See the relevant position statements on the issues in Part II, below.

discussed set of objectives.   What is significant about the NIEO is the fact that it replaces an old order (or lack of order) by a new and hopefully better one. The new order itself is not a static concept but a dynamic and evolving process.   Its defining characteristic is the attempt to eliminate economic injustice and equalise economic opportunity, conducive toward the unfolding of productive capacities capable of responding to basic needs in all parts of the world.

Beyond dependence; toward-self reliance -- these ideals define the striving toward the NIEO more than any specific demand or resolution. The formulation of NIEO objectives are subject to change and evolution; the NIEO itself is here to stay. A future without a working international economic order is not conceivable. Only future historians will know, however, whether our generation had the wisdom and the political will to bring about a working order in the late 70s and early 80s, or whether it came about later, at the cost of major crises and catastrophes.

A Note on Methodology

The NIEO constitutes a system of problems, questions, demands and objectives which forms an integral whole. An analysis of specific points connected with the NIEO necessarily violates its systemic unity. Yet if the NIEO is to be understood not only in its global and historical wholeness but also in its concrete specificity, the issues with which it deals must be discussed individually, though in awareness of their mutual relation. Following a general overview of its global and historical context, we now turn to the specific issues of relevance to the NIEO.

In the appropriate encompassing view, the world economy issues of relevance to the NIEO include issues of aid and assistance, international trade and finance, of industrialization, technology transfer and business practices, as well as social, political and institutional issues. A total of 25 such issues are distinguished in the present study, and the objectives articulated under the aegis of the NIEO are described under the heading of each.

The listing of the 25 key world economy issues follows. Part I provides a descriptive account of the documents by means of which the objectives of the NIEO were articulated in international fora on each of the issues. With due regard for the development of the formulations, and also for the relative weight of particular documents, each of the 25 sets of objectives are described first in terms of the documents most closely identified with the NIEO (Resolutions of the Sixth and Seventh Special Session of the General Assembly, Charter of Economic Rights and Duties of States and, because of their frequent endorsement, the Second United Nations Development Strategy and the Lima Declaration and Programme of Action). Then their development is traced through the work of the United Nations systems. Finally the contribution of major international bodies are considered.

Part II provides some indication of the current position of States and groups of States on the world economy issues of NIEO relevance. The here cited positions were expressed in statements and papers presented to the first regular session of the Committee of the Whole charged by General Assembly Resolution 32/174 with work relative to the NIEO.

The book consists of 25 world economy issues under six general headings, with three catgories of documents reviewed in Part I and an additional category in Part II (see Table I).

No further attempt is made in this volume to evaluate or interpret the NIEO or its objectives. The purpose of Parts I and II is to convey a clearer understanding of the state of the art of international negotiations and debates on the NIEO, with a view to helping individuals and policy-makers to make their own assessments. It is hoped that by first placing the NIEO in the appropriate historical and global perspective, and then offering a descriptive overview of the articulation of its principal objectives together with some current national and regional positions, an improved basis is provided for concerted and sustained efforts to improve the formulation and the acceptance of realistic and far-sighted objectives, in the interest of progress toward the establishment of a much needed new and equitable international economic order.

Acknowledgements

As director of the international research project "Progress in the Establishment of the New International Economic Order: Obstacles and Opportunities," in the framework of which the present volume was prepared, it is my duty, and distinct pleasure, to acknowledge the valuable collaboration of my colleagues, Robert Baker, Elliott Eisenberg and Venkata K. Raman, who have done, among them, most of the original research and drafting on Part I of this report. Further contributions were received from Ukandi Damachi of the International Institute for Labour Studies in Geneva and Jagbans Balbir of UNESCO, Paris. The UNITAR Library Staff, Alfred Moss, Harry Winton and Hideo Makiyama were most helpful in assuring access to the documentation, and Christopher Laszlo of Swarthmore College assisted in the research. Mrs. Teresita Alfonso prepared the original document files and typed the manuscript. Their assistance has been vital to our work and is deeply appreciated.

Ervin Laszlo

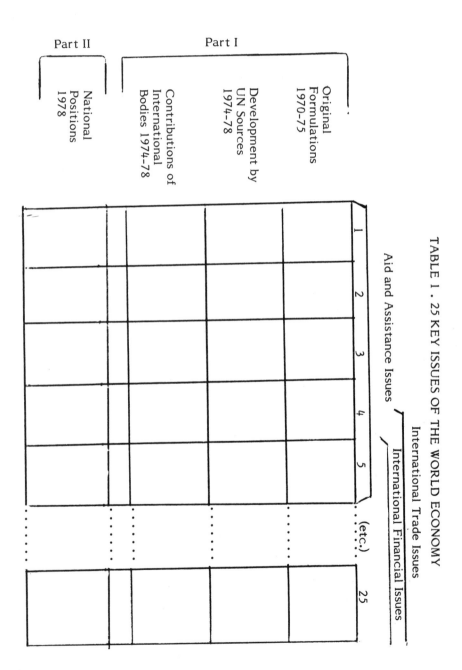

TABLE 1 . 25 KEY ISSUES OF THE WORLD ECONOMY

International Trade Issues

International Financial Issues

Aid and Assistance Issues

Part II

National
Positions
1978

Part I

Contributions of
International
Bodies 1974-78

Development by
UN Sources
1974-78

Original
Formulations
1970-75

1 2 3 4 5 (etc.) 25

Part I
The Objectives of the New
International Economic Order Concerning
25 Key Issues of the World Economy

1 Aid and Assistance Issues

WORLD ECONOMY ISSUE 1

Attaining United Nations Official Development Assistance Targets

1.1 The original formulation of the NIEO objective at the United Nations

The International Development Strategy for the Second United Nations Development Decade (2626 (XXV) 24 October 1970)* set a development assistance target of 0.7 per cent of the gross national product of developed countries:

> Each economically advanced country will progressively increase its official development assistance to the developing countries and will exert its best efforts to reach a minimum net amount of 0.7 per cent of its gross national product at market prices by the middle of the Decade.

The second IDS also requested that financial assistance be, in principle, untied, and that it be provided, to the greatest extent possible, on a long-term and continuing basis.

The Program of Action on the Establishment of a New Internatonal Economic Order (3202 (S-VI) (1 May 1974) urged the implementation at an accelerated pace by the developed countries of the time-bound programme, as already laid down in the International Development Strategy for the Second United Nations Development Decade, for the net amount of financial resource transfers to developing countries. It also urged an increase in the official component of the net amount of financial resource transfers to developing countries so as to meet and even exceed the target of the Strategy.

---

* Frequently cited documents will be subsequently cited in abbreviated form.

Development and International Economic Cooperation (3362 (S-VII) 16 September 1975) reaffirmed the ODA target and requested that:

> Developed countries confirm their continued commitment in respect of targets relating to the transfer of resources, in particular the official development assistance target of 0.7 per cent of gross national product...and adopt as their common aim an effective increase in official development assistance with a view to achieving these targets by the end of the decade. Developed countries which have not yet made a commitment in respect of these targets undertake to make their best efforts to reach these targets in the remaining part of this decade.

The same resolution also suggested that concessional financial resources to developing countries be increased substantially, their terms and conditions ameliorated, and their flow made predictable, continuous and increasingly assured.

The Lima Declaration and Plan of Action on Industrial Development and Cooperation (26 March 1975) stated that:

> the developed countries should, in particular, increase their cooperation in order to make available to developing countries the resources required to sustain the growth effort essential for accelerating their social and economic development.

> The stated targets for transfer of resources to developing countries should be fulfilled in the shortest possible time.

1.2 Specification and development of the NIEO objective at the United Nations, 1974-78

Resolution 150 (XVI) (October 1976) of the Trade and Development Board of UNCTAD reaffirm the need for developed countries to meet the 0.7 per cent target for official development assistance. The resolution urged all developed countries to prevent the volume of their ODA from being affected by budgetary difficulties or balance of payments problems.

It suggested that ODA financial resources might be raised by the use of the profits from sales of monetary gold held by the International Monetary Fund.

The resolution made, inter alia, the following recommendations:

> Developed countries should jointly study the various proposals made for altering the definition of ODA, including the proposal that development loans with a concessional element of less than 50 per cent should be excluded from the definition of such assistance;

> Each developed country should use its best endeavors to improve the financial terms of its ODA so as to achieve an over-all grant element of at least 90 per cent;

An official development assistance loan should, as a general rule, be untied and to that end multilateral arrangements for the reciprocal untying of ODA flows should be worked out as early as possible;

Official development assistance should be provided to recipient countries in the forms most appropriate to their developmental needs and priorities;

The 0.7 per cent target for official development assistance should be treated as the actual financial flow target and the one percent target for net financial resource transfer should be considered a broad indicator of financial cooperation;

All developed countries should distribute their official development assistance rationally and equitably among developing countries, without prejudice to existing bilateral and multilateral agreements between developing and developed countries;

A draft resolution submitted by Jamaica on behalf of the Group of 77 in "Texts Remitted for Further Consideration Within the Permanent Machinery of UNCTAD" (TD/L.125, October 1976) reiterated the importance of General Assembly Resolution 3362 (S-VII) mentioned above. The resolution reaffirmed that:

All developed countries should effectively increase their ODA so as to achieve the target of 0.7 per cent of GNP for such assistance as soon as possible, and in any case no later than 1980. To achieve this end and to ensure that ODA flows are predictable, continuous and assured, the following measured, inter alia, could be considered;

Introduction by developed countries of a development tax as a means of raising the required revenues, thereby avoiding discontinuity in appropriation by legislatures;

Use by the developed countries of the interest subsidy technique as a means of minimizing the budgetary burden of achieving the 0.7 per cent target and of generating a large expansion of concessional flows in a short span of time.

The 50 per cent grant principle and its definition was reiterated.

A draft resolution submitted by France on behalf of Group B urged that all donor countries increase effectively their ODA and to attempt as soon as possible to attain the target of 0.7 per cent of GNP set out in the International Development Strategy for the Second United Nations Development Decade. Official development assistance should be predictable, continuous and increasingly assured. The draft resolution agrees substantially in all other respects with the above mentioned draft resolution submitted by Jamaica, except a change appears in the overall grant element from 90 per cent to 84 per cent.

A report of the UNCTAD Secretariat on item 11 of the provisional agenda of UNCTAD IV (TD/188, 29 December 1975) insists on the necessity of both attaining the 0.7 per cent target of ODA and of distributing it among the developing countries according to objective criteria, including differences in degrees of development, capacity to usefully absorb private capital and to assure the servicing of the corresponding debts, and the necessity to assure an equitable distribution of income.   The report mentions a suggestion concerning the institution of a special development tax in the developed countries. Such tax would permit a supplementation of the amounts normally reserved for development aid and would have the further advantage of increasing at the same rate as income in the developed countries.

1.3 Contribution of major international bodies, 1974-78

The final communique of the Commonwealth Heads of Government (1975) agrees with the 0.7 per cent target and urges its speedy implementation. There occurs also an endorsement of the 84 per cent grant element (a reduction from 90 per cent). Terms of assistance for the poorer countries would be such that repayment would be at least 40 to 50 years with a grace period of at least 10 years and a maximum rate of interest not exceeding 1 per cent.

The Manila Declaration and Programme of Action (TD/195 5 May 1976) affirmed the 0.7 per cent ODA target. It also re-affirmed all other targets that were mentioned in the above cited UNCTAD document of October 1976.

There seems to be an agreement between developing and developed countries that a 0.7 per cent target must be met, according to a final report by a Commonwealth Expert Group (March 1977). The report expressed disappointment that many of the DAC countries had not met this target. In 1975, only two DAC countries, the Netherlands and Sweden had met it: Australia, Belgium, Canada, Denmark, France, Norway, and New Zealand were in a band from 0.66 to 0.52 per cent of GNP, West Germany of 0.40 per cent and Britain 0.37 per cent. Austria, Finland, Italy, Japan, Switzerland, and the United States transferred less than 0.30 per cent of GNP. The average of the whole group was 0.35 per cent. The report said that reaching the target is a matter of political will. It urged all developing countries regardless of their economic and social systems, and particularly those with per capita GNP of over $2,000 to implement the United Nations target without further delay.

WORLD ECONOMY ISSUE 2

Providing Technical Assistance For Development And Eliminating the Brain Drain

2.1 The original formulation of the NIEO objective at the United Nations

One of the principles set forth in the Declaration on the Establishment of a New International Economic Order (May 1974) is the "extension of active assistance to developing countries by the whole international community, free of any political or military conditions." This idea was endorsed in the Programme of Action on the Establishment of the NIEO (May 1974), where, in addition to stating that "the developed countries should respond favourably .... to the requests of developing countries for the financing of industrial projects," it was further specified that:

> The international community should continue and expand, with the aid of the developed countries and the international institutions, the operational and instruction-oriented technical assistance programmes, including vocational training and management development of national personnel of the developing countries, in the light of their special development requirements.

To assist these programmes, and to aid the least developed countries in general, the Programme of Action decided to establish "a Special Fund under the auspices of the United Nations, through voluntary contributions from industrialized countries and other potential contributors, ... to provide emergency relief and development assistance...."

In General Assembly Resolution 3362 (S-VII) on Development and International Economic Cooperation (September 1975), the developed countries, and those developing countries in a position to do so, were "urged to make adequate contributions to the United Nations Special Fund with a view to an early implementation of a programme of lending, preferably in 1976."

In addition to urging contributions to the Special Fund, Resolution 3362 stated that:

> Concessional financial resources to developing countries need to be increased substantially, their terms and conditions ameliorated and their flow made predictable, continuous and increasingly assured so as to facilitate the implementation by developing countries of long-term programmes for economic and social development.

Further, developed countries and international organizations should "ensure that the developing countries obtain the largest possible share in the procurement of equipment, consultants, and consultancy services." It is also stipulated that all assistance, financial and otherwise, should, as a general rule, be untied.

The Charter of Economic Rights and Duties of States (December 1974) likewise noted the importance of technical aid, stating that "the flow of development assistance resources should include economic and technical assistance."

The Lima Declaration and Plan of Action on Industrial Development and Co-operation (March 1975) called for "expanded technical assistance programmes for the benefit of the developing countries," and declared that the assistance should be such that:

(i) It contributes to the development of structures for professional training and middle management training such as institutes or centres for the training of workers, and research laboratories;

(ii) It contributes to the financing of integrated training programmes and scientific research;

(iii) It is executed and managed in the developed countries by competent organizations;

(iv) Its effectiveness is as far as possible assured by the Governments of the developed countries, especially as regards the quality of personnel;

(v) It is integrated and co-ordinated with the long-term programmes of individual developing countries;

(vi) It ensures the continuance and maintenance which are indispensable conditions for the fulfilment and functioning of the projects;

(vii) It is executed by personnel capable of accepting the living and working conditions in the developing countries concerned.

The obverse of an inflow of technical aid via consultants and consultancy services is the outflow of qualified personnel from developing to developed countries. Since this outflow "seriously hampers" the development of developing countries, Resolution 3362 asserted that "there is an urgent need to formulate national and international policies to avoid the 'brain drain' and to obviate its adverse effects."

Thus the issue of technical and financial aid and assistance embraces the issue of the outflow of qualified personnel from developing to developed countries (also called 'the brain drain' and 'the reverse transfer of technology'); a consequence of the conditions of underdevelopment that technical and financial aid and assistance is to help overcome.

2.2 Specification and Development of the NIEO Objective at the United Nations, 1974-78

Shortly after the conclusion of the General Assembly's Sixth Special Session, the Economic and Social Council adopted Resolution 1904-LVII (1 August 1974) on the outflow of trained personnel from developing to developed countries. It recommended that:

countries which benefit from the 'brain drain', particularly those which gain most from the 'brain drain' from developing countries, should consider the adoption of measures which will help, directly or indirectly, to diminish the gravity of the problem;

It further recommended that:

Member States .... consider the application of a voluntary system of data collection on this phenomenon, such as information in connection with migratory movements - persons entering and leaving the country, by profession, purpose of travel, duration of stay, and other headings - with a view to exchanging such information among themselves and transmitting it, as appropriate, to the United Nations, in order to estimate the net outflow of trained personnel from developing countries;

The resolution also urged members of the United Nations system and other concerned international organizations "to help to reverse the phenomenon of the 'brain drain' .... by promoting in the developing countries activities conducive to the creation of career possibilities, and the improvement of fellowships and other forms of encouragement for training personnel in areas of direct concern to developing countries...."

The 'brain drain' issue was also addressed in Resolution 87 "Transfer of Technology," adopted at UNCTAD-IV in May 1976. Discussed under the heading "Reverse Transfer of Technology," this resolution recommends:

that all countries, particularly those benefitting from the brain drain should .... consider what measures may be necessary to deal with the problems posed by such outflow, inter alia, refraining from adopting policies that might promote the exodus of trained personnel from developing countries, and assisting in making arrangements that contribute towards encouraging qualified personnel to remain in the developing countries....

Noting that private enterprise is imporant in the transfer of know-how, a General Assembly document (A/31/230, October 1976) suggested that Governments may wish to review the traditional forms of technical assistance programmes. It suggested that:

new forms of technical assistance might be provided, as envisaged in the Lima Declaration and Plan of Action, for instance through

a) the increased use and involvement of existing national institutions;

b) the sponsoring of more business contacts;

c) the greater involvement of private enterprises in technical assistance projects;

d) and the increased participation of nationals at the community level.

At the same time it may be advisable to consider development assistance in its entirety, combining technical assistance with investment and financial assistance.

Also in October of 1976, the Trade and Development Board of UNCTAD adopted Resolution 150 (XVI) dealing with the transfer of real resources to developing countries. Noting that "official development assistance flows should be predictable, continuous and increasingly assured," the resolution stated that "developed countries should consider adopting new and additional methods of increasing concessional flows." It re-affirmed that official development assistance loans should, as a general rule, be untied, and that those countries benefitting from increases in aid should primarily be the least developed countries and other countries with the greatest difficulties whose needs have been specifically defined on the basis of objective criteria. The resolution also suggested that technical assistance activities in the field of access to capital markets should be further expanded.

In December of 1977 Argentina, Ecuador, Iran, Jordan, Kenya, and Morocco submitted a draft resolution to the General Assembly on the Reverse Transfer of Technology (A/C.2/32/L.85). In the preamble the draft resolution reaffirmed Resolution 3362 (S-VII) on the "urgent need to formulate national and international policies to avoid the 'brain drain' and to obviate its adverse effects" (see above) and endorses Resolution 87 at UNCTAD IV (May 1976) in which the Conference recommended that "all countries, particularly those benefitting from the 'brain drain' should, ... consider what measures may be necessary to deal with the problems posed by such outflow" (see above).

After recommending and urging similar measures, the draft resolution requested:

> the Group of Governmental Experts on Reverse Transfer of Technology convened by the Secretary-General of the United Nations Conference on Trade and Development to undertake an in-depth study; exploring the possible and feasible arrangements for the establishment of an international labour compensatory facility to compensate labour-exporting countries for their loss of highly trained personnel, ... or other social arrangements taking into account any decisions regarding operational activities that may be reached in the Ad Hoc Committee on the Restructuring of the Economic and Social Sectors of the United Nations System.

2.3 Contributions of major international bodies, 1974-78

The Manila Declaration and Programme of Action, adopted by the Third Ministerial Meeting of the Group of 77 on 7 February 1976 (TD/195) decided that:

> In order to compensate for the reverse transfer of technology resulting from the exodus of trained personnel from the developing countries, now amounting to several billion dollars, arrangements should be made to provide, on a cost-free basis, the necessary financial means to create the infrastructure to retain qualified personnel in the developing countries.

WORLD ECONOMY ISSUE 3

Renegotiating The Debts Of Developing Countries

3.1 The original formulation of the NIEO objective at the United Nations

Increases in the debts of developing countries are of serious concern to the international community.

The Programme of Action on the Establishment of a New International Economic Order (May 1974) requested that "appropriate urgent measures, including international action, should be taken to mitigate adverse consequences for the current and future development of developing countries arising from the external burden of debt contracted on hard terms." The Programme of Action further requested "debt renegotiation on a case-by-case basis with a view to concluding agreements on debt cancellation moratorium, rescheduling or interest subsidization."

The Development and International Economic Cooperation resolution (September 1975) noting that "the burden of debt on developing countries is increasing to a point where the import capacity as well as reserves have come under serious strain," endorsed the decision of UNCTAD to consider at its fourth session "the need for, and the possibility of, convening as soon as possible a conference of major donor, credit countries to devise ways and means to mitigate this burden." (The Seventh Special Session also called for special attention to the plight of the most seriously affected countries - see issue 4, below).

The Lima Declaration (March 1975) in addition to viewing this matter as one calling for "rescheduling of debt-servicing of long outstanding debts," urged the consideration of the conversion of these debts, "if possible, into grants." Rescheduling was also suggested in the International Development Strategy for the Second United Nations Development Decade (October 1970). The idea that some form of action on Third World debt (be it a rescheduling, a moratorium, or even outright cancellation) should be agreed upon is evident throughout the original formulations of the NIEO documents.

3.2 Specification and development of the NIEO objective at the United Nations 1974-78.

This principle of renegotiation of Third World debts was the subject of UNCTAD Trade and Development Board Resolution 150 (XVI) (October 1975). Recalling the Programme of Action, this resolution endorsed the recommendation of an Ad Hoc Group of Governmental Experts that, "on the intitiative of debtor developing countries, ad hoc meetings may be convened, with the participation of major creditor countries concerned and of interested developing countries, to examine at the international level a debtor country's situation in a wider development context, prior to debt renegotiations in the customary forums."

The Ad Hoc Group of Governmental Experts also concluded that "past experience indicates that it is not possible to establish general criteria for debt relief applicable to all countries in all cases. On the other hand, it is generally agreed that there are certain common elements which might usefully be set forth for consideration in future debt negotiations..."

The report listed five common elements:

Debt reorganization should :

Take into account the development prospects of a debtor country, thereby enabling it to continue debt servicing payments and restore its creditor business;

Be conducted in the customary multilateral framework, concluding agreements quickly to reduce uncertainties regarding foreign exchange availabilities;

Promote the principle of equality and non-discrimination among creditors;

Take into account the anticipated long-term debt servicing capacity of the debtor country and the legitimate interests of the creditors;

Provide for flexibility to review the situation at the end of the consolidation period in the light of unforeseen circumstances.

The above were reviewed in a report by the UNCTAD Secretariat (TD/188 29 December, 1975). The report suggested that there was "some merit in the view that it is not possible to establish general criteria for debt relief applicable to all countries . . . ." However, the report continued, "The present debt-servicing difficulties of developing countries are not the result of specific external circumstances peculiar to particular countries... The problem has clearly a more general dimension since it springs from the maladjustment in the world economy and is beyond the ability of developing countries to control." Therefore, the report suggested, "the 'common elements' agreed upon by the Group could be expanded so as to include general principles that would guide . . . . multilateral debt negotiations." Two proposals were put forward:

a. The most seriously affected countries should have their debt servicing payments on official assistance loans waived for the remainder of the decade. Consideration should be given to the possibility of converting the official development assistance debt owed by least developed countries into grants.

b. Multilateral lending institutions should provide programme assistance to the most seriously affected countries in an amount not less than the debt-servicing payments by these countries to the multilateral institutions.

The report also noted that developing countries not in need of concessional debt relief are often saddled with the problem of their short-term debt coming due more or less at the same time. It was suggested that "funding of such debts, consideration should be given to the establishment of an ad hoc international fund to refinance - at commercial interest rates but with maturities of, say, 15 years - the commercial debts of developing countries in need... The participation of each developed country in the fund could be determined in the light of the commercial debt owed to it by developing countries."

In a supplement to this report (TD/188/Supp. 1) there was a further proposal that the waiver of debt-service payments for the rest of the decade be extended to all countries, not just those designated as most seriously affected.

The debt problems of developing countries were the subject of Resolution 94 (IV) at UNCTAD IV in May, 1976. At that Conference, "the governments of the developed countries pledged themselves to respond in a multilateral framework by quick and constructive consideration of individual requests with a view to taking prompt action to relieve developing countries suffering from debt-service difficulties, in particular least developed countries and most seriously affected developing countries." The resolution also invited "appropriate existing international forums to determine, before the end of 1976, what features might usefully be discerned from past operations . . . . . which could provide guidance in future operations relating to debt problems as a basis for dealing flexibly with individual cases." With regard to this resolution, it must be noted that a report by the Economic Commission for Africa issued in March, 1977 (M77-475-No. 36) stated that "no meaningful resolution" could be adopted at the fourth session of UNCTAD on the matter of Third World debt.

Third World debt problems were the subject of other resolutions as well. In December, 1976, Resolution 31/158 of the General Assembly urged "The International Conference on Economic Cooperation (CIEC) to reach an early agreement on the question of immediate and generalized debt relief of the official debts of the developing countries ... and on the reorganization of the entire system of debt renegotiations to give it a development rather than a commercial orientation." (This resolution recalls the October 1975 resolution of UNCTAD's Trade and Development Board which urged a developmental rather than a commercial orientation to the debt problems of developing countries.)

Policy issues and developments in the field of indebtedness of developing countries since UNCTAD IV were reviewed in a note by the UNCTAD Secretariat (TD/AC.2/5 30 June, 1977). The note mentioned a draft resolution (TD/L.124) submitted at UNCTAD IV which proposed "the consolidation of the commercial debts of interested developing countries over a period of twenty-five years and the establishment of a facility to fund their short-term debt." It was further stated that "in recent months, several authorities* have begun to accept the need for some form of official initiative, there being 'growing recognition' that private intermediaries may not be able to manage the required task."

Thus, the note stated, "There seems to be increasing support for a new international facility to finance part of the financial requirements of

* Cited are statements by former United States Federal Reserve Chairman Arthur Burns, Morgan Guaranty in its "World Financial Markets," the Governor of the Bank of England, and the United States Export-Import Bank.

countries' deficits." It was suggested that the IMF might be able to facilitate the establishment of such a facility. This note also asserted that there is a general consensus that "agreed guidelines relating to the renegotiation of debt would be useful." It stated that "consensus must be reached in four specific areas before detailed aspects of the guidelines can be discussed."

1. A procedure for the iniatiation of negotiations must be designed (to commit parties to serious discussions and to carry out any agreed conclusions);

2. An agreed context within which the discussions would take place (i.e., the ultimate goals of the renegotiation must be specified in detail);

3. The duties and rights of the creditor and debtor countries must be delineated within a concept of shared responsibility for the ultimate outcome;

4. Creation of a balanced institutional framework to insure that the discussions and analysis are carried out in a manner which is not prejudicial to any of the participants.

Draft Resolution TD/L.124 is also cited in a study by a regional commission, "Strategies for Development in the 1980s" (E/ESCAP/DP.2/L.10 30 November, 1977). Besides mentioning the proposed consolidation of commercial debt over a 25-year period (note above) and the Draft Proposal's suggestion that the official debts of the least developed, land-locked and island countries should be cancelled (see issue 4, below), the draft proposal was quoted to the effect that "each developing country seeking relief on its debts to developed bilateral creditors and donors was to be 'provided such relief according to a common set of factors in the form of waivers', etc." However, it was the opinion of the ESCAP study that, "the resolution adopted by the conference falls far short of the above mentioned proposal," and instead "reflects the case-by-case approach adopted by the developed market countries, which consider that the existing machinery for renegotiation of debts needs only minor improvements to enhance flexibility in dealing with individual cases." The study concluded by noting that the inability of the conference "to agree on anything more meaningful on such a critical problem undoubtedly represents a major failure."

A resolution adopted in December, 1977 by the General Assembly (Resolution 32/187) called on UNCTAD's Trade and Development Board at its ministerial sessions to reach satisfactory decisions on:

a. Generalized debt relief by the developed countries on the official debt of developing countries, in particular of the most seriously affected, least developed, land-locked, and island developing countries . . . .

b. Reorganization of the entire system of debt renegotiation to give it a developmental orientation . . . .

c. The problems created by the inadequate access of the majority of developing countries to international capital markets, in particular, the danger of the branching of repayments caused by the short maturities of such loans.

UNCTAD's Trade and Development Board held its ministerial session from 6 to 11 March 1978 and adopted Resolution 165 (S-IX) on "Debt and Development Problems of Developing Countries." The resolution stated, inter alia,

The Board notes with interest the suggestions made by the Secretary-General of UNCTAD with respect to an adjustment of terms of past bilateral official development assistance in order to bring them into line with the currently prevailing softer terms.

Developed donor countries will seek to adopt measures for such an adjustment of terms of past bilateral development assistance, or other equivalent measures, as a means of improving the net flows of official development assistance in order to enhance the development efforts of those developing countries in the light of internationally agreed objectives and conclusions on aid.

Upon undertaking such measures, each developed donor country will determine the distribution and the net flows involved within the context of its own aid policy.

The Board reviewed at its ministerial meeting the work carried out within UNCTAD and other international fora relating to the debt problem, and found that common to the varying approaches are the following basic concepts:

International consideration of the debt problem of a developing country would be initiated only at the specific request of the debtor country concerned;

Such consideration would take place in an appropriate multilateral framework consisting of the interested parties, and with the help as appropriate of relevant international institutions to ensure timely action...;

International action...would take due account of the country's economic and financial situation and performance, and of its development prospects and capabilities and of external factors...;

Debt reorganization would protect the interests of both debtors and creditors equitably in the context of international economic co-operation.

3.3 Contributions of major international bodies, 1974-78

The issue of Third World debts was discussed in several international forums. The Conference on Raw Materials at Dakar, in E/AC.62/6 April 1975, invited "the industrialized countries to agree to a moratorium for the reimbursement of debt contracted by developing countries until the objectives for which financial assistance was given are achieved." The Conference also proposed "the cancellation of re-scheduling of debts contracted on unfavorable terms."

The Manila Declaration and Programme of Action, adopted by the Group of 77 at Manila (7 February 1976) made three specific proposals on debt relief.

1. Debt relief should be provided by bilateral creditors and donors in the form, inter alia, of waivers or postponement of interest payments and/or amortization, and cancellation of principal, of official debt to developing countries seeking relief. In that framework the least developed, the developing land-locked and the developing island countries should have their official debts cancelled...

2. Multilateral development finance institutions should provide programme assistance to each developing country in an amount no less than its debt-service payments to these institutions.

3. Agreement should be reached to consolidate the commercial debts of interested developing countries and to reschedule payments over a period of at least 25 years...This would "require the establishment of suitable financial arrangements machinery, which might include, inter alia, a multilateral financial institution, such as a fund or a bank, designed to fund the short-term debts of interested developing countries."

The Conference on International Economic Cooperation (CIEC) did not, according to its report of 27 October 1976 (A.31.282), recommend any proposals like those just cited. However, it was agreed that the Commission on Financial Affairs would "formulate proposals for principles or features for debt reorganization operations." The Commission on Development would "consider other aspects of proposals on indebtedness of developing countries taking into account their development needs and external payments problems, as well as proposals for measures which would contribute to the alleviation of the existing debt burden of developing countries largely dependent on such aid." Particular emphasis was to be placed on the needs of the least developed and most seriously affected countries.

The idea that Third World debt problems should be managed via general principles was also supported in the final communique of the Ministerial Meeting of the Bureau of Non-Aligned Countries held in New Delhi (A/32/74, 7-11 April 1977).

The problem of external indebtedness should be dealt with across the board, in terms of universally applicable principles, and not on a case-by-case basis, except when the debtor country so desired. Debt relief should be regarded as transfer of resources and not as a device to meet temporary difficulties in the balance of payments.

The August 1977 Report of the CIEC (A/31/478/Add.1) responded to the CIEC of the previous year. Six general objectives of debt reorganization were presented along with a procedure for the initiation of international action, a procedure for analysis of the country's long-term economic situation, and guidelines for reorganization operations.

The general objectives of debt reorganization are:

> Policies with regard to debt reorganization should be considered in the overall context of internationally agreed development targets ...which call for an increased net transfer of resources to developing countries.

> Debt reorganization .... should be recognized as an appropriate means of increasing untied and quickly disbursable resource transfers to developing countries.

> (Recognition that) often debt problems indicate a need for augmented financial flows on appropriate terms.

> Debt relief should not be restricted to cases of so-called debt crisis....ways and means must be found for developing countries to initiate international action at an early stage of emerging difficulties.

> Mitigation of debt service difficulties...is in the interest of both debtor and developing countries.

> Debt reorganization would be carried out within an institutional framework that would ensure the application of the principles of international financial cooperation and protect the interest of debtors and creditors equitably.

The Report suggested three fundamental elements of a procedure for the initiation of international action.

> The procedure should confirm that it is the exclusive right of the debtor country to initiate the process of reorganization. It should not in any way open the possibility of international surveillance or a prior analysis.

> It should result in action...well before the problems of the developing country have reached crisis proportions and have damaged its development plan.

> After a developing country initiates the process for international action "developed creditor and donor countries will participate in the reorganization and commit themselves to contribute the necessary resources warranted by the economic analysis and the development objectives of the country."

Finally, the CIEC suggested that a set of guidelines for reorganization operations should include, inter alia, the following elements:

> Reorganization should be completed expeditiously.

Measures adopted should be consistent with an accepted minimum rate of growth of per capita income.

Policy actions adopted should be consistent with the socio-economic objectives and priorities of the country's development plan.

The provision of new flows and the terms of debt negotiation should be on a long-term basis consistent with the country's long-term financial and developmental needs as reflected in the analysis.

The terms and conditions of rescheduling the official and commercial debts should be no harsher than the softest terms prevailing for the same kind of loans at the time of reorganization.

Provisions should be included to facilitate additional financial flows, if needed, or accelerated repayments.

WORLD ECONOMY ISSUE 4

Undertaking Special Measures To Assist Land-Locked, Least Developed And Island Developing Countries

4.1   The original formation of the NIEO objective at the United Nations

The necessity to extend special treatment to the particular needs of the least developed among the developing countries (in general the land-locked and the island countries and those developing countries in particular economic difficulties) was recognized in the United Nations well before a New International Economic Order was formally called for.

Already the International Development Strategy for the Second United Nations Development Decade (October 1970) projected a variety of measures specifically aimed at developing and assisting the trade and developmental needs of the least developed countries. These include "technical assistance and financial aid " through "grants and/or exceptionally soft loans to enhance their absorptive capacity."

> Special measures ... to improve ... (their) capacity ... to expand and diversify their production structure so as to enable them to participate fully in international trade .... special consideration will be given to commodities of interest to these countries .... In the field of manufactures and semi-manufactures ... measures ... will be so devised ... to allow ... (them) to be in a position to derive equitable benefits .... special attention will also be paid .... to improve the quality of their production for export as well as of marketing techniques in order to enhance their competitive position in world markets.

Special measures in favour of land-locked developing countries:

National and international financial institutions .... extend technical and financial assistance to projects designed for the development and improvement of the transport and communications infrastructure .... All States are invited to become parties to the Convention on Transit Trade of Land-locked States of 8 July 1965 .... and take into account the relevant decisions and resolutions of UNCTAD.

Special measures in favour of the least developed among the developing countries:

......Every possible effort will be made to ensure their sustained economic and social progress ..... and to enhance their capacity to benefit fully and equitably from the policy measures for the Decade...

The Declaration on the Establishment of a New International Economic Order (May 1974) called for the "full and effective participation ..... of such countries on the basis of equality .... bearing in mind":

....the necessity to ensure the accelerated development of all the developing countries, while devoting particular attention to the adoption of special measures in favour of the least developed, land-locked and island developing countries as well as those developing countries most seriously affected by economic crises and natural calamities, without losing sight of the interests of other developing countries.

To take urgent measures to increase the import and export capability of the least developed countries and to offset the disadvantages of the adverse geographic situation of land-locked countries, particularly with regard to their transportation and transit costs, as well as developing island countries in order to increase their trading ability.

Appropriate steps should be taken to give priority to (such) developing countries and to the countries most seriously affected by economic crises and natural calamities, in the availability of loans for development purposes (on) more favourable terms and conditions.

The Programme of Action on the NIEO (May 1974) further identified a number of areas where the special needs of the least developed and land-locked countries should be borne in mind. These include (a) the formulation of an international code of conduct for the transfer of technology, (b) making available modern technology appropriate to their specific economic, social and ecological conditions, (c) assisting in the research and development of suitable indigenous technology, (d) regulating the commercial practices concerning the transfer of technology to such countries, and (e) extending international cooperation in the development, conservation and legitimate utilization of their natural resources including all sources of energy.*

The Charter of Economic Rights and Duties of States (December 1974) reiterated that:

> In furtherance of world economic development, the international community, especially its developed members, shall pay special attention to the particular needs and problems of the least developed ... land-locked ... and also island developing countries with a view to helping them to overcome their particular difficulties ...

The Seventh Special Session's resolution "Development and International Economic Cooperation" (September 1975) further reiterated,

> Special attention should be given to the particular problems in the industrialization of the least developed, land-locked and island developing countries ... to put at their disposal ... technical and financial resources as well as critical goods ... warranted by their human and material resources.

> Developed ... and developing countries in a position to do so, should provide food grains and financial assistance on most favourable terms to the most seriously affected countries to enable them to meet their food and agricultural ... requirements within the constraints of their balance of payments position.

> Special measures should be undertaken ... to assist in the structural transformation of the economy of (such) countries.

The Lima Declaration and Plan of Action on Industrial Development and Cooperation (March 1975) pointed out that the least developed countries "should enjoy a net transfer of resources from the developed countries in the form of technical and financial resources as well as capital goods ...   to accelerate their industrialization."

Noting that the least developed land-locked and island developing countries present problems which require special measures, the Lima Declaration identified the following needed for their rapid industrialization:

a. Infrastructures, inventories of natural resources and the technical and financial assistance required for the exploitation of their resources;

b. Establishment of complete industrial estates and pilot plants utilizing as far as possible local resources;

c. Creation of integrated production units including new servicing and maintenance facilities;

d. The implementation of an appropriate agrarian policy for the promotion of integrated rural development schemes;

---

* For a discussion of the general NIEO objectives under these headings, see the relevant world economy issues, below.

e. Development of cottage industries;

f. Systematic assessments of their industrialization potential;

g. The harnessing and proper conservation of water resources, especially in those countries affected by drought;

h. Preferential treatment for industrial products and processed goods through joint enterprises under regional cooperation;

i. Assistance for transport and communications;

j. Assistance in respect of their transportation and additional transit costs;

k. Assistance from UNIDO and other international organizations to accelerate their industrialization.

4.2 Specification and development of the NIEO objective at the United Nations, 1974-78

In the United Nations system, the problems of land-locked, island and least developed among the developing countries have been treated by a number of bodies. These include the General Assembly, the Economic and Social Council, UNCTAD, UNIDO, and the Office of the Secretary-General of the United Nations. Their consideration of the special measures required to promote the economic development of the land-locked, least developed and island countries includes ECOSOC Resolution 30 (LVII) of 2 August 1974, UNCTAD Resolution 62 (III) of 19 May 1972, the Secretary-General's reports on the establishment of a Special Fund for the least developed countries (15 May 1974), and UNCTAD Resolution 98 (IV) of 3 May 1976. These and a host of other enabling and follow-up resolutions of the various organs and their intergovernmental boards, constitute an impressive record of international efforts through international organizations seeking implementation of the basic NIEO objective in this area. For the most part the issues treated in the documentation include virtually every topic in the list of New International Economic Order issues.

In an initial Report of the Secretary-General of the United Nations (E/5499 15 May 1974), the following "specific arguments" were advanced for the creation of a special fund for the least developed countries:

a. The creation of a special fund would give the needed international focus to the ... problems of the least developed countries;

b. (These problems) call for a significant departure from the existing approaches, procedures, guiding principles, and institutional framework;

c. For purposes of expediting assistance;

d. To concentrate on specific projects and to combine technical and financial assistance in a useful manner;

e. For coordinating global efforts through a single mechanism and to handle their problems in an integrated and comprehensive manner;

f. To set criteria, needs and priorities and to channel bilateral assistance;

g. Such concerted efforts enable mobilization of additional funds and assistance;

h. The creation of the fund will not interfere with the developmental assistance given to other developing countries;

i. Experience shows that specific commitments made to established institutions tend to increase resource flows.

The report also points out the views of those who are opposed to the establishment of a special fund. In their view, the existing institutions, such as UNDP and IBRD, should be strengthened to perform the needed services; if existing institutions cannot make the necessary adjustments the proliferation of special purpose funds is undesirable. Furthermore, the creation of a special fund would not necessarily attract additional resources; on the contrary, it might cause hardship to Governments and unnecessarily enlarge administrative expenditure.

The Inter-Governmental Group on the Least Developed Countries, created by the Trade and Development Board of UNCTAD (Resolution 119 (XIV)) adopted a number of resolutions by which the special measures in favour of the least developed among the developing countries are to be identified (TD/B/577, 25 July 1975).

The Group urged:

a. The developed countries to endeavour to achieve the 0.7 per cent target for official development assistance ... to ensure that the least developed are among the highest priority recipients of such flows;

b. Increase financial assistance in areas of high national priorities;

c. Developed market economy countries, socialist countries of Eastern Europe and others in a position to do so, as well as multilateral development agencies to provide all future assistance in the form of grants and highly concessional forms of financial assistance;

d. the above countries to provide the local costs of development projects wherever appropriate;

e. The costs of on-going projects and maintenance costs during an appropriate phasing-out period;

f. Highly concessional debt relief arrangements ... on a case-by-case basis;

g. Reduction of aid-tying arrangements for the least-developed countries progressively with the objective of their total elimination;

h. Elimination of financial counterpart requirements in connection with technical assistance projects;

i. To assist in identifying planning and preparing both financial and technical assistance projects;

j. To assist in carrying out feasibility and pre-investment surveys and post-implementation reviews;

k&l. The creation of integrated projects aimed at expanding exports;

m. To improve the mobilization of domestic resources (taxes, savings and other fiscal mechanisms).

The Secretary-General of UNCTAD was given the responsibility to organize inter-governmental meetings in consultation with UNDP, to review and assess their assistance requirements. These meetings should also review the implementation of projects. The intergovernmental group reiterated the desire of the developing countries to establish immediately a special fund for the least-developed countries (ID/B Resolution 41 (VIII) 17 May 1974).

The Inter-Governmental Group adopted <u>inter</u> <u>alia</u> the following recommendations:

Economic Cooperation - Preferential treatment as far as possible to imports of goods produced by the least developed countries, increased technical and financial assistance and the establishment of committees for industrial cooperation for solving the special problems of those countries.

Commercial Policy Measures

1. Allocations of quotas in commodity agreements to ensure the optimal marketing of their products in order to increase their foreign earnings;

2. Special exemption from financial contribution in any future integrated programme for commodities;

3. Extension of Generalized System of Preferences to agricultural products of export interest to the least developed countries;

4. Removal of tariff and non-tariff barriers as an immediate measure to assist the least developed countries, including the removal of ceilings, quotas and safeguard clauses;

5. Liberalization of the rules of origin in respect of their products;

6. Multilateral compensatory financial and other arrangements to provide for less exacting requirements for the least developed countries;

7. Extending developed countries' assistance to them for the planning, production, transportation, and sale of their manufactures.

The Working Group recommended <u>inter</u> <u>alia</u> "grant of special treatment in the early phase of the multilateral trade negotiations, giving priority to tropical products... within the context of the Tokyo Declaration."

In "Basic Problems Facing the Least Developed Countries" (ID/Conf. 3/5, October 1974) a UNIDO study made these recommendations:

Transfer of Technology

1. Assistance should be given to the least developed countries to obtain at a minimum cost and on preferential terms the results of scientific and technological developments apporpriate to their requirements;

2. Transfer of Technology centers should be established to enhance their negotiating capabilities and to promote external collaboration;

3. To secure patented, patent-related and non-patented technologies, including know-how;

4. To develop indigenous technologies and to promote the adaptation of imported technologies to their national requirements;

5. In order to compensate reverse transfer of technology (brain drain), arrangements for the provision, on a cost-free basis, of skilled manpower to meet their particular requirements.

Shipping and Freight Rates

Ship owners and liner conferences should establish freight tariffs for the least developed countries to expand their trade and to develop promotional rates for their non-traditional exports and provide financial and technical assistance for them to acquire and expand their merchant fleets.

In respect of special measures aimed at promoting small-scale industries among the least developed countries, the Report of the Second General Conference of UNIDO (ID/Conf. 3/31, 9 May 1975) states under "Policy Principles" that the ILO/UNIDO working party ... agreed on the following type of assistance:

a. Developing national plans for industrialization and a realistic assessment of possible chances for small-scale industries, including legislation and other measures to facilitate and encourage the establishment of small-scale industries;

b. Providing factory accommodation of workshop facilities, for instance in the form of industrial estates;

c.   Identifying opportunities ... and assisting in the preparation of requests for financing;

d&e.   Establishing promotional, financial and advisory services....;

f.   Developing manpower skills ...;

g.   Choosing appropriate technologies ... including assistance in marketing and sub-contracting;

h.   Promoting industrial cooperation.

Further, in respect of a number of the special measures mentioned above, specific proposals for implementation were made by various regional economic commissions, by the Kuwait Fund for Arab Economic Development and others, in cooperation with UNIDO. By a resolution adopted at the Second General Conference of UNIDO (ID/Conf. 3, Resolution 1, 10 April 1975) it was declared

> ...that there is a need to establish...within the UNIDO, appropriate machinery ... for new, more effective and practical forms of technical and financial assistance ... required by the least developed, the land-locked and the island developing countries ...

> ...such machinery should form an integral part of any new institutional and fuctional structure of the UNIDO...

UNCTAD adopted, without dissent, a number of decisions during its fourth session held at Nairobi, concerning the least developed among the developing countries, developing island countries and developing land-locked countries. The Conference affirmed the urgency to adopt and execute both the particular and the long-term or permanent measures within the framework of the UNCTAD machinery in the fields of trade and financial policies, capital and technical assistance, shipping, insurance and transfer of technology in favour of these countries. The following are the principal decisions adopted by the conference in the above mentioned areas.

<u>Financial and Technical Assistance</u>. Bilateral and multilateral donor agencies should agree on effective measures to ensure that each least developed country receives a higher flow of assistance, as also the World Bank Group and regional institutions should give high priority to increasing their assistance. Further, strong financial support should be given through existing funds or programmes. Bilateral official development assistance (ODA) should essentially be in the form of grants, taking into account the effects of the loss of purchasing power and by making suitable adjustments in assistance strategies. Developed countries should cancel the official debts of these countries and relief on concessional terms should be provided for clearing outstanding debt burdens. Multilateral institutions should convert loans granted to them into highly concessional forms. The ODA should be provided on a predictable, continuous and increasingly assured basis. As a general rule, all ODA loans should be untied; where this is not possible,

alternative arrangements should be sought in order to offset possible
disadvantages of tying.   Aid projects should be selected in consultation with
the donor countries.   Socialist countries should grant credits on highly
concessional terms and devise forms and methods of utilization within the
framework of the International Bank for Economic Cooperation.
    The criteria for granting financial and technical assistance should take
into account "the longer-term social rate of return, including related
secondary effects in those countries." In the designing and implementation of
their programmes, the participation of the majority of the population in the
benefits of social and economic development should be substantially increased.   Public services, including projects in these countries, should be
financially assisted consistent with their national programmes and plans. The
local costs and, during the phasing out period, the recurring and maintenance
costs of both capital and technical assistance projects, should be financed
wherever the lack of adequate local resources makes this appropriate.
Increased help should be given in identifying, planning and preparing projects
and in carrying out feasibility and pre-investment surveys and post-
implementation reviews.   Finally, the highest quality technical assistance
personnel should be offered, and a rapid training of local replacement
personnel should be arranged.
    Commercial Policy. Special consideration in the context of commodity
agreements should be given to least developed countries in order to increase
foreign exchange earnings and promote the processed and semi-processed
agricultural, mineral and handicraft products and others of export interest to
them.   Reduction of tariff and non-tariff barriers envisaged in the Tokyo
Declaration should be effected.   The rules of origin and other related
measures should be liberalized. Compensatory financing facilities designed to
stablize export earnings should be made available.   Measures should be
adopted to foster the creation of industries in those countries for processing
of raw materials and food products. In adapting the Generalized System of
Preferences, the special interests of these countries should be considered.
Special measures as may be necessary should be taken in the Integrated
Programme for Commodities.   The developed countries, including the
socialist countries, should assist the expansion of the sales of their products
and encourage longer-term purchase agreements as well as their production
potentialities of food, energy and other resources, including manufactures.
    Economic Cooperation Among Developing Countries.   The developed
countries should accord preferential treatment to imports, assist their
production potentialities, extend scientific and technological assistance,
provide financial and technical assistance, promote joint ventures with least
developed countries involving transfer of equipment and technology and enter
into long-term arrangements to promote their trade.
    Shipping and Promotional Freight Rates. The freight rates for these
countries should be established so as to assist their export trade including
their non-traditional exports.   Assistance in acquiring and expanding their
national or regional merchant marines and in improving their port facilities
should be extended by the developed countries and the international financial

institutions. Special efforts to minimize the foreign exchange costs of insurance and reinsurance should be made. The least developed countries themselves should adopt appropriate legislature and other measures to promote the effectiveness of their domestic insurance operations.

Transfer of Technology. Relevant scientific and technological information should be transmitted to the least developed countries and technology should be transferred on favourable terms and conditions and appropriate to their needs. Transfer of Technology Centers should be established to ensure their proper negotiation in obtaining the relevant and needed technology, including the transfer of patented, patent-related and non-patented technology.

Developing Island Countries. Special consideration, including assistance, should be given to island countries in view of the geographical factors impeding their trade, such as the extra cost and delays in shipping their products, and the need for storage and port facilities. Governments should seek to prevent discrimination of the ships of island countries, especially their break-bulk carriers plying between islands. The special problems of archipelago countries concerning their inter-island shipping should be examined and appropriate types of ships and port facilities evolved. The developing island countries should be encouraged to form consortia of international shipping companies to develop their trade opportunities. Inter-island air services should be improved to promote foreign trade and tourism including adjustment in the freight rates and fares. Training facilities should be created for the management of air transport and the development of telecommunication links. Technical and financial assistance should be extended to island countries to fully develop their marine and sub-marine resources. The commodities of foreign exchange interest to island countries should be given special treatment in the Integrated Programme for Commodities. Problems of human environment and human settlements peculiar to the small island countries should receive special consideration.

With respect to the flow of external resources, insurance and reinsurance, the considerations outlined above for the least developed countries apply also to island countries.

Land-Locked Developing Countries. The economic and social development of the land-locked states (LLS) is usually hampered by lack of access to the sea, isolation from trading centers and markets, and by the additional transportation expenditures they have to incur. The measures recommended in UNCTAD Resolution 63 (III) should be implemented. Joint cooperation in solving each transit situation should be considered. Integrated regional transport infrastructure should be planned. In consultation with the LLS and its transit neighbours, technical and financial assistance for developing and integrating its railway system, road facilities and transport mechanisms should be granted. The international community should assist in the establishment of alternative transport routes on a competitive basis. In the restructuring of the economy of an LLS, the possibility of establishing import substitution industries which produce high-bulk, low-value goods, should be explored.

With respect to the flow of external resources, shipping freight and transit costs and related matters, the measures recommended for the least developed and island countries apply to the LLS.

The Secretary-General of UNCTAD should formulate the organizational structures of the special fund for LLS, per General Assembly Resolution 3504 (XXX) of 15 December 1975.

In the event of natural disasters in the three types of developing countries considered here, effective and speedy external relief should be extended, coordinated by UNDRO. The likelihood of such disasters should enter the economic development programmes of other countries.

(Resolution 98 (IV) 31 May 1976)

By Resolution 3504 (XXX) (December 1976) the General Assembly approved the Statute of the Special Fund for the Land-Locked Developing Countries to assist them in offsetting additional transport, transit and transhipment costs due to their geographical limitation. The General Assembly inter alia called upon all Member States and the entire international community to contribute generously to the Fund in order to make it operational in 1977.

The General Assembly also adopted Resolution L.70/32 (December 1977) by which it:

> authorizes the Administrator of UNDP to propose, in close collaboration with the Secretary-General of UNCTAD, interim arrangements to implement the aims and purposes laid down in the Statute of the Fund, until the Fund becomes operational in the manner specified in General Assembly Resolution 31/177 subject to approval of such arrangements by the Governing Council of UNDP.

ESCAP and ECWA gave regional consideration to the recommendations contained in UNCTAD Resolution 98 (IV), and in the Manila Programme of Action of 18 April 1976. In regard to access to the sea of LLS, the African regional economic group voiced the hope that "all African countries will press vigorously for the recognition of the right of access...in a spirit of solidarity and regional self-reliance." (E/CN/4/ECO/90/Rev.2).

4.3 Contributions of major international bodies, 1974-78

The Dakar Conference of Developing Countries on Raw Materials (E/AC.62/6, 15 April 1975) decided:

> ...to set up a permanent committee for technical assistance which will be responsible for the transfer of technological knowledge from the developing countries to the least developed among them.

(Resolution 8)

With respect to the land-locked developing countries, the Dakar Conference decided:

to establish a Permanent Technical Assistance Commission within the Bureau of Non-Aligned Countries to take urgent measures to offset the adverse economic effects arising from the geographic situation of land-locked developing countries.

(Resolution 9)

The Conference on International Economic Cooperation, in its final report (A/31/478/Add. 1, 9 August 1977) announced:

The developed country participants are ready to contribute ...subject to legislative approval where necessary, $1 billion, which would be .... additional and, as far as possible, quick disbursing aid through multilateral channels or through bilateral assistance or debt relief, all of comparable quality ..."

Among the participants of CIEC donor countries, specific pledges to the $1 billion fund were made by Australia, Canada, EEC, Japan, Spain, Switzerland, and the United States.

WORLD ECONOMY ISSUE 5

Using Funds from Disarmament for Development

5.1 The original formulation of the NIEO objective at the United Nations

The use of funds released through disarmament was proposed in the International Development Strategy for the Second United Nations Development Decade (October 1970).   Progress towards general and complete disarmament should release substantial additional resources for the purpose of economic and social development, in particular that of the developing countries.

According to the Charter of Economic Rights and Duties of States (December 1974) all States have the duty to promote the achievement of general and complete disarmament.   Funds released should promote the economic and social development of all countries. A substantial proportion of such funds should be released for the development needs of developing countries.

5.2 Specification and development of the NIEO objective at the United Nations 1974-78

The Third Committee of High-Level Government Experts of the Regional Commission for Latin America (E/CEPAL/1025, 30 March 1977) suggested that it is necessary to support initiatives aimed at utilizing part of the resources freed by disarmament for the advancement of the developing countries.   The same statement as cited above appeared in another report from the Regional Commission of Latin America entitled "The Guatemala Appraisal" (E/CAP/1030/Rev. I, May 1977)

A report of the Secretary-General of the United Nations (A/32/88, 12 August 1977) noted that an obvious incompatibility exists between the continuation of the arms race and the reorganization of relations among States on the basis of equality and co-operation as implied in the programmes for the establishment of a new international economic order. The arms race constitutes a most important obstacle to the development processes of the developing countries. An example given by the Secretary-General is the transfer of technology. It is clear that the transfer of technology is a prominent issue in the establishment of a new international economic order. It is equally clear that the arms race constitutes a major impediment to such transfer and expansion. The enormous diversion of scientific and technological resources from development toward military ends must be curtailed.

The effects of disarmament on the volume and framework of aid for economic development was among the topics discussed in a document of the Preparatory Committee for the Special Session on Disarmament (A/AC. 187/72, 23 August 1977). The document observed, inter alia,

The promotion of economic and social development in under-developed countries is one of the most important ways in which the resources released by disarmament could be put to use. National efforts and international cooperation in the development of the under-developed countries have so far not brought about the desired acceleration of economic growth. An acceleration of the rate of growth of under-developed countries depends upon many factors, including the adoption of appropriate national development programmes and, in many cases, social and institituional reforms. Among these programmes an important role must be assigned to encouragement of productive investment both from domestic and foreign resources. To this end world disarmament could make a major contribution. Despite the inadequacies of the available statistics, it appears that the world's military expenditures far exceed the combined gross investment expenditures of the less developed areas; they are probably at least five times as large and may be much greater. A much larger volume of resources could then be allocated to investment for productive development in these countries even if only a fraction of the resources currently devoted to military purposes were used in this way.

Disarmament could bring about a marked increase in the rate of growth of real income in the poorer parts of the world. This conclusion is reinforced by a comparison of the volume of resources now being devoted to military use with the various estimates made in recent years of the external financial needs of the under-developed countries. The total amount of foreign capital required by the under-developed areas, over and above their domestic resources devoted to investment, is estimated to range from $6 billion to $10 billion annually. These figures are based on conservative assumptions. After allowing for the present flow of foreign capital through existing institutions and arrangements, it is believed that there is a deficiency of about $3 billion a year that needs to be made good in order to achieve the modest annual rate of growth in income of 2 per cent per capita.

2 International Trade Issues

Improving The Terms And Conditions Of Trade Of Developing
Countries: Tariff and Non-Tariff Barriers, G.S.P.,
Duties And Taxes On Imports, Invisible Trade

6.1 The original formulation of the NIEO objective at the United Nations

A fundamental need for many developing countries is to earn the foreign
exchange required to pay for imports and service foreign loans. Their
capacity to earn foreign exchange is highly dependent on their ability to gain
access to world markets. For this reason the Programme of Action on the
Establishment of a New International Economic Order (May 1974) stated that
all efforts should be made to assume:

Improved access to markets in developed countries through the
progressive removal of tariff and non-tariff barriers and of
restrictive business practices.

The Programme of Action also urged:

Implementation, improvement and enlargement of the generalized
system of preferences* for exports of agricultural primary
commodities, manufactures and semi-manufactures from developing
to developed countries and consideration of its extension to

---

* The generalized system of preferences (GSP) negotiated under the
auspices of UNCTAD calls for preferential tariff treatment for exports of
manufactures and semi-manufactures of developing countries in the markets
of developed countries. The declared objectives of the system are to increase
export earnings of developing countries, promote their industrialization and
accelerate their rates of economic growth.

commodities, including those which are processed or semi-processed; developing countries which are or will be sharing their existing tariff advantages in some developed countries as the result of the introduction and eventual enlargement of the generalized system of preferences should, as a matter of urgency, be granted new openings in the markets of other developed countries which should offer them export opportunities that at least compensate for the sharing of those advantages.

Another way for developing countries to secure the needed foreign exchange is to obtain reimbursement from the monies derived by developed countries from customs duties and taxes applied to their exports. To this end the Programme of Action on the Establishment of NIEO declared that:

When the importing developed countries derive receipts from customs duties, taxes and other protective measures applied to imports of these products, consideration should be given to the claim of the developing countries that these receipts should be reimbursed in full to the exporting developing countries or devoted to providing additional resources to meet their development needs.

The resolution of the Seventh Special Session Development and International Economic Cooperation (September 1975) stipulated that:

Developed countries should take effective steps within the framework of multilateral trade negotiations for the reduction or removal, where feasible and appropriate, of non-tariff barriers affecting the products of export interest to developing countries on a differential and more favourable basis for developing countries.

Further, this resolution supported the GSP, stating that "the generalized scheme of preferences should not terminate at the end of the period of ten years originally envisaged and should be continuously improved...."

In addition, the resolution affirmed that:

Developed countries should fully implement agreed provision on the principle of standstill* as regards imports from developing countries, and any departure should be subjected to such measures as consultations and multilateral surveillance and compensation, in accordance with internationally agreed criteria and procedures.... Countervailing duties should be applied only in conformity with internationally agreed obligations.

---

*   "The standstill is one of the main elements of a programme for trade liberalization, including that of non-tariff barriers, namely, that existing import restrictions would not be intensified, nor new restrictions introduced, affecting particularly products of export interest to the developing countries." (TD/B/C.2/170, 18 May 1977)

Finally, the resolution stated that "the multilateral trade negotiations under way* should take fully into account the particular interests of developing countries with a view to providing them differential and more favourable treatment in appropriate cases."

The Development Strategy for the Second United Nations Development Decade (October 1970) devoted considerable attention to the issue of tariffs and non-tariff barriers,† much of it in language similar to the principle of standstill.

It stated, for instance, that:

Developed countries will not, ordinarily, raise existing tariff or non-tariff barriers to exports from developing countries, nor establish new tariff or non-tariff barriers or any discriminatory measures, where such action has the effect of rendering less favourable the conditions of access to the markets of manufactured and semi-manufactured products of export interest to developing countries.

Intergovernmental consultations are to be "continued and intensified with a view to giving effect....to measures for the relaxation and progressive elimination of non-tariff barriers affecting trade in manufactures and semi-manufactures of interest to developing countries."

The second IDS also expressed concern with trade in primary products, stating that:

Developed countries will accord priority to reducing or eliminating duties and other barriers to imports of primary products, including those in processed or semi-processed form, of export interest to developing countries through international joint action or unilateral action with a view to ensuring that developing countries have improved access to world markets and to market growth for products in which they are presently or potentially competitive.

The Charter of Economic Rights and Duties of States (December 1974) concerned itself mainly with certain aspects of the GSP and the question of access to markets. Developed countries should extend, improve and enlarge the system of generalized non-reciprocal and non-discriminatory tariff preferences to the developing countries....in those fields of international economic cooperation where it may be feasible.

States are also asked to help developing countries achieve a substantial increase in their foreign exchange earnings, the diversification of their exports, and the acceleration of the rate of growth of their trade, through, in

---

* This refers to the so-called Tokyo Round on multilateral trade negotiations which began in September 1973.

---

† A tariff is essentially a sales tax imposed on imported goods while non-tariff barriers are quantitative restrictions (e.g. quotas) or barriers of a qualitative nature.

the largest possible measure, "a substantial improvement in the conditions of access for products of interest to the developing countries."

The Lima Declaration and Plan of Action of Industrial Development and Cooperation (March 1975) called for the "progressive elimination or reduction of tariff and non-tariff barriers, and other obstacles to trade." The Lima Declaration also requested adherence to the fullest extent possible to the principle of the "standstill" on imports from developing countries and recognition of the need for prior consultation where feasible and appropriate in the event that special circumstances warrant a modification of the standstill.

The efforts of the developing countries to participate actively in international trade are also hampered by the structural limitations which characterize the international trade arena. These include many of the unwritten practices, monopolies obtained at a time when global trade and commerce were in the hands of a few, the high costs of transportation, insurance and other "invisible" elements of international trade. In order to promote the participation of the developing countries in the world economy, the Programme of Action on the Establishment of a New International Economic Order declared that all efforts should be made:

> to promote an increasing and equitable participation of developing countries in the world shipping tonnage;

> to arrest and reduce the ever-increasing freight rates in order to reduce the costs of imports to and exports from, the developing countries;

> to minimize the cost of insurance and reinsurance for developing countries and to assist the growth of domestic insurance and reinsurance markets in developing countries and the establishment to this end, where appropriate, of institutions in these countries or at the regional level;

> to ensure the early implementation of the code of conduct for liner conferences.

In a more general manner, the Charter of Economic Rights and Duties of States pointed out:

> World invisible trade, based on efficiency and mutual and equitable benefit, furthering the expansion of the world economy, is the common goal of all States. The role of developing countries in world invisible trade should be enhanced and strengthened consistent with the above objectives particular attention being paid to the special needs of developing countries.

> All States should cooperate with developing countries in their endeavours to increase their capacity to earn foreign exchange from invisible transactions, in accordance with the potential and needs of each developing country and consistent with the objectives mentioned above.

The International Development Strategy for the Second United Nations Development Decade identified the global objectives to be achieved in the area of invisibles including shipping to include the following:

The earnings of developing countries from invisible trade must be promoted by minimizing the net outflow of foreign exchange caused by invisible transactions including shipping. Toward this end appropriate action should be taken by the relevant inter-governmental organizations including liner conferences and shipper's councils.

a. the principle that the national shipping lines of developing countries should be admitted as full members of liner conferences operating in their national maritime trade.

b. the liner conferences should admit national shipping lines of developing countries, to way-port trades related to these countries' foreign trade on equal terms.

c. the developing countries' participation in the carriage of maritime cargoes should be promoted so as to encourage them to develop their own national and multinational merchant marine services and compete in the international freight market.

d. the liner conference system should be improved and all unfair practices and discriminations where they exist should be eliminated.

e. the liner freight rates should, in so far as it is commercially viable, be adjusted to promote the non-traditional exports of the developing countries, especially the least developed among them and to facilitate making improvements in their port conditions.

f. financial and technical assistance including training should be extended by the developed countries through the system of UNCTAD to expand the national and multi-national merchant marines of the developing countries including their tanker and bulk carrier facilities.

g. the terms and conditions of bilateral aid and commercial credit given to developing countries to purchase their shipping fleets should be kept under review by UNCTAD.

h. freight rates, conference practices and shipping facilities should be determined by those concerned only after full consultation with the developing countries.

i. concerted national and international efforts should be made to promote the development and improvement of port facilities of developing countries thus leading to a lowering of the cost of maritime transport and permitting reductions in freight rates.

j. appropriate measures should be taken to reduce the foreign exchange cost of insurance and reinsurance for developing countries, without increasing the risks involved. The growth of such insurance markets should be assisted in developing countries or at the regional level.

The developed countries should assist, by the relaxation of travel restrictions and exchange limitations, the tourist industry in developing countries.

The fundamental aspects of this NIEO objective are: preferential treatment to the exports of developing countries through a Generalized System of Preferences (GSP); a "standstill" on current trade restrictions while multilateral trade negotiations continue; reimbursement of customs duties levied on the exports of developing countries; and the increased participation of developing countries in the invisible elements of international trade.

6.2   Specification and development of the NIEO objective at the United Nations, 1974-78

In 1973, shortly before the Sixth and Seventh Special Sessions of the United Nations General Assembly, an important Declaration was issued at the beginning of the so-called Tokyo Round on Multilateral Trade Negotiations which began in Tokyo. The representatives of 102 Governments, from both developed and developing countries, unanimously adopted the Declaration of Aims and Principles, which provided the essential basis on which the multilateral negotiations were to proceed.

The points of emphasis in the Declaration, relevant to the specification and development of this NIEO objective in the years 1974 to 1978, are the following:

increasing the foreign exchange earnings of developing countries;

diversification of Third World exports;

reduction or elimination of non-tariff barriers;

non-reciprocity in conditions of trade;

improving the Generalized System of Preferences.

A report by UNIDO (ID/CONF. 3/10, 26 November 1974) also took note of GSP, stating that "the introduction of GSP in favour of developing countries is a further move towards improving access to the markets of the developed countries." The report goes on to mark the lack of progress "in liberalizing non-tariff barriers, including those affecting products of export interest to the developing countries," noting that "such liberalization is essential for securing a more rational international division of labour, and thereby the expansion of developing countries' exports of manufactures and semi-manufactures..." The report observes that proposals for multilateral solutions to non-tariff barriers have been discussed by various working groups of GATT, the two main approaches being:

establishing a set of relevant provisions based on the provisions of GATT:

drawing up detailed codes designed to prevent or minimize trade restricting or distorting effects of measures not applied primarily for commercial reasons.

The report states that "such proposals ought to be examined in the light of the special problems and difficulties facing these countries."

In another UNIDO report (ID/CONF.3/CRP/I/Add.1, 4 December 1974) the governments of developed countries are urged to:

facilitate the process of trade liberalization, make a more decisive contribution to the financing of the developing countries (especially those of relatively lower development), and reach agreement on the codes of conduct and other legal instruments which are indispensable for the equitable control of the new international order.

A joint report of UNCTAD and UNIDO (ID/CONF.3/19, February 1975) stated that:

Improved access of the manufactures of developing countries to the markets of industrialized countries is of vital importance. The generalized scheme of preferences should be fully implemented, maintained, and significantly expanded. A vigorous effort should be made to eliminate or reduce tariff and non-tariff barriers and restrictive business practices. The developing countries should participate fully in the forthcoming multilateral trade negotiations.

The Annual Report of the Economic Commission for Latin America (E/5608, 12 May 1975) suggested that the GSP was in need of improvement.

"Essential improvements that should be considered include the need for the preference schemes to cover numerous products that are subject to customs duties (especially processed agricultural goods), the elimination of quota systems, the adoption of principles and norms for resorting to escape clauses, the harmonization of the preference schemes of various countries, the adoption of more flexible criteria regarding rules of origin, the simplification of administrative formalities for taking advantage of the preferences, the extension of preferential treatment without reciprocity to non-tariff barriers, the establishment of a prior consultation system when for reasons of force majeure it becomes necessary to restrict the application of the System, and the adoption of other supplementary measures aimed not only at making better use of the various schemes, but also at institutionalizing the Generalized System of Preferences on a firm and clearly defined multilateral basis."

The ECLA report notes a potential problem: a general reduction of trade barriers in the industrialized countries achieved through multilateral trade negotiations may have an adverse effect on the preference margins of the developing countries. For this reason "it is essential that the developing countries should receive compensation for the loss of these preference margins...."

With reference to trade negotiations, the ECLA report proposed that the rules of negotiation adopted be such as to enable the developing countries to participate fully in the negotiations and in the periodic appraisals, and promote, through appropriate channels, action leading to comprehensive solutions in favour of developing countries. It further suggested that juridical amendments be introduced to the General Agreements on Tariffs and Trade "so that it includes all the principles which the developing countries prepared within UNCTAD with a view to giving the new international economic order an institutional form."

Guidelines for the negotiations on the liberalization of non-tariff barriers are proposed in a note by the Secretariat of the Economic and Social Council of Asia and the Pacific (Trade/TNG/(6)3, 22 October 1975).

It suggested that countries applying licensing schemes concerning imports may consider the following measures to liberalize imports from other countries participating in a regional cooperative venture.

Discretionary licensing based on quotas should be complemented by allocation of a specified amount or volume of imports from the region;

Liberal licensing should be automatically granted for imports from participating countries;

Imports from participating countries should be exempt from automatic licensing requirements, statistical licensing requirements, and invoices or other commercial documents for statistical purposes;

Participating countries should be allocated specific provisions of global quotas, perhaps taking into account provisions for gradual growth of imports. Provisions should also be made for new participating countries' suppliers and for carry-overs of unused quotas in preceding periods to succeeding quota periods;

Countries with bilateral quota systems which do not include participating countries may open up bilateral or regional quotas for those participating countries containing similar growth elements (as in the first paragraph above);

Where preferential quotas are opened up in favour of other participating countries, the quotas should be combined, as much as possible, with tariff preferences;

Pending the final elimination of import prohibitions and embargoes, participating countries should allow at least small quantities of imports subject to these restrictions;

Health and sanitary regulations should be removed where they no longer meet the requirements of the situation which motivated them; foreign exchange should be allocated automatically or as soon as possible for licenses issued or quotas granted for imports subject to concession. Import deposit requirements for these products should be waived or reduced.

A framework for the conduct of world trade was outlined by the "Framework Group," a new negotiating body established by the Trade Negotiations Committee in GATT (GATT Activities in 1976, Geneva 1977). The framework consists of five points:

The legal framework for differential and more favourable treatment for developing countries in relation to GATT provisions, in particular the most-favoured-nation clause;

Safeguard action for balance-of-payments and economic development purposes;

Consultations, dispute settlement and surveillance procedures under Articles XXII and XXIII of the General Agreement;

For the purpose of future trade negotiations: applicability of the principle of reciprocity in trade relations between developed and developing countries and fuller participation by the developing countries in an improved framework of rights and obligations under the GATT that takes into account their development needs;

An examination of existing GATT rules concerning the application of restrictions at the border that affect exports, taking into account the development needs of developing countries.

A report by the Secretary-General of UNCTAD (TD/B/642/Add.1, 3 March 1977) urged some improvements of existing GSP schemes by:

Extension of the product coverage to all agriculture products of export interest to developing countries;

More liberal application of limitations and safeguards;

Incorporating the GSP as a durable element of the tariff systems of developed countries;

Intensified efforts of developing countries to exploit trade advantages available to them under the GSP.

The Guatemala Appraisal (E/CEPAL/103/Rev.1, May 1977) asked that "special and differential treatment should be given to the developing countries, both in the review of the judicial framework of GATT and during the present multilateral trade negotiations." It further asserted that "voluntary restrictions on exports should not be extended or increased" and "other non-tariff barriers preventing an increase in exports of manufactured goods to developed countries should be avoided."

A report by the Secretariat of UNCTAD (TD/B/C.2/170, 18 May 1977) noted that the trade of developing countries continues to suffer from departures from the standstill. The Committee on Manufactures of the Trade and Development Board proposed therefore the following guidelines to help ensure more strict observance of the standstill as regards imports from developing countries:

Exemption, in principle, of products originating in developing countries from the scope of measures to intensify existing import restrictions or the imposition of new restrictions, including "voluntary export" restraints or "orderly marketing arrangements," particularly in cases where imports from developing countries are not the major cause for the difficulties that give rise to the measures in question;

The need for prior consultations before action is taken by the countries concerned with the developing countries likely to be affected by the import measures, in order to provide for meaningful discussions of the reasons for the action as well as the measures intended to be taken;

In cases where the import restrictions could be justified by compelling and exceptional circumstances, the countries introducing the measures should take into account the interests of developing countries by making provisions to ensure growth of imports from developing countries of the affected products and for new suppliers among developing countries;

The need for periodic review, every three or six months of the import restrictions, with a view to examining their implications for developing countries' exports, measures needed to be taken to alleviate or mitigate their adverse effects, and steps for their elimination as quickly as possible.

Since the Generalized System of Preferences was first agreed upon in 1970 there have been several general reports on the implementation of the GSP. The most recent of these, by the Trade and Development Board (TD/B/C.5/53, 12 January 1978), set forth suggestions for improving the various GSP schemes of Japan, United States and Western Europe:

The Special Committee on Preferences should consider how to make GSP concessions more secure and stable. Agreement extending the duration of GSP should be made more specific; e.g. an extension of ten years should be envisaged subject to a comprehensive review before the end of that period to determine whether the system should be further continued.

Harmonization and simplification of the differing rules of origin applied under the various schemes would make the system much more effective. This could be largely achieved by eliminating limitations on preferential imports, or at least by maintaining those limitations only on genuine sensitive products, which would otherwise be placed on the list of exceptions.

In addition, the following measures are required for a meaningful improvement of the GSP:

Extension of product coverage to all products of current export interest to developing countries, including agricultural products;

Duty-free entry for all products covered;

Substantive harmonization and liberalization of the rules of origin;

Non-discriminatory application of generalized preferences to all developing countries.

The Special Committee on Preferencs of the Trade and Development Board also offered proposals on how to protect GSP preferential margins from being eroded by the most-favoured-nation-tariff reductions sought in the current multilateral trade negotiations:

The measures for safeguarding preferential margins may comprise exclusion from MFN cuts of certain products of export interest to developing countries, or smaller-than-average tariff cuts on such products, and/or a longer period for staging such tariff reductions.

The standstill issue was again the subject of a report by the UNCTAD Secretariat (TD/B/C.2/194, 21 March 1978) in which criteria and procedures were proposed as regards future departures from standstill:

a. Save in very exceptional cases, imports of developing countries, particularly those that do not cause or threaten market disruption, should be exempted from the application of import restrictions or the intensification of existing restrictions including "voluntary export restraints" or "orderly marketing arrangements." Exceptional cases should be defined as unforeseen difficulties arising in a specific sector for which emergency action is necessary to avoid serious permanent injury to the affected factors of production.

b. Any emergency action taken under a. above should, to the fullest extent possible, be preceded by advance notice and consultations with the developing country suppliers to be affected by the measures, with a view to ensuring their least possible adverse effects on the countries concerned. Consultations should include consideration of the modalities of the import restriction, inter alia,

(i) the type of restriction to be applied;

(ii) provision for growth, including for new developing country suppliers;

(iii) the duration

(iv) the adjustment assistance measures to facilitate the gradual reduction   and final removal of the restrictions;

(v) measures by developing countries affected; and

(vi) assistance by the developed country taking the emergency.

c. Establishment of a surveillance and review mechanism to ensure that agreed measures under b. above are fully implemented and other appropriate measures as may be required are taken in a timely manner.

Turning now to United Nations work on the NIEO objective of increasing the participation of developing countries in the invisible elements of international trade, the Latin American Conference on Industrialization (ID/CONF.3/CRP/1/Add.1, 4 December 1974) recommended that agreement should be reached for the maritime transport of a substantial proportion of the industrial production of the world through the ships of the developing countries.   The ships needed for future world transport should be built in the shipyards of the developing countries.

During its Fourth Session in Nairobi, UNCTAD gave particular attention to invisible trade and adopted the following decisions (Resolution 98 (IV), May 1976):

Freight rates should be established in a manner that will encourage and assist the expansion of the export trade of the least developed among the developing countries, promote their non-traditional exports and facilitate the opening up of new markets. The developed countries and the international financial institutions should extend as a matter of priority assistance to the least developed countries in acquiring and expanding their national or regional merchant marines and in improving their port facilities and related infrastructure. To the extent that it is compatible with the effective operation of insurance and reinsurance companies, special efforts should be made by the developed countries to minimize the foreign exchange costs borne by the least developed countries and extend financial and technical assistance for developing such institutions in those countries or at the regional level.

In order to achieve these objectives the least developed countries should take appropriate legislative and administrative actions to ensure more effective supervision and regulation of the insurance operations transacted in their territories. UNCTAD and UNDP and other related agencies should render all adequate and necessary assistance in the implementation of these measures.

Special mention has been made of the applicability of these measures to island developing countries for promoting tourism as an important sector of their economic development. The shipping freights and transit costs must be established in a manner that will facilitate and encourage the export trade of the land-locked States. Adequate assistance should be provided for developing alternative transport routes to the sea and the related international conventions and legal procedures should be applied in a manner that will facilitate the transport of exports of developing land-locked countries. Further assistance should be made to develop air transport facilities to land-locked States to improve their tourism industry.

Reporting on the measures taken for the implementation of International Development Policies in the various areas of its competence, the Secretary-General of UNCTAD pointed out (TD/B/642/Add.1, 31 March 1977) that "a major step towards achieving some of the objectives of the (International Development Strategy) was the adoption of the Convention on a Code of Conduct for Liner Conferences in 1974...though the Convention has not yet come into force...many of its provisions are, in fact, being observed."

Only slight progress is noted in the achievement of increased participation of developing countries in world shipping activities. "By mid-1976, the merchant shipping fleets of developing countries represented some 7.5 per cent of the world total, compared with 7 per cent at the beginning of the decade. For dry bulk cargo vessels, the share of developing countries .... was as little as 5.5 per cent, and for tankers 5.7 per cent .... the recent recession in world trade has, at least temporarily, made it difficult to obtain loans for ship purchase ... by most developing countries..." The effectiveness of the Shippers Councils in developing countries has been limited due to "lack of adequate knowledge concerning the feasibility and cost of alternative methods of shipment."

Self-reliance in insurance received particular attention, and cooperative regional action has been suggested and reiterated at the Mexico Conference on Economic Cooperation among Developing Countries as a useful strategy. "The operations of several existing sub-regional insurance pools are expected to be complemented in 1977 by those of intergovernmental regional reinsurance corporations in both Africa and Asia ....," according to an UNCTAD report (31 March 1977).

6.3   Contributions of major international bodies, 1974-78

The NIEO concept of reimbursement of taxes and duties on exports from developing countries by the developed importing countries was already proposed by the Conference of Developing Countries on Raw Materials, held in Dakar (E/AC.6216, 15 April 1975). The concept was treated as an element relating to "access to markets" by developing countries. It was stated, inter alia, that:

Developed countries which are not in a position to eliminate internal taxes and other duties on imports from developing countries should refund the receipts derived therefrom to the developing countries concerned.

With reference to invisibles, the Manila Declaration and Programme of Action adopted by the Third Ministerial meeting of the Group of 77 (TD/195,

7 February 1976) dealt with shipping and promotional freight rates, emphasizing the need to encourage and assist the expansion of the export trade of the least developed countries to facilitate the opening of new markets and the development of trade flows. The conference decided that "links between the service sectors of the developing countries should be established or reinforced, with particular reference to interconnexion of their transportation and communications networks, and cooperation in respect of banking, insurance and credit."

The fifth Non-Aligned Conference held at Colombo (A/31/197, 8 September 1976) recommended early accession to and ratification and implementation of the convention on the Code of Conduct for Liner Conferences and the establishment of exclusive conferences and joint shipping services for developing countries. The creation of national and regional enterprises capable of competing with the merchant fleets and airlines of the developed countries and of their transnational corporations is another objective stated by the NAC conference. Joint and united action is recommended to secure financing for shipping, road and railway linkages among developing countries and for improving their port facilities.

Also included in the invisibles for joint action is the expansion and integration of existing telecommunication channels, the establishment of joint insurance arrangements, and the creation, in Yugoslavia, of an "International Centre on Public Enterprises in Developing Countries" for training and exchange of information.

Interregional cooperation is sought to be established through the creation of Regional Cooperative Pharmaceutical Production and Technology Centres in the field of health and medicine.

The Final Report of the Conference on International Economic Co-operation (A/31/478/Add.1, 9 August 1977) suggested that developed countries should improve their GSP schemes. The following measures were recommended:

Maintain the system of generalized tariff preferences in force beyond the period initially planned;

bring more security into the use of the GSP to enable the beneficiaries to orientate their industrial development plans on a satisfactory basis, by providing greater opportunities for the concerns of beneficiaries to be taken into account in the case of reduction or withdrawal of GSP advantages, including some form of prior consultations, unless impracticable or inappropriate;

make a significant effort to improve the application of the system of generalized tariff preferences by expanding product coverage, reducing restrictive stipulations and deepening tariff cuts, in the spirit of and in accordance with the relevant provisions of UNCTAD Resolution 96 (IV);

undertake concerted efforts among donor countries in adjusting their schemes and a revision of the system for a new period beyond the initial period of ten years orginally envisaged, in taking into account the real needs of the developing countries and particularly of the problems facing the poorest among them and with a view to ensuring a fair distribution of the advantages offered among the beneficiary countries;

assistance to beneficiaries to increase utilization of the existing preferential systems;

particular attention to the interests of the least developed countries.

The CIEC did not agree on a policy statement on invisible trade. Included in the respective formulations of developed and developing countries are the question of the code of conduct on liner conferences, the transportation of developing countries' raw materials, wider dissemination of appropriate market information to prevent unfair trading practices, and prevention of trading activities which cause artificial or distorted prices.

WORLD ECONOMY ISSUE 7

Adopting An Integrated Approach To Commodities:
The Integrated Programme, Buffer Stocks,
Producers' Associations, Indexation

7.1 The formulation of the original NIEO objective at the United Nations

(i)   The Integrated Programme for Commodities

In the context of the historical instability of commodity prices and its effect on developing countries, the adoption of an integrated approach to commodities is of major importance. The Programme of Action on the NIEO (Resolution 3203 (S-VI) May 1974) called for the "preparation of an over-all integrated programme, setting out guidelines and taking into account the current work in this field, for a comprehensive range of commodities of export interest to developing countries." The Sixth Special Session also requested that measures be taken "to reverse the continued trend of stagnation or decline in the real price of several commodities exported by developing countries, despite a general rise in commodity prices, resulting in a decline in the export earning of these developing countries."

Taken together these two statements constitute a strong call for an integrated commodities programme since, as is mentioned in the second statement, these pronouncements were issued at a time when the general level of commodity prices were high. The normal expectation is that the pressure for such a programme would be low during a period of generally high export revenues.

Similarly, the Charter of Economic Rights and Duties of States (December 1974) observed that "it is the duty of States to contribute to the development of international trade of goods, particularly by means of arrangements and by the conclusion of long-term multilateral commodity agreements....All States share the responsibility to promote the regular flow and access of all commercial goods traded at stable, remunerative and equitable prices, thus contributing to the equitable development of the world economy, taking into account the interests, in particular of developing countries." As in the Programme of Action there is an emphasis on "arrangements" (on programme guidelines) to improve the international trade of goods, and on the promotion of stable, equitable prices that facilitate less developed economies.

There are similar objectives expressed in Resolution 3362 (S-VII) Development and International Economic Cooperation (September 1976) in the call for "decisions on the improvement of market structures in the field of raw materials and commodities of export interest to the developing countries, including decisions with respect to an integrated programme and the applicability of elements thereof." Further, there is a request for "market arrangements for securing stable, remunerative prices for commodities of export interest to developing countries and promoting equilibrium between supply and demand, including where possible long-term multilateral commitments."

Key demands in the area of commodities, therefore, are (1) the creation of an overall programme (arrangements, guidelines on commodities) which will improve market structures and lead, ideally, to (2) stable, remunerative, and equitable prices. The creation of buffer stock through producer's associations is concerned with the first of these demands, and the idea of indexing third world export prices to tie them to the prices of the manufactured and capital exports of the developed countries is addressed to the second.

(ii) Buffer Stocks

The Programme of Action on the NIEO (May 1974) also called for:

The setting up of buffer stocks within the framework of commodity arrangements and their financing by international financial institutions, wherever necessary, by the developed countries and, when they are able to do so, by the developing countries, with the aim of favouring the producer developing and consumer developing countries and of contributing to the expansion of world trade as a whole.

In short, the Programme of Action requested that buffer stocks be financed by, in order of priority, (1) international financial institutions, (2) developed countries, and (3) developing countries. Only the first of these sources of finance was mentioned at the Seventh Special Session. Development and International Economic Cooperation (Resolution 3362 (S-VII)) asserted that "drawing under the buffer stock financing facility of the International Monetary Fund should be accorded treatment....similar to that under the compensatory financing facility." It further requested that "the fund should expedite its study of the possibility of an amendment of the

Articles of Agreement....that would permit the fund to provide assistance directly to international buffer stocks of primary products."

The International Development Strategy for the Second United Nations Development Decade (Resolution 2626-XXV, 24 October 1970) did not enumerate or emphasize any one source of financial support; it merely stated that "all possible resources for the pre-financing of buffer stocks, when necessary, will be considered while concluding or reviewing commodity agreements incorporating buffer stock mechanisms."

The focus of the documentation concerned with buffer stocks is on the financial support necessary to set up and operate the stocks.

(iii) Producers' Associations

Recognizing that one of the major factors contributing to the inability of developing countries to play their proper role in world commodity markets is the absence of proper organizations or associations of primary producers, negotiations on a New International Economic Order focused attention on the right of developing countries to associate in organizations of primary commodity producers. The Declaration on the Establishment of the New International Economic Order (May 1974) has as one of its objectives "facilitating the role which producer associations may play and .... assisting in the promotion of sustained growth of the world economy and accelerating the development of developing countries."

The Programme of Action emphasizes the need:

To facilitate the functioning and to further the aims of producers' associations, including their joint marketing arrangements, orderly commodity trading, improvement in the export income of producing developing countries and in their terms of trade, and sustained growth of the world economy for the benefit of all.

These objectives have received further recognition in the Charter of Economic Rights and Duties of States. Article 5 of the Charter states:

All States have the right to associate in organizations of primary commodity producers in order to develop their national economies, to achieve stable financing for their development and, in pursuance of their aims, to assist in the promotion of sustained growth of the world economy, in particular accelerating the development of developing countries. Correspondingly, all States have the duty to respect that right by refraining from economic and political measures that would limit it.

The right of the primary producers to form a united front for conducting negotiations vis-a-vis the developed countries received further recognition in the Lima Declaration and Plan of Action on Industrial Development and Cooperation (March 1976). In this connection it affirmed that:

the developing countries must consider all possible means of

strengthening the action of producers' associations already established, encourage the creation of other associations for the principal
commodities exported by them, and establish a mechanism for
consultation and cooperation among the various producers' associations for the purpose of the coordination of their activities and
for their mutual support, in particular as a precaution against any
economic or other form of aggression.

The Lima Declaration further emphasized that the establishment of such
primary producers' associations serves to contribute to a steady growth of the
world economy and to the acceleration of the development of the developing
coutries,

notably through the action of producers' associations of the
developing countries, by means of a continuous exchange of
experience, harmonization of their actions and mobilization of
support for any of them in case of need, so as to ensure, inter alia,
the solidarity of developing countries and their full sovereignty over
their natural resources.

The establishment of producers' associations is intended "to put an end to
speculative practices and erratic movements in prices harmful to the
harmonious development of world trade and the growth of the developing
countries."

(iv) Indexation

Still another aspect of the integrated approach to commodities is the
question of assuring an equitable relationship between the prices of the
exports and of the imports of developing countries. The Declaration on the
Establishment of a New International Order (May 1974) asserted that a new
economic order should be founded on full respect for the principle of:

Just and equitable relationship between the prices of raw materials,
primary commodities, manufactured and semi-manufactured goods
exported by developing countries and the prices of raw materials,
primary commodities, manufactures, capital goods and equipment
imported by them with the aim of bringing about sustained
improvement in their unsatisfactory terms of trade and the
expansion of the world economy.

The Programme of Action on the Establishment of a New International
Economic Order advocated "setting up general principles for pricing policy for
exports of commodities of developing countries, with a view to rectifying and
achieving satisfactory terms of trade for them." Further, the Programme of
Action stated that all efforts should be made,

To evolve a just and equitable relationship between the prices of raw
materials, primary commodities, manufactured and semi-
manufactured goods exported by developing countries and the prices

of raw materials, primary commodities, food, manufactured and semi-manufactured goods and capital equipment imported by them, and to work for a link between the prices of exports of developing countries and the prices of their imports from developed countries.

(A link between the prices of exports of developing countries and the prices of their imports from developed countries constitutes a form of "indexation" of Third World export prices by tying them to the prices of the manufactured and capital exports of developed countries.*)

The Charter of Economic Rights and Duties of States (Dec. 1974) likewise affirmed that:

> All States have the duty to cooperate in achieving adjustments in the prices of exports of developing countries in relation to prices of their imports so as to promote just and equitable terms of trade for them, in a manner which is remunerative for producers and equitable for producers and consumers.

Finally, the International Development Strategy for the Second United Nations Development Decade (October 1970) stipulates that particular attention should be paid "to securing stable, remunerative and equitable prices with a view to increasing the foreign exchange earnings from exports of primary products from the developing countries."

The above-cited documents affirm the need for an integrated programme for commodities, including the integrated programme itself as well as the creation of buffer stocks, producer associations, and the indexation of Third World export prices.

7.2 Specification and development of the NIEO objective at the United Nations, 1974-78

Considerable work has been done at the United Nations on the specification and development of the integrated programme for commodities and its related aspects, buffer stocks, producers associations, and the indexation of Third World exports.

The demand for a full-fledged integrated programme for commodities was supported by the report of the Advisory Committee to UNCTAD's Trade

---

* The idea of "indexation" is, in effect, a proposal that ways and means be found of preventing, or compensating for, declines in the real prices of the commodity exports of developing countries from agreed base levels of these prices. Prevention of a decline in the real price of a commodity implies that the actual market price of the commodity in money terms would have to rise, from its base level, at a rate not less than the rate of increase in an index of the prices of goods imported by the countries exporting the commodity, or in some other index of world inflation. Such an approach is what the Secretariat has called in its earlier studies on the subject, "direct indexation". (From a report of the Secretary-General of UNCTAD, 7 July 1975 (TD/B/563)).

and Development Board and to the Committee on Commodities (TD/B/519). The Advisory Committee concluded that there was a strong need "for the establishment of effective and durable international arrangements for a wide range of commodities of export interest to developing countries." In addition to the establshment of pricing mechanisms the Committee considered that "international arrangements for individual commodities...should cover also matters such as access to markets, diversification, research and development and marketing."

With regard to the establishment of pricing mechanisms, the indexation of prices was the subject of a study by the UNCTAD Secretariat (TD/B/503/Supp.1, July 1974). The study outlined four active or "direct" approaches to indexation.

1. A link between the prices of exports of developing countries and the prices for their imports in general or from developed countries in particular, whereby the prices of all indexed exports could be adjusted in the same proportion.*

A variant of this method is the linking of indexed primary commodity exports to the prices of manufactured exports from developing countries. As manufactured goods predominate among the imports of developing countries, application of this second version among the imports of the developing countries would approximate to the stabilization of the terms of trade of the commodity being indexed.

2. To relate the prices of primary commodities to those of the manufactured goods in which these primary commodities are incorporated. This approach could probably be applied only to industrial raw materials, and would exclude most foods and beverages, which are not subject to any further processing. (This approach has recently been applied by Jamaica to the taxation of its exports of bauxite, by linking these taxes to the prices of aluminum ingots.)

3. Indexation through linking of primary commodity prices to changes in their costs of production. (This is the approach used in the Commonwealth Sugar Agreement, which requires that the negotiated price be reasonably renumerative to efficient producers.) This might necessitate the creation of "an international diversification fund, possibly financed by an export (preferably) or import levy on foreign trade in the commodity concerned," to assist diversification by the producers. Their relatively high-costs could be subsidized by this approach.

4. Indexation could be related to changes in currency valuations, in order to protect developing exporting countries from losses in purchasing

---

*   It is this approach that was called for in the Programme of Action on the Establishment of a New International Economic Order. An example of this type of arrangement is the 1971 agreement between OPEC and the international petroleum countries, calling for a 2 1/2 cent annual upward adjustment in posted prices to take account of inflation.

power such as those occasioned by the devaluation of the dollar since 1971 and the concomitant rise in the average dollar prices of developing countries' imports from the developed countries as a whole.

The Secretary-General of UNCTAD issued a Report (TD/B/503, 6 August 1974) on the findings of the above study. This report suggested that:

The stabilization of export earnings could be achieved by means of financial transfers from developed primary commodity importing countries to developing countries exporting primary commodities, designed to compensate for adverse movements in the terms of trade of the latter countries. Transfers under this approach, which might be called "indirect" indexation, would need to be automatic, upon the satisfaction of certain criteria - which would include (and possibly be limited to) shortfalls from agreed export "norms" and non-repayable.

(It should be noted that, unlike direct indexation, indirect indexation does not attempt to influence the terms of trade of the developing countries through the regulation of the prices of individual commodities.)

Concerning direct indexation, the report observed that "for those commodities for which direct indexation on a commodity-by-commodity basis could be effected, it would be necessary to link prices of the exports of developing countries to some indicator of the purchasing power of these exports." This reference price would be established for the period in which indexation commenced and "could be based upon some agreed 'normal' terms of trade ratio for the commodity concerned, derived from historical value of that ratio, or it could be an estimate of the true equilibrium value of the price or of a 'fair' or 'renumerative' price in existing market conditions." These it was noted, "would be matters for negotiation in the initial phase of any indexation scheme." Nevertheless, whatever the method employed for determining the initial level of the reference price, its future level would be determined automatically by a simple formula relating movements in the reference price proporionately to movements in the price index of imported goods, with intervention by the appropriate bodies to ensure that the market price was kept throughout as close as possible to the reference price.

The report suggested that "the commodities for which direct indexation might be attempted are those whose supply could be effectively controlled." This control could be based on "buffer stocks, production regulation, export quotas or uniform export taxes," depending on the commodity in question, and might be achieved within the framework of international commodity agreements.

The contents of an over-all integrated programme itself were spelled out more precisely in August 1974 in a note of the Secretary-General of UNCTAD (TD/B/498) which outlined "a possible integrated programme for commodities," and indicated further steps to be taken in preparing such a programme.

An over-all integrated programme for commodities would cover a range of specific commodities for each of which appropriate action would be taken, either by producers and consumers jointly or by producers alone, to deal with price problems and other problems as necessary. The programme would be an "over-all" one in the sense that, one way or another, it would encompass the principal "problem" commodities of export interest to developing countries. It would be an "integrated" programme in the sense that it would be devised as a unified "package" and might be negotiated as such.

In addition to the traditional principle that "international commodity agreements should take due account of the interests of exporting and importing countries" the Report stressed that "co-operative action by producers should be one of the elements of an over-all integrated programme for commodities." It was suggested that while the traditional principle of a commodity-by-commodity approach "may still be necessary in some cases ... more emphasis needs to be given henceforth to a multi-commodity approach." The Report stressed a multi-commodity approach in the context of cooperative action by producers as a basic principle of an over-all integrated programme.

The major objective of an integrated programme is "the regulation of prices." The Report noted that price regulation had two aims: (1) to maintain the relative prices of commodity exports with respect to the imports of developing countries, an objective which "would involve some form of indexation," and (2) "the reduction of excessive short-term price fluctuations for the purpose of preventing wide and disruptive variations in the earnings of exporters, and in the import bills of importers, of the commodities concerned." Further objectives would be "expansion of access to markets, market promotion and the improvement of marketing and distribution systems."

As techniques and mechanisms to achieve these objectives, the Report put forth the following:

1. long-run regulation of supply via export quotas.

2. long-run regulation of supply via "the establishment of a uniform export tax by all exporting countries," the rate of which would be adjusted in order to elicit the global supply required.

3. long-run regulation of supply via "the establishment by exporting countries of a central selling agency, or international marketing board," through which all export sales would be channelled.

4. long-run regulation of supply via buffer stocks

In terms of the last proposal, the creation of buffer stocks, the Report noted that:

the resources required for the establishment of a range of buffer stocks in the context of an over-all integrated programme for commodities would be very large. Hence, close consideration needs to be given to the feasibility of establishing a central pool of finance for buffer stocks, which would minimize the capital costs involved.

A central fund, moreover, might be able to obtain loan capital more easily than would separate buffer stocks for individual commodities, since money invested in such a fund would enjoy a high degree of security.

On 31 December 1974 the Secretary-General of UNCTAD issued another report on indexation (TD/3/C.1/168). A main theme of this Report was that "a general policy of indexation would need to be co-ordinated with other international approaches to the problems of commodity trade, and in particular with the proposed integrated programme for commodities...." The report asserted that:

> unless producers alone can adopt co-ordinated policies for market management*....the administration of an indexation scheme could be carried out only under some form of internationally concerted arrangements, such as those proposed as the principal approaches in the context of an integrated programme-stocking policies, multilateral commitments in commodity trade and compensatory financing.

The Report noted that compensatory financing was referred to as indirect indexation in the Secretariat's earlier study on indexation (TD/B/503 cited above).

On the basis of the findings in a report on establishing an integrated programme for commodities (TD/B/498), UNCTAD's Trade and Development Board adopted Resolution 124 (XIV) which requests the UNCTAD Secretary-General to elaborate his proposals further. The result of this resolution was a report by the Secretary-General of UNCTAD (TD/B/C.1/166, 9 December 1974) proposing that the overall programme might consist of five key elements:

a) a series of international stocks to stabilize markets and to assure supplies;

b) a common fund for the financing of these stocks;

c) a system of multilateral supply and purchase commitments on individual commodities;

d) improved compensatory financing arrangements to stabilize the export earnings of developing countries;

e) trade measures to expand and facilitate the processing of primary commodities in developing countries.

---

* These policies would (1) effectively eliminate recurrent crises of oversupply on international markets and (2) ensure that benefits from improved productivity in the exportable commodity production sector accrue to the factors of production in the form of higher returns, as well as to the consumer in the form of lower prices.

Important ingredients of such a programme are the producer associations needed, at least initially, to manage the various international stocks. In this regard the Conference of Ministers of the Economic Commission for Africa decided to "organize meetings among African countries which are producers and exporters of the same commodities with a view to setting up or consolidating appropriate producer-exporter associations" (E/CN.14/642, 24 February 1975).

Similarly the Economic Commission for Latin America, while "urging the Governments of Latin America to ....support...existing associations of commodity producing and exporting countries and the establishment, mainly in collaboration with the Governments of the developing countries of other regions, of further associations...", invited "to set up without delay a council of commodity producer/exporter associations of developing countries." (E/CEPAL/989/Rev. 1, May 1975).

In a Report by a Group of Experts of the Economic Commission for Africa (E/CB.14/WP.1/103, 18 July 1976) (on the basis of the work which summarized the experiences of existing associations) it was recognized:

(a) That several means of intervention, some of which had not so far been utilized on a global scale, were available to existing producers' associations and to associations likely to be created in future. The Group drew up the following list of different kinds of action:

   (i) The unilateral fixing of the sales price of commodities by producers. Such action might be accompanied by an agreement at the production level;

   (ii) The building up of stocks of products either where they were consumed or where they were produced. This measure could be supplemented by purchases or sales on the various raw materials exchanges;

   (iii) The harmonization of contractual clauses, especially through the adoption of model contracts of sale by the association;

   (iv) The establishment of common marketing bodies;

   (v) Diplomatic co-operation for the purpose of inhibiting action by international agents which was deemed to be harmful, of reaching agreement with non-members or of weakening opposition;

   (vi) Scientific and technical co-operation to increase productivity and raise the quality of products;

   (vii) The exchange of information among members on various subjects of common interest;

   (viii) The establishment of mutual funds for financing, which would keep pace with the development of the world economic situation.

It was also recognized

b) That the environment puts constraints on action by producers' associations at the following four levels:

(i) Commodity markets

Markets limit producers' associations, first because of their transparency and second, because of the effectiveness of the various types of action which it was possible to take. In that connection attention was drawn to the harmful effects of the policy of distorting information now being practiced by international firms. The Group also felt that any attempt at market analysis should necessarily take the problems related to the power structure into account.

(ii) Member countries

The countries members of a producers' association could impede the work of the association owing to possible divergency among them at the ideological level, previous commitments (at the commercial and financial levels), or differences in their assessment of the future growth of demand, in the quality of their representation in the various organs of the association (professional background and training), in production costs or political costs (budgetary impact on employment) or in their political will to co-operate.

(iii) Consumer Countries

Action by consumer countries could be initiated by private firms (transnationals) and/or by public authorities. Such action generally took the following forms: Market intervention and product stocking, diversification of supplies to the detriment of the members of associations, recourse to substitutes, manipulation of information, monetary intervention, planned decreases in demand, and various kinds of diplomatic action aimed at dividing producer·countries.

(iv) Growth of co-operation within the Group of Developing Counties and between the developing and industrialized countries

The Group felt that a producers' association was necessarily bound by trends in the general climate of co-operation among nations and could not for long ignore efforts for agreement made within larger political forums, such as those in the United Nations system and the group of non-aligned countries.

c) That the consideration referred to under a) and b) above led to the conclusion that there were a great many tasks which could be performed by a producers' association. It was specified that in addition to price control, the following tasks might be considered to be a valid justification of the continuation of existing associations and/or the creation of new ones:

   (i) Mobilization of political co-operation (authority to negotiate with consumers, for example at the dialogue undertaken in implementation of the decisions taken at the fourth session of UNCTAD);

   (ii) Technical and scientific co-operation (to increase productivity and raise the quality of products);

   (iii) Trade promotion;

   (iv) Industrialization (adding value to raw materials locally);

   (v) Harmonization of investment policies and certain legal provisions (mine, tax, and other legislation);

d) That co-operation had already begun among the various producers' associations and that a greater effort should be made in future to extend and strengthen that co-operation.

The efforts of UNCTAD to implement a general integrated programme were noted by ECLA in its annual report for 1975 (E/5608). On 12 May 1975 ECLA endorsed the Chaguarmas Appraisal which suggested that "the main features of the integrated programme should include: (a) indexing of basic commodity prices; (b) guidelines for a new policy on international commodity agreements; (c) financing of buffer stocks at the national and international level; (d) compensatory financing." Specifically, it was proposed that Latin American countries, together with the developing countries of other regions, explore "the possibility of establishing producers' associations" for the purpose of implementing "a basic commodities price policy in line with the principles of fair prices for producers...". Given the desire to establish and operate buffer stocks, the Chaguarmas Appraisal noted, that "it is therefore necessary to study and suggest reforms in the existing financing machinery and to seek new sources of funds to finance buffer stocks of basic commodities of interest to developing countries".

The financing of buffer stock facilities was also discussed by the Interim Committee of the Board of Governors of the IMF Annual Report (1975). At a meeting of 15-16 January 1975, the Committee agreed that "the Executive Directors should be asked to .... study the possibility of an amendment of the Articles of Agreement that would permit the Fund to provide assistance directly to international buffer stocks of primary products." It is interesting to note that this proposal of the Interim Committe came prior to the request in the Seventh Special Session that the IMF do exactly that, i.e., provide assistance to international buffer stocks directly, rather than through and at the request of an IMF member country. (At this time the proposal is still under study.)

At its 10-11 June 1975 meeting, the Interim Committee agreed that, "after amendment (of the Articles of Agreement of the IMF) a member using the Funds' buffer stock facility would be able to retain any portion of the reserves held in the form of a reserve position in the Fund..." (IMF Annual Report 1975) The significance of this, as noted in a report by the UNCTAD Secretariat (TD/B/C.3/126/Add. 1, 7 September 1975) is that the drawing of currencies from the buffer stock facility" would be fully separate from, and additional to, drawing under the tranches, including the gold tranche.*

The amendment to the Articles of Agreement of the IMF (the second such amendment) became effective 1 April 1978 and is part of the reform of the international monetary system initiated in August 1971. The reform was linked with the issue of indexation in a report by the Economic Commission for Western Asia on the Implementation of the Declaration and Programme of Action on the Establishment of a New International Economic Order (ECWA/26, 18 April 1975). The report suggested that "a durable indexation formula .... could only be found after a complete reform of the international monetary system is achieved."

Another observation on indexing appeared in the Chaguarmas Appraisal (Annual Report of the Economic Commission for Latin America, E/5608, 12

---

* Based on a formula agreed upon at Bretton Woods in 1944, every member country of the IMF was assigned a "quota" and asked to subscribe 25% of this quota in gold and the remaining 75% in its own currency. (Countries with low reserves were granted more lenient terms with regard to the gold subscription.) The Articles of Agreement provided that member's purchases of the currencies of other members could increase the Fund's holdings of the member's currency up to 200% of quota, i.e., the Fund would as much as double its holdings of a member's currency, but not more. A member which made the normal 75% subscription in its own currency could therefore make total outstanding purchases equivalent to 125% of quota. Borrowing up to 25% was said to be in the "gold" tranche (portion) simply because 25% of the quota is normally subscribed in gold, which is a universally acceptable collateral. Purchases of currencies beyond 25% constitutes what is popularly referred to as "credit" tranche purchases since they exceeded a member's net contribution of a universally acceptable collateral, i.e., gold. (The Second Amendment to the Articles of Agreement, now in the process of receiving member approval, eliminates gold and substitutes SDR's.)

In June of 1969 the IMF established a facility to assist members in financing contributions to international buffer stocks. As matters now stand "drawings under the buffer stock facility are separate from, and additional to, general access to the Fund's resources, in the sense that they are ignored in computing the amounts that a member is normally able to draw in accordance with the Fund's ordinary tranche policies, (TD/B/C.3/126/Add.1). There is an exception, however - "a member drawing under the facility at a time when it still has gold tranche drawing rights at its disposal protanto loses those drawing rights." The significance, then, if the Interim Committee proposal of 10-11 January 1975 is adopted, is that members who still had gold tranche drawing rights would not lose them should they use the buffer fund facility.

May 1975.) Noting that the indexing of basic commodity prices is a long-established form of intervention practiced in the commodity markets of developed countries, the Chaguarmas Appraisal observed that "this policy has still not, however, been accepted at the international level." It suggested that "all the developing countries should pool their efforts in order to set up - by means of international co-operation - suitable mechanisms for applying the indexing principle in trade in basic commodities." In a further Report (TD/B/563, 7 July 1977) the SecretaryGeneral of UNCTAD noted that, since indexation can only be operationally effective when market price can be effectively "administered," this would be particularly difficult when the real price established by market forces is declining. For those cases, however, "where it could be effectively applied, direct indexation would be a sure and automatic means of maintaining the 'terms of trade' of a commodity, and a means which, in the last resort, could be employed by exporting countries acting on their own."

The UNCTAD Report also discussed indirect indexation. It noted that payments under an international scheme of this kind (financial transfers related to shortfalls in the market prices of individual commodities from indexed reference levels) are "analogous to the type of income support system for farmers employed in some developed countries." These payments are made in only one direction, however, i.e., from governments to farmers, there normally being no restitution in the reverse direction. This contrasts with an international system of indirect indexation where there might need to be provision for full or partial restitution by commodity exporting countries of any 'deficiency' payments already received if the market price of the commodity concerned exceeded its reference level. Under such a system, if the market price of a commodity showed the same trend as the reference price, payments and restitutions would tend to cancel out over the years; if the market price deteriorated in real terms, there would be a net flow of compensatory payments to exporting countries.

The Report noted that a scheme of this type could be applied with a high degree of selectivity and flexibility since "any number of commodities could be covered and eligibility for compensatory payments coud be restricted to developing countries." It suggested that compensatory payments made through the IMF would be more reliable than financial flows through individual governments.

Further work proceeded at UNCTAD throughout 1975, culminating in a Report by the Secretary-General of UNCTAD (TD/B/C.1/193, 28 October 1975). This set out four proposals recommended by the Secretary-General for the establishment of an integrated programme:

The establishment of a common fund for the financing of international stocks;

The setting up of a series of international commodity stocks;

The negotiation of other measures necessary for the attainment of the objectives of the programme within the framework of international commodity agreements;

Improved compensatory financing for the maintenance of stability in export earnings.

Of these four proposals the report concluded that "the common fund and international stocking policies are the core of the programme."

UNCTAD Resolution 93, "Integrated Programme for Commodities" (May 1976) also emphasized the common fund and international stocking policies. It set as its basic objective "the achievement of stabilization of commodity prices at levels which would be remunerative and just to producers and equitable to consumers...Such prices should promote equilibrium between supply and demand within expanding commodity trade." (A/31/230, Executive Director, UNIDO). The issue of indexation is not mentioned. Instead emphasis focused on the establishment and financing of a common fund, i.e., the institutional device originally termed a "central fund" in TD/B/498.

Indexation is mentioned in a document of the Economic Commission for Africa (E/CN.14/UNCTAD IV/I, 18 April 1976). It noted that indexation is used by developed countries "to ensure a certain equity between the different sectors of the populaiton."

Citing wages and rents adjustments "through cost-of-living escalation clauses," and "the system of parity prices of agricultural commodities adopted in the United States and the EEC" the report suggested that:

Implementation of this technique at the international level, and particularly in favour of commodities exported mainly by developing countries within the framework of international commodity agreements or through cooperation among developing exporting countries, would be of paramount interest to African countries.

In June 1976 a group of experts met in Geneva to prepare a draft agreement relating to the establishment of a council of associations of developing countries producers-exporters of raw materials. The Working Group of ECA "emphasized that when (such a Council) was established, it should have its own special functions which could not be duplicated by other organizations. The Council should be an instrument for the achievement of the ultimate broad objectives of the new international economic order..."

The institutional framework of the proposed Council should include "a conference, a governing board, two action committees and a Secretariat." The Conference would be the highest body of the Council and would comprise one official representative from each association. The Governing Board would be made up of representatives of the associations and would be in charge of managing the Council and co-ordinating the decisions adopted. A large part of the work carried out would be done by the action committees. There would be one committee for mineral producers' associations and another for agricultural producers' associations. Both of them would attempt to coordinate strategies for products. For example, the copper policy would be brought into harmony with the bauxite policy and a similar effort would be done in respect of all products that were interrelated or substitutable. The Secretariat would be in charge of the information and technical studies required and make a permanent evaluation of the effects of the measures taken on developing countries.

It was further recognized that the above developments "could not be decreed by a supreme authority but had to be accomplished in stages"; hence, the Working Group emphasized the need for in-depth studies on the matters involved. Recognizing the importance of the link between such a proposed Council - UNAPEC - and the United Nations Regional Economic Commissions, the Working Group envisaged cooperation on a more stable and permanent basis.

Note was made above of UNCTAD Resoution 93 (IV). This resolution envisaged a series of preparatory meetings between September 1976 and February 1978 to prepare draft proposals for agreements on an Integrated Programme for Commodities "for the consideration of governments and for use in commodity negotiating conferences." Thus report TD/B/IPC/CF/2 by the Secretary-General of UNCTAD was prepared for a preparatory meeting held 29 November 1976 for the negotiation of a common fund. In terms of objectives the report concluded that "a practical approach at this time may well be to agree in principle that the specific purpose of the common fund is the financing of commodity stocks and such other measures as the governing body of the fund may determine." The report also considered such issues as financing needs, capital structure, operation, organization, and management.

Resolution 93 (IV) also requested the Secretary-General of UNCTAD "to convene a negotiating conference open to all members of UNCTAD on a common fund no later than March 1977." The conference took place from 7 March to 2 April 1977. In the view of the Group of 77 "the conference was ending in complete failure," while it was the belief of the developed countries (Group B) that the Conference had "made significant progress, broadening the areas of consensus concerning some of the elements of a common fund." In summing up the results of the Conference, the President supported the statement of Group B, noting that a number of developed countries "expressed their readiness to participate in and financially support a common fund." He concluded by stating that "although it was not possible to proceed further at this session, it appears to me that there is a large consensus that a common fund should be established in accordance with Resolution 93 (IV) to serve as a main instrument of the Integrated Programme for Commodities." There was an agreement to reconvene the Conference not later than November 1977.

Also in March 1977 a report of the Economic and Social Council of Asia and the Pacific (E/ESCAP/L.5) commented that price stabilization is an objective of the establishment of all producers' associations.

> In any price stabilization scheme, the role of "indexation" needs to be considered, both directly by linking the export price of the commodity to the import price of the exporting country or to some index of world inflation, or indirectly through compensatory financial transfers related to shortfalls, from reference levels, in the export price of the commodity.

The establishment of an effective producers' association in any commodity would need coordination in a number of related areas. For instance, referring to the establishment of an International Tropical Timber Bureau, it was pointed out that the functions "will include commercial intelligence, grading and classification, distribution channels, market access, transport, production and processing and management training." For the Asian and Pacific region the ongoing negotiations regarding the integrated programme of commodities in UNCTAD could be useful in a number of commodities of regional interest, such as, cotton, tea, jute, coconut oil, palm oil, natural rubber, and rice. The Report further pointed out that:

> Convening meetings of producers of these commodities in the region will help clarify the expectations of the producers and possibilities of assistance from the Common Fund. Illustrative of the aspects of the establishment and operation of the Common Fund, which such meetings could consider, include elaboration of the Common Fund's policies and its institutional set-up; the priority requirements among commodities, some within each commodity, to be met by the Common Fund; possibilities of direct assistance to projects in a country and links with operations under international commodity agreements or with producers' associations.
>
> Also, there are obvious advantages to be gained from meetings of producing countries in the region, be they covered by international commodity agreements, like tin, cocoa, sugar or coffee, or international producers' associations, like iron ore, copper and bauxite.

The idea of a common fund was given further endorsement by the Guatemala Appraisal (E/CEPAL/1024/Rev.1) in June 1977. It was noted that "in the face of the decline in the prices of various commodities there is an urgent need to secure the establishment and operation of the Common Fund of the Integrated Programme."

As noted above, a conference was convened in March 1977 to negotiate the creation of a common fund. While not able to achieve a consensus, it did agree to reconvene not later than November 1977.

On the 7th of November 1977 the Conference did reconvene, but on 1 December the Group of 77 called "for a suspension of this session of the Conference ...because of the unwillingness of some developed countries to agree to even the fundamental aspects of a common fund consistent with the objectives of the Integrated Programme for Commodities." (TD/IPC/CF/Conf. L.2/Add.2) In summing up, the President noted that "the two issues which had proved the most difficult to resolve were the questions of measures other than stocking and direct contributions to the Fund."*

---

* Measures other than stocking refer to functions which the Group of 77 want to be handled by a Common Fund and which the developed countries believe may be best dealt with by existing international institutions such as the IMF and the World Bank. Examples of such functions would be lending to international commodity arrangements and the overall coordination of measures on the basis of a cross-commodity overview of the world commodity trade problem.

The question of direct contributions to the Fund revolves around the Group of 77's desire that the capital for the Fund consist mainly of direct contributions from all members of the international community vs. the position of the developed countries that the members of individual commodity agreements would determine the maximum financial requirement involved (for that particular commodity agreement) and would contribute 75 per cent of this amount in cash and 25 per cent in callable capital. Under this latter proposal (Group B) the developed countries would only contribute to the Fund to the extent they were involved in commodity agreements.

In concluding, the President "stressed once again the crucial importance of the negotiations on the common fund, not only for the Integrated Programme for Commodities, but also in the over-all context of international co-operation for development and the efforts to bring about a new international economic order."

7.3 Contributions of major international bodies, 1974-78

The Conference of Developing Countries on Raw Materials, held at Dakar (E/AC.62/6, February 975) invited all governments to co-operate in the elaboration and implementation of an overall integrated programme for commodities which would consist of four elements.

The establishment of international stocking and market intervention arrangements to support prices at renumerative and just levels;

The creation of an agency or fund for the financing of stocking and market intervention arrangements;

The substantial improvement of the facility for compensatory financing of export fluctuations;

A round of negotiations on international commodity arrangement including multilateral contracts and other techniques of market regulation to restructure the world market for raw materials and primary commodities.

The objective relating to the right of primary product producers to form associations also received extensive consideration at Dakar. A number of detailed resolutions were adopted which were taken up further in the various United Nations regional commissions mentioned above. Resolution VI of the Dakar conference dealt with cooperation and coordination between the associations of developing countries' producers-exporters of raw materials, and reaffirmed:

that the producers-exporters associations, as an essential element of the national commodity policies of developing countries, are designed to ensure coordination in production, research, development and marketing in order to protect their income, enhance their market positions, and successfully face the well-organized buyers from developed countries, thus ensuring fair and remunerative prices from exports of their commodities;

The same resolution decided,

> to recommend the establishment of a council of developing countries producers-exporters associations of raw materials ... such a council should have the following objectives...

> implementation of measures to recover control of resources, production, marketing and distribution;

> organization of regular exchange of experience and results between the various producers-exporters organizations making their common expertise available to any group of developing countries producing a primary product and wishing to establish a producers-exporters organization;

> harmonization of the actions of the various organizations and, if necessary, mobilization of common support for any particular organization, within the framework of solidarity among developing countries and effective exercise of their sovereignty over their natural resources, and the exploitation, processing and marketing thereof;

> defence against all forms of aggression, economic or otherwise;

> promotion of financial assistance between the various producers-exporters associations in the financing of buffer stocks and such other forms of market intervention as its activities may require;

> identification of the common measures to be taken by producers-exporters associations in order to control and regulate the activities of transnational corporations, with a view to consolidating the permanent sovereignty of developing countries over their natural resources;

> research, encouragement and assistance in the establishment of new producers-exporters associations

Later in the same year, the conference of Ministers for Foreign Affairs of the Non-Aligned Countries, meeting in Lima, Peru, resolved "to establish the Council of Associations of Developing Countries Producers-Exporters of Raw Materials."

The Fifth Conference of Heads of State or Government of Non-Aligned Countries (A/31/197) held in Colombo in 1976, "endorsed the conclusions of the Lima Conference ... welcomed the work carried out by the Inter-Governmental Group of Non-Aligned Countries..." and agreed that the following action be taken:

> the promotion of the establishment of additional producers' associations for primary commodities of export interest to developing countries;

> the adherence, to the fullest extent possible, of non-participating

producer developing countries to existing producers associations and other arrangements;

the strengthening and supporting of existing producers' associations and the application by them of effective methods of operation in order to secure just and remunerative prices for their export products and to protect and improve in real terms the purchasing power of their export earnings. In the process the interests of all developing countries should be safeguarded by means of appropriate measures. The investigations being conducted by the co-ordinator for the sector dealing with producers' associations should serve as a basis for identifying appropriate policies and measures in these areas;

the completion and approval of the statutes establishing a Council of Producers' Associations, on the basis of the draft prepared by the Group of Experts, with the purpose of achieving mutual support, co-ordination and the strengthening and promotion of producers' associations. To this effect another meeting of the group of experts should take place before September 1976 in order to prepare for a Plenipotentiary Conference. All producers' associations established at the initiative of developing countries are invited to join the Council.

The Conference also affirmed a "total commitment to the integrated programme for commodities", in particular, the determination to:

work in close concert with one another and undertake co-ordinated negotiating positions in the forthcoming preparatory meetings and negotiations to be covered by UNCTAD within the framework of the Integrated Programme for Commodities, for the establishment of the Common Fund and for the early conclusion of international commodity arrangements;

give expression to the commitment to the Integrated Programme for Commodities and to that end ensure that all member countries are invited to make specific pledges for contribution to the Common Fund before the Commencement of negotiations.

The Manila Declaration (TD/195, 7 February 1976) also supported the Programme of Action on Commodities. It listed as the objectives of an overall programme such things as improved terms of trade, commodity price supports, reduction of excessive price fluctuations, diversification, and improved market access for the exports of developing countries. The Declaration went on to enumerate the measures needed to achieve these objectives. The establishment of a common fund headed the list, followed by the setting up of international commodity stocking arrangements, the harmonization of stocking policies, the negotiation of other measures necessary for the attainment of the objectives of the programme, measures and procedures for indexing, improvement of compensatory financing facilities, and some related measures.

Support for an integrated programme in general, and for the Common Fund in particular was also voiced by the Conference on International Economic Co-operation (CIEC). Its report of 27 October 1976 (A/31/282) stated that "it is understood that improvement of the structure of commodity markets (in particular, action in support of negotiations within the Integrated Programme including The Common Fund) will be a permanent subject for all forthcoming sessions of the Commission."

Almost a year later the CIEC again expressed support for implementation of the Integrated Programme. The participating countries in the CIEC (and this includes developed industrialized countries) agreed "that a Common Fund should be established as a new entity to serve as a key instrument in attaining the agreed objectives of the Integrated Programme for Commodities as embodied in UNCTAD Resolution 93(IV)." Further, they pledged themselves "to secure a successful conclusion at the . . . . resumed session of the United Nations Negotiating Conference on a Common Fund scheduled for November 1977." The Final Communique of the Commonwealth Heads of Government Meeting (Colombo, 1977) "welcomed the agreement at CIEC that a Common Fund should be established." And the Heads of Government themselves agreed to work toward the early establishment of the Fund.

WORLD ECONOMY ISSUE 8

Developing An International Food Programme

8.1 The Original Formulation of the NIEO Objective at the United Nations

The problem of food was accorded special attention in the context of the NIEO at both the Sixth and Seventh Special Sessions of the General Assembly. While the Declaration on the Establishment of a New International Economic Order (3201, S-VI) simply stated "the need for all states to put an end to the waste of natural resources, including food products," the Programme of Action (3202, S-VI) enumerated several points for inclusion in a food programme.

Assistance should be given to developing countries to reclaim and fully utilize the vast potentialities of unexploited or under exploited land;

Concrete and speedy measures should be taken to arrest desertification, salination and damage by locusts or any other similar phenomenon involving several developing countries, particularly in Africa;

Natural resources and food resources should be protected from damage and deterioration, especially those derived from the sea, by preventing pollution and taking appropriate steps to protect and reconstitute those resources;

Policies relating to production, stocks, imports and exports of food should take full account of the interests of:

(i) Developing importing countries which cannot afford high prices for their imports

(ii) Developing exporting countries which need increased market opportunities for their exports.

Developing countries should be assured the ability to import the necessary quantity of food without undue strain on their foreign exchange resources and without unpredictable deterioration in their balance of payments;

Concrete measures (such as ensuring an increase in all available essential inputs, including fertilizers, from developed countries on favourable terms) should be taken to increase food production and storage facilities in developing countries;

Exports of food products from developing countries should be promoted by the progressive elimination of such protective and other measures as constitute unfair competition.

The resolution adopted by the Seventh Special Session (3362, S-VII) Development and International Economic Cooperation, in addition to devoting considerable attention to food, took up the issue of agricultural production in general. A succinct summary of the position taken at that Special Session is expressed in the following paragraph.

The solution to world food problems lies primarily in rapidly increasing food production in the developing countries. To this end, urgent and necessary changes in the pattern of world food production should be introduced and trade policy measures should be implemented, in order to obtain a notable increase in agricultural production and the export earnings of developing countries.

The suggested aspects of a food programme are proposed with a view to bringing about a rapid increase in food production in developing countries.

Bilateral and multilateral food aid of developed countries should be such as to avoid causing undue fluctuations in market prices or the disruption of commercial markets for exports of interest to exporting developing countries;

All countries should subscribe to the International Undertaking on World Food Security to build up and maintain world food-grain reserves....Intensive work should be continued on a priority basis in the World Food Council....in order to determine....the size of the required reserve.* Developed countries should assist developing

---

* A World Food Council proposal suggests a reserve of 30 million tons of rice and wheat.

countries....build up and maintain their agreed shares of such reserves. Pending the establishment of the world food-grain reserve, developed countries and developing countries in a position to do so should earmark stocks and/or funds to be placed at the disposal of the World Food Programme....The aim should be a target of not less than 500,000 tons;

Members of the General Assembly reaffirmed their full support for the resolutions of the World Food Conference and called upon the World Food Council to monitor the implementation of the provisions dealing with food and agriculture in this resolution;

Developed countries, and developing countries in a position to do so, should substantially increase the volume of assistance to developing countries for agriculture and food production, and that developed countries should effectively facilitate access to their markets for food and agricultural products of export interest to developing countries;

Developing countries should accord high priority to agricultural and fisheries development....and adopt policies which give adequate incentive to agricultural producers. States should promote inter-action between expansion of food production and socio-economic reforms, with a view to achieving an integrated rural development....Post-harvest food losses in developing countries should be reduced by at least 50 per cent by 1985. All countries and competent international organizations should cooperate financially and technically to achieve this objective. Particular attention should be given to improvements in the systems of distribution of food-stuffs;

Developing countries having the potential for most rapid and efficient increase of food production.... especially the countries with food deficits should be quickly identified to assist developed countries and the competent international organizations to concen-trate resources for the rapid increase of agricultural production in the developing countries.

Developed countries should adopt policies aimed at ensuring a stable supply and sufficient quantity of fertilizers and other production inputs to developing countries at reasonable prices and provide assistance to promote the efficiency of developing countries' fertilizer and agriculture input industries. Advantage should be taken of the mechanism provided by the International Fertilizer Supply Scheme;

Developed countries and developing countries in a position to do so should pledge, on a voluntary basis, substantial contributions to the proposed International Fund for Agricultural Development so as to enable it to come into being by the end of 1975, with initial resources of SDR 1,000 million;

Developed countries should support the expansion of work of the existing international agricultural research centres....strengthen their links with these....centres and with the national agricultural research centres in developing countries. Research and technological assistance should be co-ordinated and financed with respect to the improvement of the productivity and competitiveness with synthetics of non-food agricultural and forestry products;

All countries should accept both the principle of a minimum food aid target* and the concept of forward planning of food aid....They should also accept the principle that food aid should be channelled on the basis of objective assessment of requirements in the recipient countries....All countries are urged to participate in the Global Information and Early Warning System on Food and Agriculture;

Developed countries should increase the grant component of food aid, ... and should accept multilateral channeling of these resources at an expanding rate. In providing food grains and financing on soft terms to developing countries due account should be taken of the interests of the food-exporting developing countries, ensuring that wherever possible such assistance includes purchases of food from the food-exporting developing countries.

The proposed world food programme is thus composed of many parts. The chief goal of the programme is to increase agricultural production in developing countries. This is necessary not only to reduce food imports, but also to generate new or increased earnings from the sale of agricultural products. The various aspects of the programme come under four general headings and several issues under each.

Improved Production, Storage, and Distribution of Agricultural Inputs and Outputs.

better exploitation of the land;

curtailing damage through desertification, salination, insects, and other natural phenomenon;

protection of natural resources and food resources from damage and deterioration (pollution);

measures to increase food production and storage facilities, including better interaction between food production and socio-economic reforms;

reduction of post-harvest losses;

improved systems of distribution of food stuffs;

---

* A target of 10 million tons of food grains was specified for the 1975-76 season.

provision of an adequate supply of fertilizer and other agricultural inputs at affordable prices;

identification of those countries having the potential for the most rapid and efficient increases in food production;

increased contributions to establish the International Fund for Agriculture Development.

Food Aid

the ability and necessity to import food without undue strain on balance of payments;

food aid (bilateral and multilateral)without harming developing country food exporters;

increased grant component of food aid and acceptance of the multilateral channeling of these resources at an expanding rate;

adoption of the principles of a minimum food aid target and of forward planning of food aid.

Policies to Improve Market Competitiveness

the elimination of tariffs on food and other agricultural products from the developing countries;

expansion of international and national agriculture research centres coordinated to improve productivity and competitiveness with synthetics.

Food Security

the building up of a world food-grain reserve as part of a programme for World Food Security;

a Global Information and Early Warning System on food and agriculture.

8.2 Development and specification of the NIEO objective at the United Nations 1974-78*

Development and International Economic Cooperation, the resolution of the Seventh Special Session (September 1975) expressed full support for the

---

* The documentation on this NIEO issue area is particularly vast; hence this summary will be quite selective in order to avoid being overly repititious. This applies in particular to documents which are restatements of the goals enumerated above.

resolutions of the World Food Conference in Rome, 5-16 November 1974.
These resolutions constitute the chronologically first elaboration of the NIEO
objective concerning the development of an international food programme.
They, together with some relevant documents of the General Assembly, the
Food and Agriculture Organization, and the World Food Council, were
summarized by the FAO (A/AC.191/8, 21 April 1978), and the immediately
pertinent portions of these summaries are reproduced below.

Objectives and Strategies of Food Production

FAO in consultation with UNDP and other organizations to
formulate programmes and projects for additional food production
and indicate ways and means for carrying them out.
World Bank, regional banks, UNDP, FAO, UNIDO and other
international agencies to substantially increase their assistance for
agriculture and fisheries, giving priority to progammes for poorest
groups of population.

Priorities for Agriculture and Rural Development

UNDP, IBRD, FAO and other international and bilateral agencies
to review their criteria for financial, technical and other assistance
for integrated rural development; to give greater importance to
social criteria so as to implement broader and longer-range
programmes of rural development; and if necessary improve their
technical and administrative capacity for implementing these
programmes.
Governments, UNDP and the other international and bilateral
agencies to co-operate in accelerating the planning and implementation of integrated rural development programmes and to devote
greatly expanded resources to these activities.
FAO and other United Nations organizations concerned to
collect, evaluate and disseminate the results and experience from
past and ongoing rural development programmes, to determine the
suitability of these programmes in bringing about both expanding
agricultural production and social integration.

Fertilizers

International organizations and bilateral aid agencies significantly intensify their effort to meet the needs of developing countries,
particularly the least developed and those most seriously affected by
economic crisis, through increased material and financial support to
the International Fertilizer Supply Scheme and by stepping up
bilateral efforts, so as to bridge the gap in supply as estimated by
the Scheme from time to time. The needs of MSA countries for
fertilizer nutrients in 1975/76 were estimated at 1 million tons.

FAO, UNDP and World Bank to jointly organize a programme to assist developing countries to improve the efficiency of their fertilizer plant operations.

International institutions, developed countries and others in a position to do so to provide financial assistance, technical assistance, technology and equipment on favourable terms, to build required additional fertilizer production capacities in appropriate developing countries, and to assist all developing countries with storage facilities, distribution services and other related infrastructures.

FAO in collaboration with other international organizations, such as UNIDO and the World Bank, and Governments to undertake analysis of long-term fertilizer supply and demand aimed at ensuring adequate supply at stable and reasonable prices in order to provide the elements of a world fertilizer policy.

Intensification of international efforts in the transfer of technical knowledge, particularly on the intermediate level, in order to increase production and to make more effective use of fertilizers, including the improvement of extension services and training of farmers in all countries.

Food and Agriculture Research, Extension and Training

FAO undertake the systematic collection, and dissemination of data on current research.

Agricultural Research, co-sponsored by FAO, UNDP and the World Bank, be substantially enlarged to enable it to augment the number and scope of international and regional research programmes in and for the developing countries.

FAO, UNDP and the World Bank to consider establishing a co-ordinated programme for the improvement of extension systems.

Policies and Programmes to Improve Nutrition

FAO, in cooperation with WHO, UNICEF, WFP, IBRD, UNDP and UNESCO, assisted by PAG to prepare a project proposal for assisting Governments to develop intersectoral food and nutrition plans.

The international agencies, non-governmental agencies and countries which are in a position to provide funds and foods for this purpose, should provide assistance to Governments who will request such aid in order to introduce in the period 1975-1976, emergency programmes for supplementary feeding of a substantial number of the malnourished children with due attention to basic health and other essential services for the welfare of all children at risk.

FAO, in association with other international and non-governmental organizations concerned, to undertake an inventory of vegetable food resources other than cereals, such as roots, tubers, legumes, vegetables and fruits, including those from unconventional sources, and to study the possibility of increasing their production and consumption, particularly in countries where malnutrition prevails.

Governments to take action to strengthen and modernize consumer education services, food legislation and food control programmes and the relevant aspects of marketing practices, aiming at the protection of the consumer (avoiding false and misleading information from mass-media and commercial fraud) and to increase their support of the Codex Alimentarius Commission.

The joint FAO/WHO food contamination monitoring programme, in cooperation with UNEP, to be further developed in order to provide early information to the national authorities for appropriate action.

A global nutrition surveillance system to be established by FAO, WHO and UNICEF to monitor the food and nutrition conditions of the disadvantaged groups of the population at risk, and to provide a method of rapid and permanent assessment of all factors which influence food consumption pattern and nutritional status.

Governments to consider establishing facilities and funds for applied nutrition research related to economic, cultural, social and medical aspects of production, processing, preservation, storage, distribution and utilization of food, and FAO, WHO and UNICEF to arrange for an internationally coordinated programme in applied nutritional research including establishing priorities, identifying appropriate research centres and generating the necessary funding.

World Soil Charter and Land Capabiity Assessment

Food and Agriculture Organization of the United Nations to select the most appropriate ways and means to establish a World Soil Charter.

FAO, UNESCO and UNEP, in accordance with WMO, and other competent international organizations, and in consultation with Governments concerned, to prepare without delay an assessment of the lands that can still be brought into cultivation, taking proper account of forestry for the protection of catchment areas of land required for alternative uses.

Scientific Water Management: Irrigation, Drainage and Flood Control

International institutions and bilateral and multilateral aid agencies to provide substantially increased external assistance to enable the developing countries to undertake rapidly urgent action on technical measures which Governments and international agencies such as FAO and WMO were requested to take.

Pesticides

FAO in cooperation with UNEP, WHO and UNIDO to convene an ad hoc consultation, including member Governments and industry, to recommend ways and means to give effect to the intentions of the resolution on pesticides.

Programme for the Control of African Animal Trypanosomiasis

FAO in cooperation with the Governments of the countries concerned, interested international organizations and specialized research institutes and with the support of bilateral and multilateral assistance agencies to launch as a matter of urgency a long-term programme for the control of African animal trypanosomiasis as a project of high priority.

FAO to take immediately the necessary steps to mobilize the funds and services required for the programme.

Immediate establishment of a small coordinating unit at FAO headquarters to start the first phase of the programme devoted to training, pilot field control projects and applied research, in preparation for future large-scale operations.

International Fund for Agricultural Development

An International Fund for Agricultural Development should be established immediately to finance agricultural development projects primarily for food production in the developing countries.

All developed countries and all those developing countries that are in a position to contribute to this Fund should do so on a voluntary basis.

The disbursements from the Fund should be carried out through existing international and/or regional institutions in accordance with the regulations and criteria to be established by the Governing Boards.

The Secretary-General of the United Nations to convene urgently a meeting of all interested countries and institutions to work out the details, including the size of, and commitments to, the Fund.

Reduction of Military Expenditures for the
Purpose of Increasing Food Production

States to take measures for the most rapid implementation of resolutions pertaining to reduction of military expenditures on behalf of development, and to allocate a growing proportion of the sums so released to the financing of food production in developing countries and the establishment of reserves to deal with emergency cases.

Food Aid to Victims of Colonial Wars in Africa

The Director-General of FAO and the Executive Director of WFP to take immediate action to intensify food aid to the populations of Angola, Cape Verde, Guinea Bissau, Mozambique, Principe and Sao Tome.

The Secretary-General of the United Nations and all the executive heads of organizations within the United Nations system to take all necessary measures to assist the national liberation movements or the Governments of these countries to formulate a comprehensive plan of national reconstruction.

Global Information and Early Warning System on Food and Agriculture

A Global Information and Early Warning System on Food and Agriculture to be established and FAO, as the most appropriate organization, to operate and supervise the System.

FAO, in co-operation with other concerned international organizations, particularly the International Wheat Council, to formulate arrangements necessary for the establishment of the System, and submit them for final approval by Governments participating in the System.

All Governments to participate in the System and extend full cooperation, on a voluntary and regular basis, by furnishing as much current information and forecasts as possible, initially on basic food products, including in particular, wheat, rice, coarse grains, soybeans, and livestock products and, to the extent practicable, other important food products and other relevant aspects.

Governments to take steps to amplify and improve their data collection and dissemination services in these fields; and FAO, WMO, WHO, the Intergovernmental Bureau for Information and other multilateral and bilateral sources urgently to assist interested Governments with technical and financial assistance, and coordinate this action with that of the World Food Council.

Information thus collected to be fully analysed and disseminated periodically to all participating Governments, and for their exclusive use; it being understood that, where requested, certain information provided by Governments would be disseminated in aggregate form particularly in order to avoid unfavourable market repercussions.

World Meterological Organization, in co-operation with FAO (a) to provide regular assessments of current and recent weather on the basis of information presently assembled through the World Weather Watch; (b) to expand and establish joint research projects to investigate weather/crop relationships; (c) to strengthen present global weather monitoring systems at national and regional levels; and (d) to encourage investigations on assessment of probability of adverse weather conditions occuring in various agricultural areas, and on a better understanding of causes of climatic variations.

International Undertaking on Food Security

All countries concerned to adopt objectives and main elements of the International Undertaking on World Food Security.

Early completion by FAO bodies of operational and other practical arrangements required for implementation of the proposed international undertaking, including examination of practical economic and administrative problems involved.

Governments and concerned international and regional organizations to provide necessary technical, financial and food assistance in the form of grants or on specially favourable terms to develop and implement appropriate national food stocks policies in developing countries.

An Improved Policy for Food Aid

Need for continuity of a minimum level of food aid in physical terms, in order to insulate food aid programmes from the effects of excessive fluctuations in production and prices, and all donor countries, traditional and potential, to make all efforts to provide commodities and/or financial assistance that will ensure in physical terms at least 10 million tons of grains as food aid a year starting from 1975 and also adequate quantities of other food commodities, to ensure that the minimum target is reached by 1977/78.

All donor countries to accept and implement the concept of forward planning of food aid, and those which have not yet done so should make every effort to ensure as soon as possible the forward planning of food aid supplies.

Interested cereals-exporting and importing countries as well as current and potential financial contributions to meet as soon as possible to take cognizance of the needs and to consider ways and means to increase food availability and financing facilities during 1975 and 1976 for the affected developing countries and, in particular, for those most seriously affected by the current food problem.

All donor countries to (a) channel a more significant proportion of food aid through the World Food Programme, (b) consider increasing progressively the grant component in their bilateral food aid programmes, (c) consider contributing part of any food aid repayments for supplementary nutrition programmes and emergency relief, (d) provide, as appropriate, additional cash resources to food aid programmes for commodity purchases from developing countries to the maximum extent possible.

Intergovernmental Committee of the World Food Programme, reconstituted as recommended, to be entrusted with the task of formulating proposals for more effective co-ordination of multi-lateral, bilateral and non-governmental food aid programmes and of co-ordinating emergency food aid.

International guidelines for emergency stocks to be developed as a part of the proposed undertaking to provide for an effective coordination of emergency stocks and to ensure that food relief reaches the neediest and most vulnerable groups.

International Emergency Food Reserve

Pending establishment of world food grain reserve, developed countries and developing countries in a position to do so should earmark stocks and/or funds to be placed at the disposal of the World Food Programme as an emergency reserve to strengthen capacity of the programme to deal with crisis situations in developing countries. The aim should be a target of not less than 500,000 tons.

International Trade, Stabilization and Agricultural Adjustment

Governments to devise in the appropriate organizations effective steps for dealing with the problem of stabilizing world markets particularly for food-stuffs and specially through international arrangements aimed, *inter alia*, at increasing food production, particularly in developing countries.

UNCTAD to intensify its efforts in considering new approaches to international commodity problems and policies and in elaborating further proposals for an overall integrated programme for commodities.

Responsible international bodies to give highest possible priority to speed up consultations and negotiations within agreed time-limits for reaching agreements on reduction or elimination of barriers and restrictions in international trade and enabling substantially improved access of agricultural and food products of developing countries to the markets of developed countries.

FAO to take full account of discussions and decisions of the World Food Conference in formulating and implementing the proposed strategy of international agricultural adjustment.

Governments of developed countries and international organizations concerned to increase the field assistance to developing countries in export promotion activities and mechanisms, and in training of agricultural marketing and trade personnel taking due account of the diversification process and development needs.

Countries and organizations concerned to devote special

attention to the solution of the problems facing developing countries in the matter of transportation of food-stuffs.

Developed countries and the international organizations concerned to maintain and expand their support for economic co-operation among developing countries.

World Food Programme and other international organizations concerned to give priority to use of cash resources available for multilateral or bilateral food aid for purchases in developing countries at competitive world market prices and terms.

International organizations concerned....to give the highest possible priority and the most favourable terms to the least developed, land-locked and island developing countries and to developing countries most seriously affected by economic crises.

The FAO Conference held its 18th session 8-27 November 1975. As summarized by the FAO (op.cit.) the Conference decided that with reference to agriculture adjustment, increased and improved food aid, and the integration of women in rural development,

> FAO should review from an agricultural standpoint the relationship between prices of agricultural products and other commodities and industrial products, in particular how to achieve greater price stability and improved access to agricultural commodities markets by exports of developing countries.

> Donor countries which provide food aid on a credit basis should increase the element of concessionality in their aid and substantially enlarge the proportion of food aid given on a grant basis, especially to developing countries in serious economic difficulties.

> All Member States of the United Nations and its specialized agencies to support measures ensuring that women share in the benefits of development in the rural sector, particularly through the recognition of their full legal equality and the adoption of measures implementing such equality.

In April 1976 the World Food Council set forth specific proposals with respect to an international system of food security (WFC/22, 12 April 1976). These include the following:

> Reaffirm the decision of the General Assembly to create an International Reserve for Emergencies (IRE) with an initial target of 500,000 tons /.../

> Urge all donor countries to earmark a part of their national stocks as "Reserves for Emergencies and Food Aid," for use in providing emergency relief, food aid and in special cases, the uncovered commercial import requirements of most seriously affected developing countries...The normal size of such a reserve at the beginning of each year should preferably be 25 per cent above the annual food aid programme of the country concerned.

Accept, in principle, the creation of a Food Security Reserve of 15 to 20 million tons to protect the world against well defined exigencies and to prevent abnormal fluctuations in grain prices, and urge governments to work out operational and other arrangements for such a reserve. /.../

The WFC noted that "if current international efforts to conclude international grain arrangements with stock and price provisions are successful, the developing countries would have a certain measure of food security." In the absence of such arrangements, however, the developing countries would have to consider some alternative approaches to safeguard their economies and populations from sudden and unexpected food shortages.

The WFC offered as one suggestion a partial pooling of food reserves by developing countries in an "International Food Reserve for Developing Countries."

Each developing country participating in the Reserve, might contribute in kind or in cash, a premium, for instance one percent of its annual consumption of grains, to the Reserve for a period of three years.

The contribution of each country to the Reserve will be physically located in that country and will constitute its "basic quota," which it can draw at any time in consultation with the Reserve, for replenishment within the specified period.

Each participating country will acquire a preferential right to buy grain from the Reserve on a commercial basis and in very exceptional cases of well defined national contingencies (large crop failures), or international crises (large price increases). This right, called the "supplementary quota" will not normally exceed two-times the basic quota of each country and would be dependent on the total quantities available in relation to total demand on the Reserve. Any advance indication by a member country to use its "supplementary quota" facility will enable the Reserve to acquire advance options on certain quantities in the market, probably giving preference to developing exporting countries.

In case a member country wishes to make a larger contribution to the Reserve in cash or kind, it could do so, but this would not extend its supplementary quota beyond 6 per cent of its annual consumption.

The Reserve will provide grains only to developing member countries but may accept voluntary contributions in cash or kind from interested developed countries.

Further, the Executive Director of the World Food Council drew up a report on increasing food production in developing countries (WFC/20, 14 April 1976). He offered the following proposals and recommendations:

To formulate agreed criteria for determining the nature and magnitude of the food problem facing different countries or groups of countries and to agree as a first step to the identification of a group of "Food Priority countries" /.../

To recommend that special attention be paid to the food problems of the "Food Priority countries" as so far identified through such measures as: early determination of requirements of internal and external resources, policy and other constraints that have to be overcome, and the most effective means of fully utilizing the human and physical resources of these countries.

To call upon bilateral and multilateral donors to further expand their external assistance to agriculture, particularly to food production so that these resources can reach an annual average of $7-8 billion (in constant 1974 prices) during 1976-80 and to improve considerably the terms of such assistance by increasing the proportion of concessional assistance from 66 percent in 1974 to at least 75 percent by 1980.

To emphasize the need for improved lending criteria to direct the flow of resources to specific priorities, needs and objectives and to ensure inter alia that these resources reach the poorest segments of populations in developing countries.

To support the efforts of FAO, World Bank, Regional Banks and the CGFPI* and other Regional Consultative Groups to engage in more intensive evaluations of the policy and other constraints on food production in interested countries and formulate comprehensive proposals to overcome them in the shortest possible time and direct the World Food Council secretariat to prepare, in consultation with those agencies, a report on the progress of these consultations for the third session of the Council.

To request the FAO and other agencies concerned, to develop the elements of a practical and realistic strategy for attaining the proposed food production targets over the next decade and direct the World Food Council secretariat to prepare, in consultation with these agencies, a report on the progress of these activities for the third session of the Council.

Other objectives of food aid policies and programmes were set forth by the Executive Director (WFC/21,22 April 1976) as follows,

To direct future food aid programmes towards three important spheres:

---

* Consultative Group on Food Production and Investment in Developing Countries.

(i) providing emergency relief to counteract famines or acute food shortages arising from adverse natural conditions or other emergencies;

(ii) combating hunger and malnutrition through direct subsidized distribution of food to vulnerable groups;

(iii) promoting economic development through labour-intensive development projects (including food-for-work projects) and by easing constraints of budgetary and foreign exchange resources hampering food imports by developing countries;

To ensure a reasonable degree of continuity in food aid supplies from year to year through the acceptance and implementation of the concept of forward planning of food aid, and by securing assurance of a necessary minimum level of food aid in physical terms;

To provide food aid in a manner that would not interfere with the development objectives of developing countries, and would avoid disincentive effects on food production in recipient countries and on trade in food products of interest to food exporting developing countries.

A report by the Economic Commission for Latin America (E/CEPAL/1025, 30 March 1977) suggested that the preparation and wider use of proteins from non-conventional sources (single-cell proteins derived from hydrocarbons) should be given due consideration by developing countries in cooperation with UNIDO, FAO and WHO, and with developed countries possessing the know-how for such processes.

The Executive Director of the World Food Council offered some suggestions with respect to food trade (WFC/42, 30 March 1977). His report advocated special measures, such as access agreements and guarantees of stability and market security, to overcome protective policies in the importation of food products by developed countries from developing countries. He further emphasized that international agreements are needed to develop more precise and binding rules for the conduct of food trade and suggested that developing countries should be provided with limited but gradually increasing access to developed country markets for specific food products.

The third session of the World Food Council (A/32/19 -Supplement No. 19, 20-24 June 1977) recommended that international research institutes should assist the seed development programmes of developing countries by expanding their research activities for the development of high-yielding, early-maturing seed varieties suitable for rain-fed, dry land, irrigated, and other conditions.

In June 1976 the World Food Council submitted several recommendations to the relevant bodies and agencies of the United Nations and the Governments of Member States for consideration (A/31/19/ - Supplement No. 19, 14-17 June 1976). With regard to increasing food production in developing countries, the Council recommended that food production in 'food priority countries' (criteria and guidelines for determining which countries should be so designated is currently under discussion) should be accelerated by at least 4 per cent a year. To achieve this annual increase in agricultural production, bilateral donors and multilateral agencies should continue to expand their assistance and improve the terms of their assistance so that concessional assistance reaches an average of 75 per cent by 1980.

The following recommendations concern food aid targets and policies:

Reaffirm that all donor countries accept and implement the concept of forward planning for food;

Recommend that food aid should continue to be an integral part of a new grains agreement;

Emphasize that increasing amounts of food aid should be channelled through the World Food Programme;

Stress the need to supply food aid in such a way as not to interfere with the development objectives of developing countries, avoiding in particular any effect which would discourage food production in recipient countries.

With respect to an international system of food security, the Council accepted in principle (with one delegation reserving its position on the matter) "the concept of a food security reserve to protect the world against well defined exigencies and to prevent abnormal fluctuations in grain prices..."

With reference to international food reserves, the WFC stated:

these reserves should operate under rules which ensure fair and just prices to consumers and remunerative prices to producers to encorage continued production. The size and cost-sharing formula between exporting and importing countries, ...should be determined through negotiations.

The Council further urged that immediate steps should be taken by governments and appropriate international agencies to determine a minimum package of agricultural inputs in support of the expanded programmes of food priority countries to achieve the targeted minimum annual growth rate of 4 per cent. The minimum package of inputs should include fertilizers, pesticides, high-yielding varieties of seeds which are pest and disease resistant, improved breeds of livestock, credit to small farmers, irrigation equipment and selective and appropriate implements for mechanization.

8.3 Contributions of major international bodies

The final communique of the Commonwealth Heads of Government meeting at Jamaica (May 1975) affirmed that the problems of rural development and food production should be attacked in an integrated manner and should receive high priority from individual governments and aid agencies. The need for aid-providing agencies to adopt their practices and programmes to - meet the special needs of food production and rural development was emphasized. The Heads of Governments endorsed the proposal to establish a food production and rural development division within the secretariat, and welcomed efforts, in the Commonwealth and elsewhere, to provide adequate supplies of fertilizer at reduced costs and called for similar efforts with respect to farm machinery, feed stuffs and other agricultural inputs.

Other international bodies, including the CIEC at its June 1977 meeting, discussed, reiterated and affirmed several of the above-enumerated aspects of an international food programme, but did not add basically new elements to it.

WORLD ECONOMY ISSUE 9

Adjusting the Economic Policies of Developed
Countries To Facilitate The Expansion And Diversification
Of The Exports Of Developing Countries

9.1   The original formulation of the NIEO objective at the United Nations

A number of objectives advanced under the aegis of the NIEO, especially in the areas of trade and industrialization, presuppose appropriate adjustments in the economic policies of the developed countries. In view of this, the Programme of Action on the Establishment of a New International Economic Order (May 1974) called for "appropriate adjustments in (the developed countries') economies" to observe the principles of non-reciprocity and preferential treatment of developing countries in multilateral trade negotiations -- so as to achieve a substantial increase in their foreign exchange earnings, diversification of their exports and acceleration of the rate of their economic growth. Such adjustments are also needed to "provide a fair and reasonable opportunity to developing countries to share in the growth of the market" and thus support the creation of a "rational, just and equitable international division of labour."

Already the International Development Strategy for the Second United Nations Development Decade (October 1970) called for developed countries to "undertake an objective and critical examination of their present policies and make appropriate changes in such policies so as to faciiitate the expansion and diversification of imports from developing countries." Developed countries should adopt "measures and where possible...a programme early in the Decade for assisting the adaptation and adjustmeant of industries and workers in situations where they are adversely affected by increased imports of manufactures and semi-manufactures from developing countries."

9.2 Specification and development of the NIEO objective at the United Nations 1974-78

At UNCTAD IV a resolution of 30 May 1976, under the heading "Adjustment Assistance Measures," suggests that:

> Developed countries should facilitate the development of new policies and strengthen existing policies that would encourage domestic factors of production to move progressively from the lines of production which are less competitive internationally, especially where the long-term comparative advantage lies in favour of developing countries, thus providing, inter alia, larger export possibilities for the developing countries and contributing to the attainment of their development objectives. The development and strengthening of such policies would encourage the redeployment of the industries of the developed countries which are less competitive internationally to developing countries, thus leading to structural adjustments in the former countries and a higher degree of utilization of natural and human resources in the latter. Such policies may take into account the economic structure and the economic, social and security objectives of the developed countries and the need for such industries to move into more viable lines of production or into other sectors of the economy.

The UNCTAD IV resolution on Manufactures and Semi-manufactures (31 May 1976) notes that "access to markets of developed countries for manufactures and semi-manufactures of developing countries should be improved, particularly in the following areas: (A) Generalized system of preferences, (B) Tariff reclassification, (C) Non-tariff measures, and (D) Adjustment assistance measures. Industrial development and co-operation should be promoted by the international community through concerted measures at the national, subregional, regional, interregional, and inter-national levels with a view to benefiting the economies of the developing countries." The measures should be achieved through long-term industriali-zation goals, plans and strategies in favour of developing countries.

The Third Biennial Report and Appraisal of Progress in the Implemen-tation of the International Development Strategy (E/ECWA/49, March 1977) notes that "among the obstacles that have hindered the process of exports diversificiation, ... the narrowness of the industrial production base and the inward-looking orientation that the development of manufacturing industrial (has taken) are the most important.

The Report of the Intergovernmental Group of Experts on Trade Opportunities (TD/B/680, November 1977) records that "the expert of a developed market-economy country, speaking on behalf of the participating countries members of Group B, stated that these countries were prepared to collaborate constructively in the work of the Intergovernmental Group, sharing their practical experience in trade and economic relations with the

CMEA member countries." He stressed the need for a comprehensive integrated approach to strengthen the developng countries' economic structures and capacities. He also outlined the main features of tripartite industrial co-operation, suggesting that these arrangements tended to be more successful when the developing country concerned was able to participate as an equal partner.

Many United Nations bodies and agencies dealt with the issue of adjustments in the economic policies of developed countries in view of improving the exports of developing countries under the rubric of aid and assistance, and international trade issues.* The principal objectives that emerge from these considerations are, to assure by the developed countries:

access to markets for manufactures and semi-manufactures from developing countries;

reduction and eventual elimination of tariff and non-tariff barriers;

extension of preferential treatment to developing countries on a non-reciprocal and non-discriminatory basis;

moving domestic lines of production into areas where the long-term comparative advantage is in favour of developing countries;

consideration of specific issues deemed important by the developing countries;

measures to meet ODA targets and other assistance levels in conformity with United Nations resolutions and principles.

In recent years the question of appropriate adjustments in developed countries was frequently tied to the discussion of eliminating protectionist measures having negative impact on the diversification and growth of the exports of developing countries. The spread of protectionism was discussed by GATT in "International Trade 1976/77" (Geneva, 1977). The GATT document noted that while during 1973-76 industrial production in developed countries was stagnating, industrial capacity, production and exports continued to grow in the developing countries. This situation made for the rise of demands for protection in the developed countries.

The GATT report commented:

A willingness on the part of so many governments to give effect to these demands is more difficult to understand ... since in so doing they have become involved in contradictions between their stated policy objectives and actual policy conduct; /.../

The spread of protectionist pressures may well prove to be the most important current development in international economic policies, for it has reached a point at which the continued existence of an international order based on agreed and observed rules may be said to be open to question; /.../

---

* Cf. World Economy Issues 1 through 8, above

Without a basic change in the present trend of international trade policy - that is, without a clear return to more liberal trade practices, accompanied by the necessary adjustment measures - the stage would appear to be set for a further cumulation of economic difficulties.

9.3   Contributions of major international bodies, 1974-78

Concern with appropriate adjustments in the economies of developed countries in general was voiced in a number of major international fora, including the Dakar Conference on Raw Materials (February 1975), the Manila Declaration and Programme of Action (February 1976), the report of the Commonwealth Experts Group (March 1977) and the Conference on International Economic Co-Operation (June 1977). (The recommendations of these fora are listed under the specific issues 1 through 8, above.)

WORLD ECONOMY ISSUE 10

Improving And Intensifying Trade Relations Between
Countries Having Different Social And Economic Systems

The original documents stating the objectives of the NIEO do not make special reference to the above issue, but consider it under the general heading of trade relations between developed and developing countries. In subsequent fora the distinction between developed market economies and socialist countries, in reference to their trade and other relationships to developing countries, was increasingly introduced. The distinction is due not only to marked differences in the net flows between socialist and developing countries compared to those between developed market economies and developing countries, but also to the desire of socialist countries (in this context, this refers to the CMEA countries of Eastern Europe) to be considered independently of other developed countries in the discussion of the new international economic order. Further details on this are given in Part II, under the corresponding heading.)

10.1&2   Formulation and development of the NIEO objective in the United Nations 1974-78

Before UNCTAD IV, where the major formulation of the relevant NIEO objective was achieved, three fora dealt with the issue in specific terms. At the first (ID/CONF.3/10, November 1974), the UNCTAD Secretariat was given the task to undertake studies concerning measures for the expansion of trade between developing countries and the centrally planned economies of Eastern Europe (UNCTAD Resolution 76 (III)). Accordingly, the Secretariat prepared a preliminary factual study on import regimes in selected centrally planned economies. In light of this study and later consultations between countries having different economic and social systems, it was generally recognized that they contributed greatly to a better understanding of the persisting problems and to the possibilities of finding mutually advantageous solutions to these problems, including in particular facilitating the access of developing countries' manufactures and semi-manufactures to the centrally planned economies of Eastern Europe. The second conference was TD/B/539 of UNCTAD on Trade Expansion, Economic Co-operation, and Regional Integration Among Developing Countries held in January 1975. Paragraph 30 specifies recommendations made by experts on trade relations between countries having different economic and social systems. The first group of recommendations is concerned with increasing the volume of studies and reports with a view to inceasing mutual understanding as a basis for some form of linkage or multilateral collaboration. The second and third group of recommendations is concerned with operative measures, such as bettering financial transaction terms, transfer of technology, and the possibility of joint research efforts.

The third and last conference preceding UNCTAD IV was ID/CONF.3/19 on Industry and Trade in the Process of Development (Secretariat of UNCTAD and UNIDO) in February 1975. The conference noted that "despite the considerable increase in the exports of manfactures from the developing countries to the centrally planned economies of Eastern Europe in recent years, these exports are still at a low level whether measured in terms of absolute value, as a percentage of the total imports of manufactures by the centrally planned economies, as a percentage of GDP, or as a percentage of industrial production." The conference stressed the fact that "there is considerable potential for the expansion of exports of manufactures from the developing countries to the centrally planned economies."

At UNCTAD IV, Resolution 95 (31 May 1976) spelled out in detail the objectives concerning trade relations among countries having different economic and social systems. The resolution's recommendations include, inter alia, the following measures concerning relations between the socialist countries of Eastern Europe and the developing countries:

Extend the practice where found mutually beneficial, of concluding medium-term and long-term agreements on trade, economic, scientific and tchnical cooperation;

Extend the practice of concluding medium-term and long-term co-operation programmes in specific areas of trade, industry, science and technology;

Make wider use of the practice of concluding compensatory agreements aimed at developing the export sectors in the developing countries continue where appropriate, to make provision in agreements and contracts for deliveries against credits granted and also for the purchase, on commercial terms, of the products of enterprises set up with the assistance of the socialist countries of Eastern Europe;

Improve, jointly with their partners, the co-operation mechanism, by expanding, where appropriate, the functions of bilatral intergovernmental commissions in the field of economic, scientific and technical co-operation, and by increasing the volume and improving the quality of economic and corresponding administrative information;

The socialist countries are asked to:

Widen the areas of economic co-operation through the identification and adoption of measures to promote an increase of exchanges with developing countries without prejudice to previously contracted commitments;

Progressively reduce, and whenever possible eliminate, their tariff barriers on imports from developing countries, and this will continue to be on the basis of non-reciprocity and non-discrimination;

Further implement other, non-tariff measures of a preferential character on a non-reciprocal and non-discriminatory basis in accordance with the modalities of their foreign trade system

Expand and improve their schemes of generalized preferences with respect to the products of vital importance for developing countries and the list of beneficiary developing countries /.../

Give due consideration to the trade needs of developing countries when their national economic development plans are being formulated and later co-ordinated within the Council for Mutual Economic Assistance (CMEA) particularly by making appropriate provisions in their plans for an increasing volume of imports from the developing countries, especially in processed and semi-processed forms;

Continue to intensify policies and measures aimed at increasing their imports from developing countraies;

In order to facilitate their trade with developing countries:

Take specific measures so that products imported from developing countries are not re-exported to third countries, unless it is with the express agreement of the developing country concerned;

Seek, together with the developing countries, additional possibilities for the expansion of their mutual trade, while taking into account the interests of the developing countries to increase their exports to the markets of the socialist countries of Eastern Europe. To this end, these flows of trade should not necessarily and always be conducted on the basis of equivalent volumes of exports and imports;

Cover trade with interested developing countries, upon their request, by appropriate payments arrangements and, if necessary upon request, examine provisions for the convertibility of the surplus balances of developing countries into convertible currencies;

Expand the present CMEA payments arrangements in transferable roubles so as to take into account the trade needs of the developing countries; in the case of conclusion of trade agreements between developing countries and CMEA member countries in transferable roubles, the International Bank for Economic Co-operation will aid the developing countries to utilize the surplus, using the positive balance with one CMEA member country for settling accounts with another;

Take steps to:

Provide adequate opportunity to developing countries to participate in the realization of common projects in third countries;

Where appropriate, carry out, on considerations of the international division of labour with the developing countries on a long-term, stable basis, structural changes in favour of developing countries on mutually acceptable conditions in those branches of their national economy in which the comparative advantages lie with the developing countries, including those which involve processing of raw materials, by these countries;

Continue to co-operate in establishing production capacities in developing countries, as appropriate, and to focus their efforts in the sphere of economic and technical assistance to developing countries on the development of production forces according to appropriate modalities, in particular in the State sector;

Provide interested developing countries with assistance in elaborating economic development plans and programmes for various sectors, including the foreign trade sector;

Take appropriate steps to increase effectively and substantially economic and technical assistance to developing countries in order to assist them in their development efforts, and to this end:

Cooperate with interested developing countries with a view to assisting them to arrive at a comprehensive solution of major economic tasks and to join efforts in resolving these tasks, in particular in areas where complementarity in economic structures is apparent; assist interested developing countries in the development of their national resources;

Continue to co-operate with developing countries on a bilateral, as well as a multilateral basis, having regard to their particular situation, in seeking mutually acceptable solutions with regard to the volume and terms of technical and economic assistance and the accompanying credits, including questions relating to their repayment;

Examine the state of trade and economic relations with developing countries at the sixteenth session of the Trade and

Development Board and, if it proves necessary, undertake to submit to the Board at its seventeenth session concrete proposals so as to give a new impetus to these relations;

Resolution 95 (IV) asks the developing countries in turn to

Continue their efforts with a view to increasing their trade and economic co-operation with the socialist countries of Eastern Europe and to creating, for that purpose, conditions which are no worse than those normally granted to their trading partners among the developed market-economy countries;

Increase their efforts in studying the markets of the socialist countries of Eastern Europe, adapt as much as possible their export production to the latter's specific needs, and study ways of expanding purchases of goods in the socialist countries of Eastern Europe.

The Secretary-General of UNCTAD is requested, in particular, to "continue and intensify the present technical assistance activities of UNCTAD as an executing agency of the United Nations Development Programme in the fields of training and the dissemination of information on questions of economic and trade co-operation with the socialist countries of Eastern Europe, in close co-operation with the regional commissions of the United Nations."

In a Joint Statement (TD/211), the socialist countries reaffirmed their willingness to improve trade relations with the developing countries. The areas of an integrated commodities programme, the transfer of technology, manufactures and semi-manufactures, the machinery for co-operation, and monetary and financial matters are dealt with. Also, UNCTAD is requested to assist the socialist countries by "the expansion of the section of the UNCTAD Secretariat which deals with the problem of trade between countries having different systems" in particular.

In the October 1976 meeting of an intergovernmental group of experts on opportunities for trade between developing countries and CMEA countries (TD/B/620), areas for consultation on trade opportunities for the developing countries are identified in detail.

A later report of the intergovernmental group of experts for the UNCTAD Eighteenth Session (TD/B/680, October 1977) deals in detail with trade relations between countries members of CMEA and developing countries. A number of experts, in particular the spokesman for the Group of 77, considered an examination of concrete issues within the subject of important trade relations, and held that UNCTAD Resolution 95 (IV) was insufficiently specific concerning such issues. Various experts from developing countries said that their trade relations with CMEA countries had improved in recent years, but recommended that CMEA countries might:

buy more processed goods from developing countries;

increase representation and sales promotion with developing

countries;

offer capital goods, which is not the case at present;

ameliorate the situation concerning payments arrrangements.

Some experts from developing countries expressed their desire to see an increase in the availability and exchange of information concerning the experience of other developing countries co-operating with the CMEA. The experts from the countries members of the CMEA reaffirmed their countries' willingness to expand and intensify their trade and economic relations with countries having different economic and social systems, especially with developing countries, both on a bilateral and a multilateral basis. The representative of the CMEA Secretariat noted that provision was being made for the partial or complete participation of any non-CMEA member country in the implementation of the Comprehensive Programme (for Socialist Economic Integration, 1971).

A Trade and Development Board review of the present state of payments between developing countries and socialist countries of Eastern Europe (TD/B/AC.22/2 November 1977) describes a number of objectives to be achieved in the framework of UNCTAD Activities and especially through a consultative machinery. These include, in paraticular, (a) the introduction of additional flexibility in existing payments arrangements, and (b) the achievement of multilateral settling of balances emerging in trade between developing countries and the socialist countries of Eastern Europe.

10.3   Contributions of major international bodies

The Manila Declation and Programme of Action (February 1976) laid the groundwork for the work of UNCTAD IV in the area of multilateral action objectives for expanding trade and economic relation between countries having different economic and social systems. Section Eight outlines the major steps discussed in detail in UNCTAD Resolution 95 (IV) (see above).

WORLD ECONOMY ISSUE 11

Strengthening Economic and Technical Cooperation
Among Developing Countries

11.1   The original formulation of the NIEO objective at the United Nations

The Programme of Action on the Establishment of a New International Economic Order (May 1974) proposed inter alia the following measures for co-operation between developing countries:

the establishment or strengthening of economic integration at the regional and sub-regional levels;

the increase of imports from other developing countries;

preferential treatment for imports from other developing countries;

the promotion of close cooperation in the fields of finance, credit relations and monetary issues;

the promotion and establishment of effective instruments of co-operation in the fields of industry, science and technology, transport, shipping and mass communication media.

The Charter of Economic Rights and Duties of States (December 1974) reiterated the need for States to participate in sub-regional, regional and inter-regional co-operation in the pursuit of their economic and social development. According to Development and International Economic Cooperation, the resolution of the Seventh Special Session of the General Assembly (September 1975), co-operation among developing countries should include :

utilization of know-how, skills, natural resource and technology within developing countries for promotion of investments in industry, agriculture, transport and communications;

trade liberalization measures;

transfer of technology.

11.2   Specification and development of the NIEO objective at the United Nations 1974-78

The Working Group on Technical Co-operation Among Developing Countries (TCDC) , in its Report on the Third Session (DP/69, 20 May 1974) stressed the fact that developing countries were increasingly participating in one or another form of technical cooperation among themselves. However, the capacities existing in these countries and the potentialities of such co-operation are yet to be adequately perceived and utilized. The gap is particularly striking at the interregional level. Technical co-operation among developing countries should lead to:

the use of experience and capacity already existing and the development of new capacities in developing countries;

the opening of additional channels of communication among developing countries;

the promotion and strengthening iof economic integration among developing countries on as wide a geographic basis as possible;

the enhancement of the multiplier effect of technical co-operation already being provided through bilateral and multilateral channels;

the fostering of economic, scientific and technological self-reliance;

the improvement of knowledge and confidence in the capacities available in developing countries;

the co-ordination of their policies on the international transfer of technology;

the development of indigenous technology and the introduction of techniques better suited to local needs, particularly in the subsistence sectors;

the promotion, inter alia, of:

national science and technology plans;

economic and social planning;

linkage of research and development with economic growth project planning and evaluation;

utilization of human and natural resources potential;

modern management and administration;

technical, scientific and administrative manpower cadres;

accelerated professional training at different levels.

"Preliminary Notes for the Preparation of a Plan of Action on Industrialization," UNIDO Secretariat (10/B/C.3/27, October 14, 1974) reitereated the principles stated in the Programme of Action on the NIEO. Developing countries, with a view to expanding co-operation at the regional, sub-regional and inter-regional levels, should:

take further steps to promote, establish and strengthen economic integration at the regional and sub-regional levels;

give (wherever possible) preferential treatment to imports from other developing countries in order to increase such imports considerably;

promote and establish effective instruments of co-operation in the field of industry.

The basic principles on which industrial cooperation among developing countries should develop in the future were stated as follows:

a joint approach to industrial development is needed by most developing countries to help overcome the obstacles posed by the small size of each individual country's domestic market;

the benefits to be derived from specialization in manufacturing industry based on agreed plans of industrial co-operation should be sought for both, through industrial integration in subregional groups of neighbouring countries, and through schemes of industrial cooperation within wider regional groups and between countries in different regions;

in order to facilitate the participation of less developed countries, the more industrialized developing countries should make special efforts to import manufactured goods produced by the less developed countries including non-reciprocal trade preferences and to give to these countries special treatment in the industrial co-operation schemes;

developing countries, particularly the least developed countries, can and should benefit from an exchange of experience on various aspects of industrial development.

The Plan of Action should first re-emphasize the need for closer economic cooperation at the sub-regional levels. At the regional level developing countries in cooperation with UNIDO and the respective regional economic commissions should jointly prepare the regional contribution to the proposed system of consultations at the world level. The Plan of Action may also recommend the creation of instruments to foster industrial co-operation among developing countries of the region. The African Conference of Ministers, for instance, recommended the creation of multinational African enterprises where capital and inputs would come from various countries of the region. The same formula might be applied to other regions.

Industrial cooperation among developing countries was also discussed in "Industrialization of the Developing Countries: Basic Problems and Issues for Action." (UNIDO Secretariat, (ID/CONF. 3/5, 21 October, 1974). The extent of integration planning and co-operation will be dicated by:

the range of overlapping domestic objectives of participating members;

the existing and potential structural integration of economic activities.

Cooperation among developing countries should not be restricted to integration schemes alone. The common interests of developing countries cut across regional lines. In this regard, new efforts are required in the area of important industrial and raw material commodities that are of vital interest to the industrialization programmes of these countries. Increased consultations among Governments are required to insure that planning, investment decisions and financing shall be consistent with their mutual objectives.

The Latin American Conference on Industrialization (ID/CONF.3/CRP/Y Add. 1 4 December 1974) recommended the following measures to enhance cooperation among developing countries:

the expansion of trade and the promotion of co-operation in fields such as -

joint investments;

the exchange of experience in the field of science and technology, including experience in negotiations with sources of technology;

the exchange of experience regarding transnational corporations, including experience on negotiations with these;

reciprocal financing.

The establishment of institutional machinery to facilitate economic co-operation through periodic consultation, particularly in the field of industry.

The fostering of joint action to defend fair, remunerative, and stable prices for the export products of developing countries on international markets, including the establishment of producers organizations.

In a note on "Technical Co-operation Among Developing Countries" (E/AC.62/10, May 13, 1975) the Secretary-General of the United Nations pointed out that technical cooperation among developing countries has been recognized as the prime responsibility of the developing countries themselves as a part of their accelerated progress towards self-reliance. Their efforts should be supported by developing countries and the United Nations development system as a whole.

The Secretary-General of UNCTAD suggested that the potential of strengthening the links among developing countries is unlikely to be realized without a political commitment to a development strategy inspired by the concept of collective self-reliance. ("Trade Expansion, Economic Co-operation and Regional Integration Among Developing Countries." (TD/B/557, 24 June 1975). Such a strategy would require a new orientation in national policies designed to intensify commercial, technological, monetary and financial links among developing countries supported by appropriate institutional arrangement. The first element in such a policy reorientation should be based on the principle of preferential treatment by individual developing countries in their economic relations with other developing countries. A new initiative is therefore required on the part of developing countries not only to evolve a set of policies designed to expand their mutual trade, but also to create the necessary institutional and infrastructure support. Such a new initiative could be based on the negotiation of a system of preferences covering trade among developing countries, designed to promote existing and new patterns of specialization. Such a preferential system, to be fully effective, would have to cover both tariff and non-tariff preferences, and be extended to primary commodities as well as manufactured goods and to services such as banking, shipping and insurance facilities.

Provisions for economic cooperation among developing countries were set forth in UNCTAD, Resolution 92 (IV) (1976). Developed countries and the United Nations system are to provide, when requested, support and assistance to developing countries in strengthening and enlarging their mutual cooperation. To this end:

The developed countries, both the developed market-economy countries and the socialist countries of Eastern Europe, commit themselves to abstain as appropriate from adopting any kind of measures or action which could adversely affect the decisions of developing countries in favour of the strengthening of their economic cooperation and the diversification of their production structures;

The developed countries, both the developed market-economy countries and the socialist countries of Eastern Europe, agree to support and facilitate the implementation of legitimate decisions taken by the developing countries in order to ensure fulfillment of their programmes of economic cooperation, including the following measures:

Support for existing and new programmes of inter-regional, regional and subregional economic co-operation and integration among developing countries, including those aimed at full economic integration as well as those with more limited trade, monetary and sectoral objectives;

Support for developing countries in the setting up and functioning of their multinational marketing enterprises. This support should include the removal of any restraints, where they exist, or of any future restraints which would adversely affect their operation;

Allocation of funds within their development assistance programmes for the promotion of multinational ventures of developing countries, such funds to be applied to the financing of feasibility studies, project inventories and the building up and assessment of available technologies and technological research;

Consideration of measures by developed countries, in furtherance of the programme of economic cooperation among developing countries, to reduce further the interest cost of loans to recipient developing countries, particularly in the context of multilateral development financing;

Support, including financial support, for programmes of economic and technical cooperation of developing countries;

Facilitating the participation of developing countries, on a subcontracting basis, in projects undertaken by the developed countries;

The developed market-economy countries should, in particular

Support preferential trade arrangements among developing countries, including those of limited scope, through technical assistance and through appropriate policy measures in international trade organizations;

Facilitate in every way possible the conclusion of separate sales contracts, where feasible, for equipment and technological components, so as to encourage importation of technology by developing countries from other developing countries;

Provide technical support for the establishment of financial and capital markets in developing countries so as to help strengthen direct financial links between surplus and deficit developing countries;

In order to encourage economic co-operation among developing countries, and to meet capital needs arising in that context, actively implement their undertakings in General Assembly Resolution 3362 (S-VII) by adopting specific actions to grant developing countries increased access, on favourable terms, to the capital markets of the developed market-economy countries, to the extent that the possibilities in each of these countries allow;

Consider the expansion of existing, and the creation of new, export credit finance and guarantee schemes by the World Bank and regional and subregional development banks in the light of existing studies and of on-going studies which are being undertaken by international institutions on this subject and which should be expeditiously finalized;

The socialist countries of Eastern Europe should lend their support in particular through:

The provision of technical assistance for the setting up and operation of State import and export enterprises of the developing countries, at both the national and multinational levels;

The promotion of links, wherever appropriate, between the transferable rouble system of the International Bank of Economic Cooperation and sub-regional and regional payments arrangements of developing countries;

Technical assistance to developing countries engaged in the formulation of joint investment programmes of developing countries in the productive sectors, as well as technical, commercial and financial support to those countries in the implementation of such programmes. In this context there should also be a sharing with developing countries of the experience of the socialist countries of Eastern Europe;

International financial institutions, including regional and sub-regional ones, should, within the framework of their statutory provisions and potential to evolve further, give their strongest support for the programme of economic co-operation among developing countries, particularly by:

Adjusting their internal operational and financial policies so as to take specific account of the particular difficulties involved in the promotion of multinational projects. This may be achieved by:

- the creation of special promotional units within these institutions;
- the creation of pre-investment funds for the preparation and promotion of multinational investment projects; and
Making use of part of their resources for equity or other forms of financing of multinational enterprises set up by developing member States.

UNCTAD should strengthen its capability commensurate with its expanding role as executing agency for technical assistance to developing countries, in the promotion and implementation of their programmes of economic cooperation at the subregional, regional and interregional levels;

The United Nations system, and in particular the United Nations Development Programme, should devote a larger proportion of technical assistance resources, and UNCTAD should devote a larger portion of any funds in trust it may have available for that purpose, to projects related to economic cooperation among developing countries, especially those programmes which include, or are negotiated among, least developed, land-locked and island developing countries. To that end, donor countries should favourably consider providing direct contributions, inter alia in the form of trust funds for specific projects of technical assistance undertaken by UNCTAD and other bodies of the United Nations system in the field of economic cooperation among developing countries;

Donor countries should increase their voluntary contributions to the United Nations Development Programme, with a view, inter alia, to enable it to meet the increasing technical assistance requirements of developing countries in the implementation of their programmes of economic cooperation at the subregional, regional and inter-regional levels.

Several regional commissions reported on the continuing necessity for cooperation among developing countries. A report from ESCAP entitled "The Developing ESCAP Region in the Mid-1970's Retrospect and Prospect" (E/ESCAP/55, 25 March 1977), characterized the emergence of TCDC as one of the most important developments at the regional and interregional levels in recent years with respect to collective self-reliance among Third World countries. The concept of technical cooperation among developing ESCAP countries and those of other regions is not intended to replace technical and financial assistance from other sources. TCDC has been recognized as an eminently practical approach to social and economic development, which should compliment and stimulate progress toward other forms of economic integration.

A report from ECWA entitled "The Role of Regional Commissions in Promoting Co-operation Among the Developing Countries" (E/ECWA/52, 28 March 1977) suggested:

measures of support of concomitant action at the interregional level to be implemented by the developing countries as whole;

establishment of links among the regional and sub-regional groupings;

facilitation of participation in co-operation and integration schemes of countries that are at present outside such schemes;

consideration of a possible mechanism or a consultative body, whichever is appropriate, to coordinate and promote their activities with regard to the above-mentioned areas.

In order to secure the continuing effectiveness of Third World cooperation at the subregional, regional and interregional levels, the restructuring process at the United Nations might involve the following:

the designation of the regional economic commissions as team leaders with responsibility for co-operation and co-ordination of intersectoral programmes at the regional level;

the designation of the commissions as executive agencies of the UNDP for future United Nations inter-sectoral, subregional, regional and interregional projects;

the delegation in full of the executive agency functions to the regional commissions of existing inter-sectoral regional and sub-regional operational activities.

According to a report by the Administrative Committee on Coordination "Economic Cooperation Among Developing Countries" (E/AC.51/86, 24 May 1977) the concept of economic cooperation among developing countries (ECDC) encompasses the entire development effort and the measures envisaged to promote such cooperation cover almost all fields of economic and social development. The programme of economic co-operation adopted in Manila (see below) emphasizes in particular the need to promote ECDC in respect of food, agriculture and rural development, raw materials and commodities, trade and finance, industrial development, transfer and development of technology, energy, transport and communications. The measures to promote ECDC range from the establishment and/or strengthening of economic integration between developing countries, to the establishment of consultative procedures with a view to promoting new forms of joint action. Approaches to ECDC include:

the "market sharing" approach comprising exchange of information, experience and expertise;

joint programming and development of resources including strengthening of complementarities and the provision of common fora to serve common objectives;

schemes of integration and other forms of institutionalized cooperation.

The report discusses TCDC, the new dimension recently added to international cooperation for development. TCDC involves the sharing of capacities and skills between two or more developing countries. It includes development programmes, projects and activities in which expertise, consultancy services, training facilities, equipment and supplies are provided by developing countries to one another. It is viewed as a means through which developing countries can build the individual and collective self-reliance required by them to solve their development problems and as an effort to enhance the total availability of assistance for development.

TCDC is an integral component of ECDC and both are clearly interdependent. ECDC includes technical co-operation but provides a broader framework for cooperation to promote economic and social development. Technical cooperation is an essential instrument to secure the viability of schemes for ECDC.

UNIDO Resolution 47 (XI) (June 1977) urges the fostering of technological co-operation among developing countries and their institutions through bilateral and multilateral arrangements that will permit:

exchange of information as appropriate to the conditions that govern the transfer of technology;

joint preparation, financing and execution of research projects that are of interest to several countries;

exchange of experts, expertise and trainees;

utilization by a country of the laboratories and installations of another, in order to promote a better use of human and material resources;

formulation of joint agreements on technology in order to benefit from the economics of scale, to exchange the experiences obtained in the implementation of common technologies;

creation of specialized technological centres.

The Secretariat of CEPAL, in a note entitled "Operational Policies of CEPAL in Connexion with Technical Co-operation and with the Implementation of TCDC among Latin American Countries and Among Developing Regions of Different Geographical Areas" (E/CEPAL/L.169. November 1977) suggested the following in connection with promoting and putting into effect an effective intraregional network of TCDC:

Provide an integrated view of the genuine development problems of the countries of the region. This can be the basis of TCDC activities geared to the real needs of the developing countries and carried out in the light of their socio-cultural features;

co-ordinate TCDC activities at the sectoral level through an effective integrated view of the action carried out by the United Nations bodies at the regional levels;

gather and distribute information on TCDC matters and provide inputs for the UNDP electronic data system (TCDC/INRES);

exercise the operational role required in formulating and implementing TCDC activities of an intra-regional character;

provide member governments, in close collaboration with other regional organizations and institutions, as appropriate, with a forum for exchanging experience, identifying TCDC programmes and projects, and exercising the political will to adopt and implement such programmes and projects.

The Secretary-General of the United Nations Conference on Technical Cooperation Among Developing Countries (A/Conf. 79/PC/24, 3 April 1978) proposed a series of 33 recommendations concerning TCDC for consideration by the Conference. These deal with such issues as the capacities of national institutions for participation in TCDC; use of the developing countries' own experience in application to other developing countries; joint commissions and mechanisms for TCDC; international guidelines for TCDC implementation; information systems for communicating development experience; long-term programmes to be incorporated by governments in national development plans; technological self-reliance through developing indigenous technologies; the role of corporations, professional, technical and other private institutions, as well as of intergovernmental and international organizations; national educational policy; financing of TCDC activities; the role and financing of UNDP and other relevant United Nations agencies, programmes and organizations; the aid practices and procedures of developed countries; the migration of professional and skilled labour among developing countries; the problem of the "brain drain"; and the establishment of an infrastructural network of developing countries comprising transport, communications, and other means of international exchange.

11.3   Contributions of major international bodies 1974-78

The Fifth Conference of Heads of States or Government of Non-Aligned Countries (NAC/Conf.5/S.2, 21 August 1976) reviewed many of the aspects of TCDC and placed particular emphasis on cooperation to achieve self-reliance in agriculture. Among its recommendations are to:

promote preferential trading arrangements sub-regionally, regionally and on the widest feasible basis among non-aligned and other developing countries;

establish machinery to identify areas where agricultural output can be increased through rationalizing production on a sub-regional, regional or wider basis;

promote consultative groups to identify possibilities of co-operative ventures between food exporting and potential food exporting developing countries on one hand and oil exporting countries on the other;

co-operate in multinational projects in food production and processing in the manufacture of fertilizers and other agricultural inputs,
counteracting desertification and elimination of pests, diseases and
other physical disabilities which reduce the land available for
cultivation;

re-orient, nationally, regionally and globally, to the extent feasible,
from export agriculture primarily dependent on developed country
markets, to food production for developing country consumption so
as to attain a more balanced and self-reliant agriculture;

examine the feasibility of bulk purchase of agriculture inputs on a
multinational basis, utilizing such bulk purchasing both to obtain
better prices for participating countries as well as to encourage the
development of new production and trade in and among non-aligned
and other developing countries;

in the field of research and development to promote co-operative
measures that would lead to an unrestricted flow of agricultural
technology among developing countries and the promotion of
measures for the improvement and expansion of national, regional
and international research institutions in developing countries;

co-operate and share experience, knowledge and facilities in:

undertaking research;

the planning and management of large-scale agricultural and
development projects;

the design and management of small, medium and large-scale
irrigation systems;

methods, equipment, processing, harvesting, handling, storing,
preserving of foods, particularly grains and perishable food
items;

promoting the consumption of nationally produced food;

training extension workers and farmers;

the creation of food security stocks by non-aligned countries in co-
operation with other developing countries, individually or collectively, to stabilize supplies and prices of import requirements of
developing countries.

Regarding economic co-operation among developing countries, the
Commonwealth Heads of Government (CW/London/1977) endorsed the view of
the Commonwealth Group of Experts that schemes of regional economic and
functional co-operation among developing countries should increasingly
became a focal point of international development strategy to promote social
and economic transformation and development in developing countries on the
basis of self-reliance. The Heads of Government also agreed that in working
toward their ODA targets, donor countries should be asked to give particular

attention to the financing of multi-national projects that would promote the process of regional economic integration and cooperation.

The following measures for ECDC were adopted at the Third Ministerial meeting of the group of 77 at Manila (February 1976). It suggested that the developed countries (both the developed market-economy countries and the socialist countries of Eastern Europe) take the following measures:

promotion and financing of multilateral interest subsidization schemes by developed countries to reduce the cost of loans by surplus developing countries;

remove restrictions, taxes and other obstacles that discriminate between borrowing developing countries and domestic borrowers seeking access to their capital markets;

support the expansion of existing and the creation of a new export credit finance and guarantee schemes by the World Bank and regional and subregional development banks.

It further suggested that the socialist countries of Eastern Europe lend their support, in particular through:

"technical assistance to developing countries engaged in the formulation of joint investment programmes in the productive sectors, as well as technical, commercial and financial support to those countries in the complementation of such programmes."

These measures are an elaboration of UNCTAD Resolution 92 (IV) 1976 cited above. All other measures recommended in the UNCTAD resolution were reiterated here.

The participants of the Conference on International Economic Co-operation (A/31/478/Add. 1, 9 August 1977) agreed to give their support to a programme of economic cooperation among developing countries by measures such as:

establishing units with the purpose of promoting multinational projects of developing countries;

establishing pre-investment funds for the preparation and promotion of multinational projects of developing countries;

providing resources for giving loans for multinational projects of developing countries;

making use of their resources for the equity and/or other forms of financing of multinational projects established by developing countries;

stimulating, by giving financial support, the establishment of multinational projects of developing countries for the marketing and transport of goods and commodities;

providing financing for joint economic development schemes and projects of developing countries at the subregional, regional and interregional levels;

establishing new and expanding the existing export credit finance and export credit insurance schemes for increasing trade among developing countries; whenever feasible;

supporting the establishment and strengthening of joint banks, funds and other financial institutions and regional financial markets of developing countries.

It was agreed at the conference that the developed countries should support and implement the following proposals:

Support efforts of cooperation among developing countries and abstain as appropriate from adopting any kind of measures or action which could adversely affect the decisions of developing countries in favour of the strengthening of their economic cooperation and the diversification of their production structures;

Support and facilitate as appropriate efforts of cooperation among developing countries with inter alia the following measures:

give support, including financial support, to programmes of economic and technical cooperation among developing countries;

contribute within their development assistance programmes for the promotion of joint enterprises of developing countries to the financing of feasibility studies, technological research and evaluation of available technology;

consider measures in furtherance of the programme of economic cooperation among developing countries to reduce further the interest cost of loans to recipient developing countries, particularly in the context of multilateral development financing;

support actions taken by the international organizations with the aim of promoting economic and financial cooperation among developing countries;

facilitate the participation of developing countries on a subcontractual basis in projects undertaken by the developed countries in developing countries.

3 International Financial Issues

WORLD ECONOMY ISSUE 12

Reforming the International Monetary System:
Using Special Drawing Rights for Development Assistance and as the Central
Reserve Asset of the International Monetary System, Promoting Stable Rates
Of Exchange and Protection From the Effects of Inflation

12.1   The original formulation of the NIEO objective at the United Nations

The Declaration and Programme of Action on the Establishment of a
New International Economic Order (May 1974) followed several years of
disorder in the international monetary system; this was dominated by pressure
on the world's principal reserve currency, the United States dollar, and a
consequent concern as to the adequacy of the system creating the international reserves needed for world trade.   As a result, the Programme of
Action called for the "adequate and orderly creation of additional liquidity...
through the additional allocation of special drawing rights based on the
concept of world liquidity needs."

The Programme of Action further stipulated that there should be "early
establishment of a link between special drawing rights and additional development financing in the interest of developing countries."   This principle of
utilizing SDR's as the central reserve of the international monetary system
and linking the creation of SDRs to development assistance was reaffirmed in
the Seventh Special Session.   Specifically, the General Assembly resolution on
Development and International Economic Co-operation (Sept. 1975) stressed
that the "role of national currencies should be reduced and the special
drawing rights should become the central reserve asset of the international
monetary system."   Concurrent with this, the IMF was requested to consider
"the establishment of a link between the SDR and additional development
finance for the benefit of all developing countries."   This was called for as

104

early as 24 October 1970 in Resolution 2626 (XXV) International Development Strategy for the Second United Nations Development Decade.

The disruption in the international monetary system was compounded by instability in international exchange rates, the transmission of inflation from developed to developing countries, and severe depreciations in the value of two international reserve currencies: the United States dollar, and the United Kingdom pound.

In response, the Programme of Action on the Establishment of the NIEO called for "measures to eliminate the instability of the international monetary system; in particular, the uncertainty of exchange rates."   There was also a call for "maintenance of the real value of the currency reserves of the developing countries by preventing their erosion from inflation and exchange rate depreciation of reserve currencies."

12.2   Specifications and development of the NIEO objective at the United Nations, 1974-78

Because of the considerable interest in SDR, significant research on this issue started already before the Sixth Special Session.   A very important example is furnished by the report of a technical group in the Documents of the Committee of Twenty, 9 July 1973, in which various pros and cons on an SDR/aid link are presented.   Those against the link expressed concern in several areas, some of which are:

Worry that the linking of "allocations of SDRs to the financing of economic development"...would exacerbate the difficulties of building up confidence "in a new system centered on the SDR;

Fear that "the establishment of a link would tend to increase expansionary pressure in an already inflationary environment..." since SDRs acquired through link allocations would be spent rather than held;

Doubts "whether the aggregate net flow of financial resources for development would increase by anything close to the full amount of SDR allocations under a link" since "there would be strong pressures in some national legislatures to deduct from conventional aid appropriations a large part of any allocations under an SDR/aid link."

Those in sympathy to the link countered that:

"Developing countries have been net users of SDR's allocated between 1970 and 1972 without detracting in any way from confidence in SDRs."

"It is improbable that the introduction of a link would involve any upward bias in SDR allocations" and in any case "developed countries have, and will retain in a reformed system, a strong majority voting position in the Fund;"

It is difficult to see why such recognition of the problems of developing countries implied by the approval of an SDR/aid link by national legislatures "should be nullified or deprived of content by

subsequent reductions in conventional aid appropriations as an offset
to the contributions of developed countries through the link."

An intermediate view saw "no inherent incompatibility between reserve
creation and resource transfer through SDR allocations" but, at least beyond
a certain point, it would attach greater weight to the argument against a link,
the more so the larger the amount of link allocations and the higher the
proportion of such allocations to total SDR allocations.

The discussion of the expert group focused on three main link schemes.

Scheme B)   direct allocations to developing countries "would in-
             volve the adoption of a new formula for the allocation
             of SDRs among countries that would channel to the
             developing countries a larger share of total allocations
             that corresponds to their share in Fund quotas."

Scheme A)   direct allocations to development finance institutions
             "would involve making available to development fi-
             nance institutions a portion of SDRs created, deter-
             mined either as a percentage of the total SDR
             allocation or as an absolute amount."

Scheme D)   indirect allocations to development finance
             institutions "would leave unaltered the principle of
             SDR allocations to participants on a basis strictly
             proportional to Fund quotas, but would be
             complemented by agreement among developed
             countries to transfer to development finance
             institutions either part of the SDRs allocated to them
             or the equivalent in currencies."

Developing countries favored Scheme B, i.e., direct country allocations,
whereas the developed countries, to the extent they favored any link at all,
favored Scheme D, indirect country allocations, which would leave the
present principle of SDR allocations intact.

Since the Programme of Action on the Establishment of the NIEO, there
have been many statements reaffirming the desirability of an SDR/aid link.
For instance, the Latin American Conference on Industrialization (ID/CONF.
3/CRP/I/Add.1, 4 Dec. 1974) declared that measures adopted to reform the
international monetary system should include "the use of Special Drawing
Rights to finance industrial development in the developing countries..." At
the same time General Assembly Resolution 3347 (XXXIX) (December 1974)
emphasized that a "political decision on the link between development
finance and special drawing rights allocation will have to be reached without
further delay..." The resolution also welcomed "the agreement of the Ad Hoc
Committee on Reform of the International Monetary System and Related
Issues to utilize the special drawing rights as the principal reserve asset..."

A report prepared by the Economic Commission for Western Asia
(E/ECWA/26, 18 April 1975) asserted that "the concept of utilizing an
'international currency' created through international multilateral

mechanisms, as the principal reserve asset of the reformed monetary system seems to have been agreed upon."

The SDR is such an international currency. A report by the UNCTAD Secretariat (TD/B/C.3/127, 24 September 1975) notes, however, that "SDR's have not been created since 1972 and recent developments appear to have weakened the case for further creation in the near future." This refers to "a rapid growth in international liquidity in the form of national currencies (e.g. dollars, marks and yen), a growth which is not directly under the control of monetary authorities." This has implications for the implementation of an SDR/Aid link since, as is noted by the UNCTAD report, "the question of the link is related to that of establishing a viable role for SDR's in the international monetary system." As to the concept of the link itself, the UNCTAD report observes that "although the rationale of the link is widely accepted, there is not as yet a consensus in favour of establishing the link."
The topic of international liquidity was the subject of a report by the Committee for Development Planning (E/5793/Supp. 6, 29 March-7 April 1976). This report asserted that "the creation of international liquidity has taken place in a haphazard fashion" with traditional reserve assets and other strong currencies "being used extensively as reserve assets..." It was the opinion of the Committee that:

> Notwithstanding the new developments...the importance of reserve creation under international auspices, with proper safeguards and rules, remains unchanged. Hence, it is important that the creation of SDRs should be kept on the agenda along with the issue of their link with development finance.

A report by the Economic Commission for Africa (E/CN.14/UNCTAD IV/1, 18 April 1976) endorsed this point of view:

> It is necessary to see to it that the role of the SDR in the international monetary system is strengthened and that provision is made in the IMF Articles of Agreement for the link between SDRs and development financing, which has long been sought by the Association of African Central Banks.

Making the SDR the principle reserve asset in the international monetary system was affirmed in the IMF Annual Report of 1976. To help achieve this goal the SDR replaced "gold as the means of payment by members to the Fund and by the Fund to members."

In May 1977 the Guatemala Appraisal (E/CEPAL/1030/Rev. 1) supported "the introduction of a new international monetary system based on Special Drawing Rights (SDR)" that would be "linked to development financing. "Also in May of 1977 the Ministers of the Group of 24, finance ministers from the Group of 77 countries, indicated support for this NIEO objective. In a press communique on 2 May 1977 the committee stated:

> A second allocation of SDR should be considered imperative both in the context of the present international liquidity position and in moving toward the objective of making the SDR the principal

reserve asset of the international monetary system. Appropriate steps should be taken to enchance the reserve characteristics of the SDR.

Serious consideration should be given to the establishment of a link between SDR allocation and the provision of financial resources to developing countries.

The IMF decision to replace gold by SDR as the means of payment within the Fund received comment in a report by the Economic Commission for Africa (E/CN.14/AMA/96, August 1977). Noting that the industrialized countries can acquire gold with ease through the Bank for International Settlement "it is an open question," the report stated "whether SDR would be required by these countries in any substantial amounts with the risk that this may militate against any possible expansion of the SDR and their substitution of the present reserve currencies as the principal reserve asset." The report also noted that "the reform of the international monetary system fell short of the expectations of African countries," not only in establishing the SDR as the principle reserve asset but in the failure to establish the required link between the creation of SDR and development finance.

Efforts to establish the SDR as the central international reserve asset were not advanced by actions of the IMF in 1977. According to the IMF Annual Report of 1977:

On June 29, 1977 the Managing Director, after consulting with the Executive Directors, reported to the Board of Governors that there was no proposal for a new allocation that can be considered to be consistent with the provisions of the Articles that has broad support among participants.

The date upon which additional SDR allocations could be made, 1 January 1978, has passed without the allocation of additional SDR. The Managing Director did note that "if the outstanding questions can be resolved" he will "submit a proposal for an SDR allocation as soon as ((he is)) satisfied that one can be made that will be consistent with the requirements of the Articles."

The "outstanding questions to be resolved" concern the need for, and control of, additional international liquidity via the creation of new SDRs, given a situation of floating exchange rates. (Theoretically, with floating exchange rates there is no need for an international reserve currency to be augmented periodically. Currencies of the various countries exchange directly for one another on foreign markets, the price being determined by the supply and demand for a currency at any given time).

The reduced need for the creation of SDRs, however, does not mean a reduced role for the IMF. Almost as soon as the Sixth Special Session of the General Assembly concluded, the IMF took some action in the area of exchange rates. On 13 June 1974, it adopted guidelines for the management of floating rates to aid IMF members "collaborate with the Fund to promote exchange stability to maintain orderly exchange arrangements with other members and to avoid competitive exchange alterations."

Exchange rate adjustments are the subject of General Assembly

Resolution 3347 (XXIX) (December 1974).   This resolution endorsed "the concept of an adjustment process in which adequate methods to assure timely and effective balance-of-payments adjustments will be assisted by improved international consultation within the International Monetary Fund." In fact, a study by the Economic Commission for Western Asia observed that "the absence of an effective and proper international monetary management could mean exchange controls, competitive depreciations, trade restrictions, freezing of assets and other arbitrary and discriminatory actions." As for the present situation, a report of the UNCTAD Secretariat (TD/B/665, 15 August 1977) noted that "the process of liquidity creation and balance-of-payments finance has been increasingly passed on to the private sector...arrangements... reminiscent of the earlier day's domestic credit system without a central bank." (This has happened in recent years as the commercial banks in the developed countries have become more and more willing to lend to developing countries for balance-of-payment purposes, thereby earning higher rates of interest than are often possible for domestic loans. These loans add to international liquidity and further reduce any need for the creation of additional SDR.   Thereby they compound the problem of controlling international inflation.)

The need for exchange rate guidelines was also sounded by the Economic and Social Commission for Asia and the Pacific.   A document entitled "Strategies for Development in the 1980's" (E/ESCAP/DP.2/L.10, 30 November 1977) suggests that guidelines could be developed at a regional level for official interventions in foreign exchange markets and for the development of better adjustment policies.

In response to provisions of Article IV of the proposed Second Amendment to the Articles of Agreement of the IMF, its Executive Board worked intensively on developing principles for the guidance of members with respect to their exchange rate policies and procedures for the Fund surveillance over these policies. The set of principles and procedures which resulted, entitled "Surveillance over Exchange Rate Policies," was adopted 29 April 1977. The general tenor of this document is best summed up by the following: "A member shall avoid manipulating exchange rates or the international monetary system in order to prevent effective balance of payments adjustment or to gain an unfair competitive advantage over other members." (In other words, a member should not attempt to maintain an exchange rate which is clearly counter to market forces). It is also stated that the surveillance of exchange rate policies "shall be adopted to the needs of international adjustment as they develop," meaning that exogenous events with international ramifications (such as the dramatic increase in oil prices in 1973) may necessitate patience and originality in dealing with cases of persistent balance-of-payment difficulty. It is further stipulated that "each member shall notify the Fund in appropriate detail within thirty days after the Second Amendment becomes effective of the exchange arrangements it intends to apply in fulfillment of its obligations under Article IV, Section 1." Members are also obliged to notify the Fund promptly of any changes in their exchange arrangements.

12.3   Contributions of major international bodies, 1974-78

The NIEO objective of an SDR/Aid Link and the use of SDR as the central international reserve asset were discussed in a number of international fora.

The final communique of the Commonwealth Heads of Government meeting (May 1975) took a position "that developing countries should have priority call on Special Drawing Rights (SDR's) through some form of 'link' mechanism."

The final report by a Commonwealth Expert's Group (March 1977) expressed similar views and reaffirmed the principle of building up the SDR as the principal reserve asset of the international monetary system. The final communique of the Commonwealth Heads of Government Meeting (June 1977) also supported this principle by agreeing "they would work for an acceleration of the process of international monetary reform, including implementation of the decision to make the SDR the principal reserve asset in the monetary system."

The Manila Declaration (TD/195, 7 February 1976) strongly endorsed the principle of promoting stable rates of exchange by its call for "increased consistency in exchange rate policies and greater stability in the exchange rates of the major currencies," and the strengthening of existing mechanisms to protect developing countries from being adversely affected "by internal maladjustments in developed countries."

WORLD ECONOMY ISSUE 13

Assuring Adequate Participation By Developing Countries
In World Bank and IMF Decision Making

13.1 The Original Formulation of the NIEO Objective at the United Nations

The Declaration and Programme of Action on the Establishment of a New International Economic Order (May 1974) called for the "full and effective participation of developing countries in all phases of decision-making for the formulation of an equitable and durable monetary system." This principle was also expressed in the request for "more effective participation by developing countries ... in the decision-making process in the competent organs of the International Bank for Reconstruction and Development (and) the International Monetary Fund ."

The need for more effective participation by developing countries was reiterated by the General Assembly at its Seventh Special Session in Resolution 3362, "Development and International Co-operation." The reso-lution stated that any increase in participation by developing countries in the decision making process should not affect adversely "the broad geographic representation of developing countries" and be "in accordance with the existing and evolving rules."

The Lima Declaration and Plan of Action on Industrial Development and Co-operation (March 1975) likewise called for the "full and effective participation of the developing countries in all bodies entrusted with this reform (of the international monetary system), particularly in the Board of Governors of the International Monetary Fund, in accordance with the existing and evolving rules of such bodies"

13.2 Specification and development of the NIEO objective at the United Nations 1974-78

The increased participation of developing countries in the decision-making process of the IMF was the subject of General Assembly Resolution 3347 (XXIX), December 1974. With regard to reconsideration of the quota system of the IMF, this resolution stressed the following needs:

a. to take fully into account the requirements of developing countries for, and their ability to contribute to, balance-of-payments finance;

b. to reflect recent changes in balance-of-payments position and creditor positions of the members of the Fund;

c. to increase the overall participation of developing countries in the decision-making process of the Fund, bearing in mind the measures referred to in sub-paragraphs (a) and (b) above.

The involvement of developing countries in the international monetary system is emphasized in a report by an UNCTAD Group of Experts (TD/B/579, March 1976). It noted that "the developing countries would clearly suffer from a prolonged recession in the developed market economy countries but they would also lose from a renewed acceleration of inflation in those countries." It was with this reasoning in mind that "the Group agreed on the importance of international consultations on monetary and fiscal policies, and noted that it is particularly important that such consultations should involve the developing countries."

As noted above, one way to ensure that developing countries are consulted is to increase their representation in the decision-making process of such international institutions as the IMF and the World Bank. There has been some progress in this. On 22 March 1976 the Executive Directors of the IMF "agreed that the quotas of the major oil exporters should be substantially increased by doubling their share as a group in the enlarged Fund, and that the collective share of all other developing countries should not be allowed to fall below its present level." (IMF Annual Report 1976).

The IMF's decision on quotas is duplicated by the World Bank since "it is a long-standing policy of the Bank that when increases in IMF quotas are received, members are also expected to request increases in their sub-scriptions to the capital of the Bank." (World Bank, Annual Report 1977)

(It should be noted that this action will not materially alter present voting power wherein "a combination of the largest shareholders (Canada, France, Germany, Japan, the United Kingdom, and the United States) could together defeat an issue requiring a simple majority of the votes, the normal requirement for decisions." ("Questions and Answers," A World Bank publication.))

13.3 Contributions of major international bodies, 1974-78

The NIEO objective of increased participation by developing countries in the decision-making process has received considerable support in international fora. The Final Communique of the 1975 Commonwealth Heads of Government Meeting recommended that "Commonwealth Finance Ministers should at the next meeting of their Boards of Governors take up the question of securing changes in the voting rights and managerial structures of the IBRD and the IMF, so as to give the developing countries greater participation in the decision-making in these institutions."

The Manila Declaration by the Group of 77 (TD/195, 7 February 1976, voiced the same sentiment, stating that "the system of voting in the IMF and the World Bank should be reformed so as to accord developing countries greater representation and weight in decision-making in these institutions."

The notion of increased participation was strongly supported in a report on the implications for African countries of provisions contained in the Manila Programme of Action (E/CN/UNCTAD IV/I). The report noted that:

The full and effective participation of representatives of African countries in all phases of decision-making for the establishment of an equitable and durable monetary system should be insisted upon. What is of cardinal importance is to ensure that the state of affairs witnessed in the last few years in which "developing countries remained largely 'off-stage' as the world liquidity problem emerged, successive crises affected the currencies of the major industrial nations, urgent international consultations were conducted and a variety of instruments were introduced to patch up the existing international monetary system without their interests being taken into account during this period," is not allowed to continue.

WORLD ECONOMY ISSUE 14

Increasing The Transfer Of Resources Through The World Bank And IMF

14.1   The original formulation of the NIEO objective at the United Nations

The Declaration and Programme of Action on the Establishment of a New International Economic Order (May 1974) followed several years of chaos in the international monetary system. The Declaration (3201, S-VI) requested that one of the main aims of a reformed international monetary system

should be "the promotion of the development of the developing countries and
the adequate flow of real resources to them."

The Programme of Action (3202, S-VI) noted a "need for improvement in
practices of international financial institutions in regard to, inter alia,
development financing and international monetary problems." As an example
the Programme of Action suggested "improved compensatory financing
schemes," and review of IMF terms for credit repayments, 'stand-by'
arrangements and the financing of buffer stocks.

The resolution on Development and International Economic Cooperation
(3362, S-VII) noted that:

> in order to enlarge the pool of resources available for financing
> development, there is an urgent need to increase substantially
> the capital of the World Bank Group, in particular the resources
> of International Development Association, to enable it to make
> additional capital available to the poorest countries on highly
> concessional terms.

In addition, the World Bank Group was "invited to consider new ways of
supplementing its financing with private management, skills, technology and
capital."

Resolution 3362 (S-VII) also stated that:

> Developing countries should be granted increased access on favour-
> able terms to the capital markets of developed countries. To this
> end, the joint Development Committee of the International Mone-
> tary Fund and the International Bank for Reconstruction and
> Development should progress as rapidly as possible in its work.

Hence, it was suggested that consideration "be given to the examination of an
international investment trust and to the expansion of the International
Finance Corporation capital" without prejudice to the increase in finance
from other intergovernmental institutions and procedures.

The Seventh Special Session also supported the call of the Programme of
Action on the Establishment of the NIEO for expansion and liberalization of
"the compensatory financing facility now available through the International
Monetary Fund." In this connection it was suggested that methods should be
devised "which would mitigate export earnings shortfalls of developing
countries, with special regard to the poorest countries." Further it was
thought appropriate that:

> Early consideration should also be given by the International
> Monetary Fund to proposals to expand and liberalize its coverage of
> current transactions to include manufactures and services, to ensure
> that whenever possible, compensation for export shortfalls takes
> place at the same time they occur, to take into account, in
> determining the quantum of compensation, movements in import
> prices, and to lengthen the repayment period.

In other words, Resolution 3362 (S-VII) called for a lengthening of the repayment period for balance-of-payment deficits, with the financing being provided by the IMF, possibly through its compensatory financing facility. It should be noted that already the International Development Strategy for the Second United Nations Development Decade (2626,XXV, October 1970) requested the World Bank "to pursue its efforts at working out a scheme of supplementary financing."

14.2   Specification and development of the NIEO objective at the United Nations 1974-78

On 1 August 1974 the Secretary-General of UNCTAD reported (TD/B/495) that the Committee of Twenty agreed "to recommend the establishment jointly by IBRD and IMF of a Ministerial Committee on the Transfer of Real Resources to Developing Countries." This committee was established in the interim between the sixth and seventh special sessions.

The role of compensatory financing was among the subjects discussed in a report by the Secretary-General of UNCTAD (TD/B/C.1/166/Supp.4, 13 December 1974). Noting that "the expansion and liberalization of the IMF facility would be of considerable help to developing countries" at the present time, the report outlined the principal features of the IMF facility that would seem to require attention if it were to undertake an expanded role.

The need for more flexible conditions as regards the balance-of-payments criterion for assistance whereby broader account could be taken of the impact of commodity trade developments on the economy and hence the longer-term payments situation of a developing country, and also more particularly of the problems of individual commodity sectors in difficulty.

Relaxation of the limits on the amounts of compensation available, as determined by IMF quotas, to take account of the size of shortfalls in export earnings.

Easier requirements with regard to provision of the statistical data on which a request for compensatory assistance is based.

The repayment of compensatory loans could be more clearly linked to recovery in the level of exports. Extension of the repayment period beyond the present obligation to make complete repayments within 3-5 years would help to ensure that the difficulties caused by a temporary shortfall had been eliminated by market development or met through corrective measures.

Account to be taken in the determination of compensation of changes in the import purchasing power of a country's exports.

A report by the Economic Commission for Western Asia (E/ECWA/26, 18 April 1975) took note of agreement by the IMF to study the opportunity of establishing a Special Trust Fund to extend some $3.5 billion annually of development assistance to developing countries at low interest.

Compensatory financing was discussed in the Chaguarmas Appraisal, contained in the Annual Report of the Economic Commission for Latin America (E/5608, 12 May 1975). The Appraisal stated that "the policy of compensatory financing should be aimed at protecting the developing countries against the harmful effects of decreases or shortfalls in their export earnings for reasons beyond their control." The reason for such financing is to ensure an adequate flow of development finance. A report by the UNCTAD Secretariat on the flow of financial resources (TD/B/C.3/127, 24 September 1975) suggested that enlargement of the "third window" of the World Bank, and establishment of "third windows" in regional development banks or similar national programmes could play an important role in boosting rapidly the flow of concessional finance.

The Committee for Development Planning in its Twelfth Session (29 March - 7 April 1976), while praising the decision of the IMF to increase the upper limit on drawings in this facility from 50 to 75 per cent of a country's quota in the Fund, objected to the fact that "repayments are still obligatory at the usual rates of interest in three to five years, regardless of a recovery in export earnings." The Committee also noted that "the requirements for foreign exchange are not related to the need for a stable rate of economic growth but to short-term balance-of-payment difficulties." It was the view of the Committtee that the components of a reasonable and more comprehensive compensatory policy should include the following characteristics:

All shortfalls in export earnings below a reference level should be compensated. The reference level should include an adequate growth factor;

Shortfalls should be defined in real terms to take account of adverse movements in terms of trade brought about by rising import prices;

The magnitude of compensatory finance should be related to a certain percentage of shortfalls rather than quotas;

Compensation would not be repaid until exports recover above the reference level;even then, repayments should be on a long-term basis and terms of repayment should be related to the poverty and the long-term trade prospects of the country concerned.

The decision of the IMF to increase the upper limit of drawings on its compensatory financing facility, taken on 24 December 1975, "also introduced the possibility of basing export shortfalls on partially estimated data for up to six months of the shortfall year.

This provision is designed to serve the twin objectives of (a) improving the timeliness of assistance through the possibility of a drawing being made before the end of the shortfall year, and (b) extending the possible use of the facility to members previously denied access to it because their trade data are more than six months in arrears." (1976 IMF Annual Report)

The Executive Directors of the IMF made another decision on 5 May 1976, to establish a trust fund "for the purpose of providing special balance-of-payments assistance to developing members with the profits from the sale of gold, and with any financing that may be available from voluntary contributions or from loans." The balance-of-payments assistance provided by the Trust Fund on concessional terms will be "to support the efforts of eligible members that qualify for assistance to carry out programs of balance-of-payments adjustment." The concessional terms are loans with interest rate of one-half of 1 per cent per annum to be repaid in ten equal semi-annual installments starting after five years from the date of the loan. There is also provision for rescheduling should repayment on the due date result in serious hardship.

The transfer of resources to developing countries was the subject of a draft resolution submitted at UNCTAD-IV by the Group of 77. This resolution (TD/L.126) requested the IMF to:

> make its policies more flexible so as to provide adequate longer term assistance at low interest rates and free of policy conditions to developing countries for the specific purpose of compensating them for shortfalls in export earnings and rising prices for essential imports resulting from the economic situation in the developed countries.

The resolution further requested that the IMF consider making the following changes with regard to its compensatory financing facility:

> Export shortfalls should be calculated taking into account changes in import prices and with due account for a growth factor;

> The quota limitations should be either abolished or raised to a point at which they cover the entire shortfall;

> Repayments should be triggered by "overages," just as drawings are triggered by "shortfalls";

> Countries should be given the choice of basing the calculation of their shortfalls on their total commodity earnings, or total merchandise exports, or services, or on all current account receipts, and to draw against the shortfall without basing their claim entirely on balance-of-payments criteria;

> Increased import volume resulting from climatic or other factors beyond the control of the country concerned should also be included in the calculation of the shortfalls;

> In appropriate cases, drawings under the facility should take the form of grants.

The Group of 77 asked that the IMF "undertake an early further review of its tranche policies with a view to enlarging substantially the first credit tranche and reducing the conditionality attached to drawings under the subsequent tranches."

Eighteen months after the Seventh Special Session, a report by the Secretary-General of UNCTAD (TD/642/Add.1, 31 March 1977) reviewed the implementation of international development policies. The report endorsed the "positive steps taken in recent years to expand and liberalize the compensatory financing facility of the IMF," the establishment of the Trust Fund, and the additional funds "made available under the oil facility established in 1975 to assist non-oil-exporting countries in meeting the additional costs of oil imports..." (This facility lapsed after the middle of 1976.) It was felt, however, that these measures fell short of what is required since:

1) the enlargement and addition of IMF facilities undertaken so far represents an increase of only some $2.5 billion in the amount of financing available to developing countries on other than stringent conditions regarding expenditure;

2) the total amount of IMF balance-of-payment support represents only a small proportion of the aggregate payments deficit of the non-oil-exporting developing countries;

3) IMF Lending is subject to repayment within a limited period, usually 3-5 years, a condition which severely reduces its usefulness for many developing countries suffering from shortfalls in their export purchasing power resulting essentially from external factors which are not likely to be reversed fully within a short span of time. Further expansion and liberalization of existing facilities are required.

The joint Ministerial Committee of the Boards of Governors of the Bank and Fund on the Transfer of Real Resources to Developing Countries, established in the interim between the Sixth and Seventh Special Session of the General Assembly, presented a report of its activities for the period July 1976-June 1977. The report indicated agreement that capital market countries would endeavor, as far as possible, to move toward liberalization of capital movements, and, in the meantime would afford favorable treatment to the bond issues of the developing countries. In addition it was recognized that "most of the resources needed to meet the projected current account deficits of low-income countries must come from official sources and be on concessional terms." There was also "a consensus that the World Bank and the regional development banks should be prepared to consider requests for guarantees of bond issues from interested developing countries." And in a final note of interest, the Committee considered a suggestion for the establishment of an International Investment Trust "to encourage additional portfolio investments in the securities of developing countries." According to the report the consensus of the Committee was that further consultations on the idea were needed with both developed and developing countries.

In August of 1977 the Economic Commission for Africa looked at recent developments in international finance and monetary problems (E/CN14/AMA/96, 8 August 1977). In addition to noting the procedures of the newly established IMF Trust Fund, the ECA report stated that "access to the Trust Fund should be less conditional than in the case of traditional credit tranches." It was further suggested that available funds should be provided on non-repayable grants as far as could be possible so that low per-capita income members of the Fund may derive full benefit. It was the opinion of the ECA that access to Fund resources under the various facilities has been very much below actual requirements of the African and other developing regions; therefore there should be a general review of the Fund policies to enable African and other developing countries to secure more adequate balance-of-payments support from the Fund on reasonable terms.

14.3 Contributions of major international bodies, 1974-78

The Manila Declaration and Programme of Action adopted by the Third Ministerial Meeting of the Group of 77 (TD/195, February 1976) considered the topic of resource transfers to developing countries and reommended that;

> The multilateral development finance institutions should increase substantially their lending to developing countries. To make this possible, contributions of developed countries to these institutions should be increased immediately. Contributions to the World Bank's "third window" should be increased substantially and without prejudice to the regular lending programme of IBRD, to IDA, and to the soft-loan windows of the regional banks.

It was also suggested that "provision should be made for replenishing the resources of IDA on a continuous and automatic basis." The Manila Declaration also put forth some suggestions on how to assure the orderly and adequate financing of the balance-of-payments deficits of developing countries. (These were the same suggestions contained in the draft resolution of the Group of 77 presented at UNCTAD-IV. (See above.)

The Conference on International Economic Cooperation (A/31/478/Add.1, 9 August 1977) discussed, among other things, compensatory financing, developing country access to capital markets, and other financial flows. Aside from noting the liberalization in the drawing rights of the IMF Compensatory Financing Facility in December 1975, and hence its greater use, the participants at the Conference were not able to agree on future measures.

With regard to developing country access to capital markets, the Conference participants noted and indicated their support for recommendations of the IBRD-IMF Joint Development Committee concerning the liberalization of capital market regulations and measures to improve the access of developing countries to those markets. The participants also welcomed the decision of the IMF to include in its regular consultations of their staff with the capital market countries concerned, "a review of the progress of the respective countries in implementing the Development

Committee's recommendations." The Conference participants were of the opinion that in its consultations on the subject, the Joint Development Committee should give particular attention to the restrictaive effect of the following:

Authorization and approval requirements for security issues;

The use of issue calendars;

Fixed ceilings on foreign borrowings;

Constraints by strong currency country governments on their banks being lead managers for issues in third countries;*

Security registration requirements;

Limitations on foreign investments by institutional investors.

The participants recommended that the results of the IMF consultations with respect to capital market access be made availalbe on a regular basis to the Development Committee for review and evaluation and be included, as appropriate, in the IMF Annual Report.

The Conference also recommended that the Development Committee ask its Working Group to consider the usefulness and feasibility of establishing an information system on capital markets attached to an existing international financial institution. Further, the CIEC supported the efforts of the Development Committee to:

complete its work on the subject of multilateral guarantees;

complete its studies on the proposed International Investment Trust which would have the role of improving portfolio investment flows to developing countries and also of facilitating the placement of long-term bond issues at appropriate terms;

explore ways to improve capital flows to developing countries in general.

Finally, with regard to other financial flows, the Conference took note of the analysis made by the Interim Committee of the IMF "and agrees that the resources of the IMF should be increased." The Conference strongly supported initiatives being taken by the IMF to establish a supplementary credit facility.

---

* This refers to constraints on commercial and investment banks to act as principal underwriters of security issues for sale in third countries, i.e., in a country other than that of the underwriting institution.

4 Issues of Industrialization, Technology Transfer and Business Practices

WORLD ECONOMY ISSUE 15

Negotiating The Redeployment Of Industrial
Productive Capacities To Developing Countries

15.1 The original formulation of the NIEO objective at the United Nations

The proposal for shifting some part of the industrial productive capacities of developed countries to the Third World appears in the resolution of the Seventh Special Session "Development and International Economic Co-operation" (September 1975) under the heading of Industrialization. Developed countries should facilitate the development of new policies and strengthen existing policies, including labour market policies, which would encourage the redeployment of industries which are less competitive internationally to developing countries, leading to structural adjustments in the former and a higher degree of utilization of natural and human resources in the latter. The above policies should take into account the economic structure and the economic, social, and security objectives of the developed countries concerned, and the need for such industries to move into more viable lines of production or into other sectors of the economy.

A system of consultations should be established at the global, regional, interregional and sectoral levels to facilitate the achievement of the goals set forth in the field of industrialization. In particular, this would enhance the redeployment of certain productive capacities existing in developed countries. UNIDO should serve as a forum for negotiation of agreements in the field of industry. (See issue 24, below.)

The Lima Declaration and Plan of Action on Industrial Development and Co-Operation (March 1975) proposes redeployment policies in the same sense as the resolution of the Seventh Special Session.

15.2 Specification and development of the NIEO objective at the United Nations 1974-78

The criteria for redeployment should not be identical for all situations, according to a UNIDO expert group (ID / 132, June 1974). The new economic structure should not be imposed from abroad by theoretical calculations, but should be reached progressively through a process of negotiation.   Each country should establish its own criteria and attempt to reach agreement by stages.   Industries processing renewable resources are the most likely candidates for redeployment.   Other industries to engage in the process of consultation and redeployment are engineering industries, including spare parts, the production of machine tools, and other capital goods.   These industries are of particular interest for developing countries because of their labour content, their capacity for generating research, and their linkage with other national industries.

A report issued by the Secretariat of UNIDO (ID/B/C.3/27, October 1974) stated that the new economic structure resulting from deployment policies should be fashioned through intensive negotiations.

The aim of such negotiations should be to help developing countries achieve their industrialization objectives.   Through consultation and negotiation among the respective governments, these objectives would be adjusted to the mutual benefit of the participants.

Although industries that will lend themselves to important restructuring cannot be completely specified in advance of the negotiations, nevertheless, certain broad sectors appear to be obvious:

1. Industries having a high labour content;

2. Industries requiring natural resources e.g. shipyards, petro-chemical plants, and steel mills;

3. Industries processing locally available raw materials or consuming vast quantities of energy.

In the process of co-operation particular attention should be given to the industries that developing countries have designated as having top priority in their overall development plans.   These industries would reflect such characteristics as labour content, research generation possibilities, and significant linkages.   For example, engineering industries, production of machine tools and spare parts, and capital goods offer important possibilities for co-operation.

On the other hand, the developed countries should also recognize that in some cases they may benefit (through lower consumer prices and repatriation of profits) from the relocation of domestic industries to developing countries.

The UNIDO Secretariat reported in a note (ID/B/190, April 1977) that it was discovered through a series of questionnaires that the concept of redeployment was open to broad interpretation.   Of the 7,682 companies approached, 2,391 responded from Australia, Austria, Belgium, the Federal Republic of Germany, New Zealand, Sweden, Switzerland, and the United States of America. Redeployment was interpreted in the following manner:

The establishment of subsidiaries in developing countries;

The sale of technology and know-how to developing countries;

The sale of equipment, including used equipment, to the developing countries;

The training of nationals from developing countries;

The provision of management services to the developing countries;

The transfer of existing plants or units to the developing countries;

Capital investment in developing countries.

The note suggested the need to refine the concept of redeployment, owing to the broad range of interpretation, and particularly since neither the Lima Declaration and Plan of Action, nor General Assembly Resolutions 3362 (S-VII) and 31/163 elaborated upon the concept in detail.

The following issues were raised for consideration in order to enhance the discussion on refining the concept of redeployment:

Redeployment should be more closely linked to the achievement of the industrial production target as well as to the negotiations and consultations provided for in the Lima Declaration;

Redeployment should be an intrinsic component of the evolutionary industrial restructuring taking place in the industrialized countries;

Rather than be regarded as an ad hoc activity on the part of individual entrepreneurs, redeployment might be seen as a government policy stemming from a deliberate endeavour and genuine desire to phase out certain industrial activities or to limit the expansion of selected industrial sectors in favour of the developing countries;

Redeployment might be seen to involve decision-making in the industrialized countries at two levels: a) a decision by the entrepreneur to transfer productive capacity to a developing country, thereby contributing to its development; b) a decision by the government to establish a climate conducive to redeployment by offering appropriate incentives.

Redeployment should embrace more than the redeployment of certain existing physical units. It should include the deployment from industrialized countries to developing countries of technology, know-how, equipment, capital and other production factors essential to the creation of new industrial capacities in those countries.

Redeployment would help to increase the developing countries' share in world industrial production and, in turn, in world trade. Mobility of goods can thus be seen to be an essential feature of the redeployment concept.

The companies were also asked to report on the obstacles which they foresaw in their future redeployment activities. The crucial problem was seen to be financing and particularly a lack of funds. Import restrictions in the developing countries were also cited as a major obstacle.

A further significant obstacle was the shortage of skilled workers in developing countries. In many cases, the socio-political conditions of the recipient country were reported to constitute a further constraint, most frequently encountered in the form of political instability, state intervention in private business, cumbersome administrative procedures for company registration, and restrictions of profit transfers.

The preliminary surveys indicated that among the companies responding positively to the idea of redeployment, the medium-sized and small companies predominated slightly. The investigation revealed that the establishment of direct contacts between industries in developed and developing countries helped significantly to stimulate redeployment. The preliminary findings also seemed to confirm that government policies had a decisive effect upon the pace of structural adjustment and, by implication, upon redeployment of industries to developing countries.

The note concluded by suggesting that redeployment investigations might be extended to other industrialized countries, including those with centrally planned economies. As for the implementation of redeployment in an international setting, a monitoring system could be established to measure experience gained and progress achieved once contacts have been established between the industrialized and developing countries.

The UNIDO note cited above was reissued by the Regional Commission for Asia and the Pacific (E/ESCAP/IHT/MI/9 September 1977) with some changes and additions. It was noted that the earlier concept of redeployment defined a process that implies that certain productive capacities would move progressively to developing countries. These capacities are those which become less viable in developed countries due to long-term changes in factors such as raw materials, environmental production and social costs, and in demand. As such capacities are redeployed, developed countries move into other activities in their industrial and economic sectors. This concept is in need of further clarification in light of the survey.

The ESCAP report noted that redeployment is primarily conceived as a transfer process involving interaction between industrial entrepreneurs in developed and developing countries. It may be propagated under different forms and various types of mechanisms may apply, a predominant one being direct contact between industrial entrepreneurs in developed and developing countries. In the long run, redeployment may also develop among developing countries themselves. The process of redeployment will hardly come about by means of the market forces alone. Entrepreneurs in both developed and host developing countries need support and assistance if the process is to have significant impact. Such support may be rendered by national authorities in both developed and in host countries, and by international organizations. The ultimate aim of redeployment is the achievement of a better international division of labour.

15.3 Contributions of major international bodies 1974-78

The London Communique of the Commonwealth Heads of Government (June 1977) reported that Heads of Government commended the action of one developed member of the Commonwealth in deciding not to proceed with the establishment of an industry of substantial importance to several developing countries, and urged developed countries to take account of this principle in respect of other major industries in the trade of developing countries.

The Conference on International Economic Cooperation (CCEI-OM-6, June 1977) discussed the issue of redeployment but did not reach agreement on the formulation of the objectives. Both the group of developed and the group of developing countries agreed that "the establishment of new and improved forms of relationship between developed and developing countries within a liberalized world trading system" should include the "urgent adoption and strengthening by developed countries of adjustment assistance policies and measures." These measures should include labour market policies, according to the group of developed countries, but not according to the developing countries. The measures "would enable (the developed countries') industries progressively to move into viable lines of production and ... would alleviate adverse effects on industry and labour in the developed countries." The developing countries stated that the measures would "encourage (the developed countries') domestic industries to move progressively out of lines of production in which they are less competitive internationally and alleviate adverse effects on industry and labour." This would lead, according to the developing countries, to "structural adjustment in the developed countries and redeployment of productive capacities for such industries to developing countries while taking into account the economic, social and security interests of the developed countries." The group of developed countries adopted a revised formulation which does not make reference to the concept of redeployment: (the measures allow) "structural adjustments in the developed countries and (allow) the developing countries to make full use of long-term comparative advantages" while taking into account the above-mentioned interests of the developed countries.

WORLD ECONOMY ISSUE 16

Establishing Mechanisms For The Transfer Of
Technology To Developing Countries

16.1 The original formulation of the NIEO objective at the United Nations

Access to modern and appropriate technology by developing countries is essential for the fulfillment of their development objectives. Recognizing the need to regulate the international transfer of technology to better serve social and economic development objectives, the International Development Strategy for the Second United Nations Development Decade (October 1970) called for:

the review of international conventions on patents;

the identification and reduction of obstacles to the transfer of technology to developing countries;

facilitating access to patented and non-patented technology for developing countries under fair and reasonable terms and conditions;

facilitating the utilization of technology transferred to developing countries in order to assist these countries in attaining their trade and development objectives;

the development of technology suited to the productive structures of developing countries and measures to accelerate the development of indigenous technology.

The Programme of Action on the Establishment of the New International Economic Order (May 1974) devoted a separate heading to the issue of technology transfer, affirming that all efforts should be made:

To formulate an international code of conduct for the transfer of technology corresponding to needs and conditions prevalent in developing countries;

To give access on improved terms to modern technology and to adapt that technology, as appropriate to specific economic, social and ecological conditions and varying stages of development in developing countries;

To expand significantly the assistance from developed countries to developing countries in research and development programmes and in the creation of suitable indigenous technology;

To adapt commercial practices governing transfer of technology to the requirements of the developing countries and to prevent abuse of the rights of the sellers.

The Charter of Economic Rights and Duties of States (December 1974) reiterated the need for all States to facilitate the access of developing countries to the achievements of modern science and technology, including the transfer of technology and the creation of indigenous technology for the benefit of developing countries.

Development and International Economic Co-operation (Resolution 3362 September 1975) disussed the establishment of an industrial technological information bank with the possibility of regional and sectoral banks. This would allow for the greater flow to developing countries of information permitting the selection of technologies, in particular, advanced technologies. The Seventh Special Session also affirmed the need for more assistance from the developed to the developing countries in the area of science and technology programmes, in research and development, and in the creation of suitable indigenous technology. All States should co-operate in evolving an international code of conduct for the transfer of technology, corresponding in particular, to the special needs of the developing countries. Concomitant with the above, national patent systems should, without delay, be brought into line with the international patent system in its revised form. Developed countries should give developing countries the freest and fullest possible access to technologies whose transfer is not subject to private decision.

16.2 Specification and development of the NIEO objective at the United Nations 1974-78

A report by the UNCTAD Secretariat (TD/B/AC.11/10/Rev. 1 April 1974) stated that institutions connected with the transfer of technology from developed to developing countries should inter alia:

Be responsible for the registration, deposit, review and approval of agreements involving transfer of technology in the public and private sectors;

Undertake or assist in the evaluation, negotiation or renegotiation of contracts involving the transfer of technology;

Assist domestic enterprises in finding alternative potential suppliers of technology in accordance with the priorities of national development planning;

Make arrangements for the training of personnel to staff institutions concerned with the transfer of technology.

According to a report issued by the UNIDO Secretariat (ID/B/C.3/27, October 1974) each developing country needs to develop its own policy on the transfer of technology, surveillance over the flow of technology and foreign investment, and long-term technological development leading towards greater self-reliance and training of national personnel. An overall review of the impact of patent and licensing practices on the industrialization of developing countries is in order, together with an examination of the practice of developed countries of taxing earnings from the sale of technology to developing countries.

The Regional Commission of Africa, dealing with the Implementation of a New International Economic Order (E/CN.14/ECO/74, November 1974) discussed the substance of General Assembly resolutions concerning the transfer of technology. Technology transfer is possible only when a certain threshold of scientific and technical infrastraucture is given, in the form of institutions and manpower. This threshold could be reached by promoting the establishment of institutions for research and development in different sectors of the African economies, so as to provide a continuous flow of technology and technical services for production activities. It is also necessary to develop contacts between the science and engineering communities in African countries so as to promote joint action and collaboration in research and training and in tackling problems of multinational interest in science and technology.

According to another regional commission report from Western Asia (E/ECWA/21, April 1975), countries of the region should pay increased attention to the transfer of technology so as to acquire a suitable form of technology which is easily adaptable to their specific needs and which is obtained on reasonable terms and conditions. The countries of the region should realize the importance of establishing industrial research and development institutions, in order to lessen their dependence on imported technology. As with the above cited regional report from Africa, the need for a stronger infrastructure was mentioned. The availability of technology transfers to the region depends to a large extent on an adequate supply of skilled personnel, including production engineers, product and machinery designers, and top echelon managers.

A further regional commission report issued by Latin America (E/15608, May 1975) stressed the regional nature of technology transfer, and the promotion of a regional information pool on technology marketing techniques in order to favour individual or joint negotiations on technological know-how. It called for the provision of incentives at the regional level for the generation and development of national technology and the substitution of imported technology.

A progress report on the transfer of technology issued by the UNCTAD Secretariat (TD/B/C.6/9/Add. 3 November 1975) emphasized the need to improve the terms of transfer and of indigenous technology capacity in order to meet the target developing countries have set for themselves, of producing a quarter of the world's industrial output by the end of the century. The report lists the following objectives of a technology policy:

development of a technological capacity to produce goods and services;

the ability to make autonomous decisions in the field of technology;

control over the import of technology;

increased capacity to apply technology;

progressive redirection of demand for technology from foreign to domestic sources;

development of ability to create technology.

The report continues indicating six main and interlinked areas of policy and institutions affecting the transfer and development of technology:
development strategy;

attitude to foreign investment;

contractual arrangements directly related to transfer of technology;

research and development;

industrial project preparation;

education and training.

As for regional and subregional issues regarding technology transfer, the report states that such centres need support at the global level. First and foremost effective information systems are required on the availability and sources of alternative technologies, their nature, costs, and the conditions attached to their transfer. Guidelines for both developing and developed countries in the area of transfer of technology, were offered by the UNCTAD Secretariat in a report (TD/190/Supp. February, 1976). Developing countries should establish their own policies and institutions, their own technological plans, with national centres as the first step. These centres would be progressively linked subregionally, regionally, inter-regionally and by sectors, within the framework of national and collective self-reliance.

The report suggested that developed countries might promote the transfer to and development of technology in developing countries by taking a more active part in guiding the policies of transnational corporations and by encouraging public sector enterprises in developed countries to assist developing countries in this area. Governments in the developed countries could make available the particulars of small and medium-sized firms through their export promotion machinery and should encourage linkages between Research and Development institutes in developed and developing countries through the World Association of Industrial and Technological Research Organizations.

According to UNCTAD Resolution (98(IV) May 1976), developed countries and competent international institutions should assist the institutions of least developed countries in obtaining the results of scientific and technological development appropriate to their requirements. Transfer of technology should be on terms favourable to the least developed countries. Assistance in the establishment of transfer of technology centres designed to obtain necessary technological information, to select from available alternatives and to negotiate proper terms and conditions for external collaboration is urged. Furthermore, it is urged that developed countries facilitate the transfer of patented, patent-related and non-patented technology, including know-how, suited to the economic conditions of the least developed countries. They should also provide the necessary assistance for establishing institutions of applied technology, with the aim of developing indigenous technologies and promoting the adaption of imported technologies to national requirements, and consider appropriate linkages with international and regional centres of technology and research.

The Secretary-General of the United Nations, in a report on the Establishment of a Network for the Exchange of Technological Information (E/5839, June 1976), submitted the following recommendations:

That Governments give attention to the importance of national arrangements for the intake and use of technological information for the transfer and development of technology at the national level;

That programmes, projects, systems and services in the area of information exchange for the transfer and development of technology be given priority by financing and executing agencies and organizations of the United Nations system with emphasis on the strengthening of relevant national infrastructures and training opportunities;

That regional commissions and other relevant parts of the United Nations system examine, in close consultation with the member States concerned, their role and contribution with regard to the envisaged network;

That meetings be organized at the regional level to identify more clearly the needs of the developing countries in the respective regions. These meetings should also allow for a listing and consideration of the information resources of each region with regard to their capacity to meet the needs of users in the various sectors;

That high-level expert missions to developing countries be undertaken to explore the potential relationship between the network and governmental policies;

That, in line with the request of General Assembly Resolution 3507 (XXX) use be made of the widest possible expertise and that the Advisory Committee on the Application of Science and Technology to Development be consulted at its forthcoming twenty-second and possibly twenty-third sessions as to its views with regard to the establishment of the envisaged network;

That the widest possible coverage be given, notably by the Office of Public Information and the Centre for Economic and Social Information, to the need for establishing a world-wide exchange network for the transfer of technological information as well as the various initiatives under way which would lead to its early implementation.

The Western Asia Regional Commission (F/ECWA/50 March, 1977) emphasized that the other commissions, ESCAP, ECA and ECLA have aimed at establishing regional centres for the transfer and development of technology. The Economic Commission for Western Asia consulted with UNCTAD for the purpose of initiating a concrete regional programme contributing to and arriving at a gradual reduction of technological dependence of Western Asia countries by establishing the appropriate mechanisms such as a Western Asia Centre for the Transfer and Development of Technology.

The Economic Commission for Latin America (E/CEPAL/1030/PEV.1 77-5-1064)1977) stressed the adoption of an international code of conduct of a binding nature on the transfer of technology and the revision of the Paris Convention for the Protection of Intellectual Property. It suggested that all efforts should be made to accelerate action on the following matters:

The establishment in the countries of the region of appropriate institutional machinery; especially national centres for the development and transfer of technology;

The strengthening of the region's own capacity for technological adaptation and creation, an objective which, together with that of the transfer of technology from outside, should be brought about in the conditions required by the development of each country and in accordance with the guidelines laid down at the national level;

The establishment and improvement of public sector machinery to help to locate and disseminate technologies suited to these conditions and to enable the State to fulfill its responsibility to secure suitable technologies for development on the world market;

The preparation of preferential agreements for the development and transfer of technology between Latin America and other developing regions;

The establishment in Latin America or strengthening of subregional and regional centres for the development and transfer of technology which can serve as a link with the national centres of the other developing countries;

The establishment or strengthening of subregional, regional and interregional centres in Latin America for the development and transfer of technology in specific and critical sectors.

The Commission recognized that a significant degree of technical progress had been reached in Latin America and that the countries of the region should take steps to actively stimulate the transfer and dissemination of technologies among themselves in areas that would enhance balanced economic and social development.

UNIDO Resolution 47 (XI) (June 1977) noted that in order to create an integrated programme in the field of development and transfer of industrial technology that would give developing countries access to the requisite information on alternate industrial technologies, costs, and suppliers, the following areas need to be strengthened:

The formulation and implementation of national technology plans and programmes and the identification and implementation of measures for improving them;

the elaboration of policies on the development and transfer of industrial technology;

the establishment, improvement and interlinking of national, subregional, regional and interregional centres, including special attention to strengthening technological extension and field services, with emphasis on the transfer, development and practical application of industrial technology; and the interlinking of such centres along with the Industrial and Technological Information Bank into the network for the exchange of technological information as provided in General Assembly Resolution 31/183;

the promotion of dissemination and exports, as widely as possible, of technologies from developing countries;

The selection of available industrial technology, the adaptation of that technology to local economic and social conditions and the development of indigenous and appropriate technology;

the examination and evaluation of the technical, economic, commercial and development implications of industrial technology transfers;

training programmes at national, regional, subregional and international levels, seminars and exchange of personnel in technical activities, especially aimed at providing the capability to acquire, evaluate and manage industrial technology for personnel in developing countries and for the better utilization and development of skilled personnel within and between developing countries;

studies and the publication of their conclusions on ways and means to promote technological and industrial co-operation among developing countries, including co-operative projects that can be implemented with the technical resoures of those countries;

the initiation of specific co-operation activities among the developing countries which will cover the exchange of personnel for purposes of providing advice or receiving training, and the facilitation of institutional co-operation involving, inter alia, research institutes and enterprises that carry out engineering studies and provide consulting services;

the intensification of courses on technological and industrial management, including industrial technological information in accordance with the needs of each country.

An international code of conduct of technology transfer was discussed at UNCTAD (TD/AC.1/9, 25 July - 2 August 1977). It was affirmed that the code should be universally applicable and therefore all countries should ensure that their enterprises, whether private or public, should conform in all respects to the provisions of this code. Furthermore, an international legally binding instrument is the only form capable of effectively regulating the transfer of technology. An international transfer of technology occurs when technology of a proprietary or non-proprietary nature and/or rights related thereto is transferred across national boundaries from a Supplying Party to an Acquiring Party. Transfer of technology is the transfer of production, management or marketing technologies by any means is not limited to transactions involving the sale of goods. Transfer of technology comprises any or all of the following:

Assignment, sale and licensing transactions, arrangements or agreements covering all forms of industrial property including patents, inventors' certificates, utility models, industrial designs, trade marks, service names, and trade names, legally protected inventions and other forms of industrial property insofar as they are an integral part of transactions involving technology transfers. Such industrial property as inventions protected by patents or inventors' certificates, utility models, industrial design, as well as trade marks, service names and trade names insofar as they are part of the technology transfer transaction.

Arrangements covering the provision of know-how and technical expertise in the form of feasibility studies, plans, diagrams, models, instructions, guides, formulae, supply of services, specifications and/or involving technical advisory and managerial personnel, and personnel training as well as equipment for training.

The technological contents of transactions, arrangements or agreements covering the provision of basic or detailed engineering designs, the installation, operation and functioning of plant and equipment, and turn-key agreements.

The technological contents of purchases, leases and other forms of acquistion of machinery, equipment, intermediate goods and/or raw materials insofar as they are an integral part of transactions, arrangements or agreements involving technology transfers.

The technological contents of industrial and technical co-operation arrangements of any kind including turn-key agreements, international subcontracting as well as provision of management and marketing services.

In another report of an inter-governmental group of experts on the Code of Conduct issued by UNCTAD (TD/AC.1/11, November 1977), specific measures for the special treatment for developing countries were spelled out. Developing countries should be given the fullest possible access to technologies whose transfer is not subject to private decision. Encouragement of the training of personnel from developing countries and the adaptation of research and development to local conditions was also stressed. Assistance should be rendered in the strengthening of technological capacity, particularly in the basic sectors of national economics and in the assessment of existing technologies to available scientific and industrial research data. The growth of innovative capacities and the estalishment of technology transfer centres were designated as areas which require cooperation.

The report enunciated items that should be taken into account by developed countries in their technology related policies. Contributions to the development of national technologies by providing experts under development assistance and research exchange programmes were stressed, along with provisions for training in research, engineering and design. Developed countries should further undertake the development of technologies appropriate to the needs of developing countries.

16.3 Contributions of major international bodies

The third Ministerial Conference of the Group of 77 (TD/195, February 1976) reiterated the need for the establishment of regional centres for the development and transfer of technology, to serve as essential links with national centres in developing countries. The need for technical assistance through the exchange of experts, advisory services and training courses was reiterated, along with the need for collective efforts at joint projects among the developing countries themselves.

The requisite section of the Manila Declaration (TD/195 7 February 1976), dealing with transfer of technology, put forth suggestions for the developing countries at the national level:

Formulation of a technology plan as an integral part of their national development plans, as well as the co-ordination of policies in a number of interrelated areas, including licensing arrangements, transfer, development and adaptation of technology, industrial property laws and practices, foreign investments, research and development;

Establishment of appropriate institutional machinery, including national centres for the development and transfer of technology with urgent attention being paid to defining the role and functions of such centres, including the principal linkages which need to be established with other national bodies or institutions;

Elabaoration of all necessary measures to ensure optimum utilization of their qualified manpower resources.

The Manila Declaration also stated that developed countries should grant the developing   countries unrestricted access to existing technology irrespective of the ownership of such technology.   Together with the developed countries, competent international institutions should

Assist the institutions of least developed countries to obtain, under preferential terms and conditions and at a minimum cost, the results of scientific and technological developments appropriate to their requirements;

In order to overcome the technological and negotiating weaknesses of the least developed countries, assist in the establishment and transfer of technology centres designed to obtain necessary technological information, to select from available alternatives and to negotiate proper terms and conditions for external collaboration;

Make arrangements for the grant of patented, patent-related and non-patented technologies, including know-how, suited to the economic conditions of the least developed countries;

Provide the necessary assistance for establishing institutions of applied technology, with the aim of developing indigenous technologies and promoting the adaptation of imported technologies to national requirements.

The Declaration on International Investment and Multinational Enterprises, issued by OECD on 21 June 1976, stated that enterprises should:

endeavor to ensure that their activities fit satisfactorily into the scientific and technological policies and plans of the countries in which they operate, and contribute to the development of national scientific and technological capacities, including as far as appropriate the establishment and improvement in host countries of their capacity to innovate;

to the fullest extent practicable, adopt in the course of their business activities practices which permit the rapid diffusion of technologies with due regard to the protection of industrial and intellectual property rights;

when granting licenses for the use of industrial property rights or when otherwise transferring technology do so on reasonable terms and conditions.

Participants in the Conference on International Economic Cooperation (A/31/478/Add.1, August 1977) agreed that the Paris Convention for the Protection of Industrial Property should be revised in WIPO, taking fully into account the interests of the developing countries. It would be necessary to strengthen the ability of developing countries to select, adapt, develop, and apply technology, including its institutional aspects and training as well as promotion of developing countries' exports of technology.

The Final Communique of the Commonwealth Heads of Government Meeting (June 1977) asked for the establishment of new mechanisms for financing industrial development, and the transfer, development and diffusion of appropriate technology. Measures should be taken to promote the development of specific industries, where the developing countries in commonwealth countries have developed or will develop a comparative advantage.

WORLD ECONOMY ISSUE 17

Regulating and Supervising the Activities of Transactional Enterprises and Eliminating Restrictive Business Practices

17.1 The original formulation of the NIEO objective at the United Nations

The program of Action on the Establshment of a NIEO (May 1974) laid the ground work for this issue of vital interest, especially to developing countries, with the following proposals:

All efforts should be made to formulate, adopt and implement an international code of conduct for transnational corporations:

(a) To prevent interference in the internal affairs of the countries where they operate and their collaboration with racist regimes and colonial administrations;

(b) To regulate their activities in host countries to eliminate restrictive business practices and to conform to the national development plan and objectives of developing countries, and in this context facilitate, as necessary, the review and revision of previously concluded arrangements;

(c) To bring about assistance, transfer of technology and management skills to developing countries on equitable and favourable terms;

(d) To regulate the repatriation of the profits accruing from their operations, taking into account the legitimate interests of all parties concerned;

(e) To promote reinvestment of their profits in developing countries.

Development and International Economic Co-operation, the resolution of the Seventh Special Session (September 1975) elaborated on the objective concerning restrictive business practices:

Restrictive business practices adversely affecting international trade, particularly that of developing countries, should be eliminated and efforts should be made at the national and international levels with the objective of negotiating a set of equitable principles and rules.

Earlier, the International Development Strategy for the Second United National Development Decade (October 1970) recognized the need to identify the various types of restrictive business practices with a view to the consideration of appropriate remedial measures early in the decade.

(Among restrictive business practices are those designed to prohibit the market allocation of exports from developing countries, and those aimed at securing the domination of key sectors in developing countries through anti-competitive acquisitions; others concern abuses of industrial property rights and discriminatory pricing arrangements.)

The Charter of Economic Rights and Duties of States (December 1974) declared that each State has the right to regulate and supervise the activities of transnational corporations, in order to ensure that activities of TNC's corporations shall not intervene in the internal affairs of a host State.

The Lima Declaration and Programme of Action (March 1975) reiterated the proposal for an international code of conduct in regulating and supervising the affairs of transnational corporations, in order to ensure that activities of TNC's are compatible with the development plans and policies of host countries.

17.2 Specification and development of the NIEO objective at the United Nations, 1974-78

The following lines of inquiry were suggested by the UNCTAD Secretariat (TD/B/C.2/160, 1 May 1975) for a systematic study of restrictive business practices:

What particular objective of restrictive business practice legislation are pertinent to the conditions and economic structures in developing countries?

What type of restrictive practices governments tend to control? Are such controls practicable, desirable and adequate for developing countries?

What types of administrative machinery are at present employed to implement and enforce national legislation and what types of mechanisms are needed for achieving the results in the developing countries?

The UNCTAD report pointed out that existing legislations regulating restrictive practices vary depending upon the objectives sought and the economic, social and political conditions prevailing in each country. Among the common objectives present in existing legislation are the following:

The attainment of greater economic efficiency and an improved allocation of resources, especially through the creation and maintenance of competition, control of dominant economic power, concentration of capital, control of prices and profits, consumer protection through the control of unfair trading practices, protection of small-scale enterprise and maintnenace of employment opportunities. . .

(As is evident from the above, to achieve a balance between the varying objectives is often a delicate matter, since basic conflicts may exist even within a single nation. In respect of a number of specific issues mentioned above, there are some national legislations in both the developing and developed countries which have common objectives. For example, a primary objective of a number of restrictive business practice laws is the avoidance of undue concentration of financial power with a view to securing a more equal distribution of income and wealth.)

The UNCTAD report further pointed out that:

Restrictive practices which governments control relate primarily to activities within the domestic market, namely to the manufacture, distribution and sale of products and to a lesser extent to provision of services. . . . They also seek to control the fixing of volumes of production, for example by means of quotas and the allocation of production areas on an exclusive or non-exclusive basis; the fixing of volumes or prices of sales and the allocation of sales territory both domestic and foreign; acquisition of dominant market power through mergers, takeovers and partial acquisitions or by having common directorships. The restrictive practices also include (a) boycott arrangements (refusals to supply or sell); (b) tied purchasing arrangements in respect of materials, intermediate products and finished products and (c) tied selling arrangements.

Recognizing the inter-relationship between the specific objectives to be followed at the national level, as well as the need for cooperative action at the international level for establishing effective measures to eliminate restrictive business practices, UNCTAD noted during its fourth session (Resolution 96 (IV), 31 May 1976) that:

> Action should be taken by countries in a mutually reinforcing manner at the national, regional and international levels to eliminate or effectively deal with restrictive business practices, including those of transnational corporations, adversely affecting international trade, particularly that of developing countries, and the economic development of these countries.

> . . . . Action should be taken by all countries, particularly by developed countries, to institute or improve appropriate procedures for notification of restrictive business practices.

> . . . . Action should be taken . . . . within the framework for UNCTAD . . . . to (hold) negotiations with the objectives of formulating a set of multilaterially agreed equitable principles and rules for the control of restrictive business practices . . . .

> Collection and dissemination of information . . . . by the UNCTAD secretariat and in close cooperation with the Information and Research Centre on Transnational Corporations;

> Provision of technical assistance of developing countries. . . . especially in respect of training of their officials;

> Elaboration of a model law or laws on restrictive business practices . . . . in order to assist developing countries in devising appropriate legislation.

In respect of the preparation of a Model Law or Laws, an ad hoc intergovernmental group of experts on restrictive business practices has been formed.

Simultaneously, the Commission of Transnational Corporations has also been concerned with the subject of restrictive business practices as one of the elements to be included in the proposed Code of Conduct for Transnational Corporations. In a background report prepared by the United Nations Centre for Transnational Corporations (20 July 1976) the issues involved were raised for consideration. These include "transfer pricing" of goods and services which are traded between various affiliates - or between parent and affiliate - located in different countries.

These intracorporate transfer prices may be unilaterally set by the corporation at levels that do not correspond to international prices, or they may be disadvantageous to a particular country . . . . In some cases, arbitrary transfer prices are set because international prices exist for similar products. Often the effect of transfer pricing is a loss of tax revenues and increased flows of funds out of the country in which the affiliate operates.

In the area of transfer pricing, some degree of intergovernmental cooperation (exchange of information or specific agreement) appears desirable...

The wide differences in the objective of anti-trust legislation and regulations around the world and the varying concepts of "reasonableness" of business restrictions or dominant patterns, as well as the different conceptions of "abuse" of a dominant position, sometimes make detailed regulations difficult. However, TNC's could be made responsible for reporting any use of restrictive business practices to local governments, and appropriate corporate disclosure regulations would make it possible to do much towards controlling abuses.

In a note prepared by the UNCTAD Secretariat on the considerations involved in the drafting of a Model Law or Laws on restrictive business practices (6 September 1976), it was suggested that "to be of assistance to developing countries, generally, it must be designed to meet a wide diversity in economic and social structures and in levels of economic development." Consequently "any single approach to the control of restrictive business practices seems unlikely to be suitable for all developing countries . . . . It might therefore be useful to envisage a comprehensive Model Law setting out the broad spectrum of practices which can be of concern to developing countries and a range of possible approaches to the control of such practices."

"Transnational Corporations: Issues Involved in the Formulation of a Code of Conduct" (E/.CN/CTNC/2, 28 January 1977) suggested that the purpose of a Code of Conduct for TNC's is "to ensure that TNC activities are consonant with host country objectives," and "to formulate specific policies and laws on TNCs by providing internationally acceptable models and suggesting patterns of legislation" -- leading to a harmonization of national laws, thus reducing the ability of TNCs to take advantage of differences between national regulations in optimizing their global activities.

In drafting provisions of the code the different types of transnational enterprises should be taken into consideration (extractive, agri-business, finance, manufacturing, shipping, commercial, tourism, etc.) as well as their objectives for locating in a country (such as markets, resources, or least-cost production).

Three categories of legal instruments might be used for a code of conduct:

An international multilateral convention, signed and ratified by sovereign States;

A declaration of principles (and rules), adopted at an international conference by participating sovereign States;

A resolution of an organ of an international organization (United Nations General Assembly, Economic and Social Council).

The language of any legal instrument used should be precise and specific and allow little leeway for differing interpretations.

Main issues of the code should cover: observances of local laws; adherence to economic goals and development objectives of host countries; adherence to socio-cultural objectives and values of host countries; and respect for human rights and fundamental freedoms.

Political issues should include prohibition of interference in national political affairs, interference in intergovernmental relations, and illicit payments.

Economic and commercial issues   should include full permanent sovereignty of all States over their resources; a clearly defined and announced statement by host countries of the areas and conditions under which they are ready to accept foreign investment; the obligation of TNC's to help alleviate balance-of-payment problems (such as by increasing local processing and thus contributing to the diversification and expansion of exports); close attention to inter-company transactions associated with transnationals; international co-ordination and agreement on taxation; elimination of restrictive business practices; reasonable terms and conditions for rapid technology transfer commensurate with development needs; right of trade unions as respresentatives of workers; protection of the rights of employees and the conditions of employment; training and promotion of local workers; consumer protection by revealing sales prohibitions imposed by home or other host countries; co-operation of TNC's with host Governments for environmental protection; and detailed financial accounts and other data not only for the branch in any particular country but also for the parent company available to Governments, unions, and the general public.

Member countries should treat TNCs and domestic enterprises equitably and in accordance with international law; yet allowing for "preferential and non-reciprocal treatment for developing countries, whenever feasible."

Countries should refrain from extraterritorial application of their domestic legislation, unless it is exercised under bilateral or, preferably, multilateral agreements.

Unless arbitration is mutually agreed upon, the jurisdiction of the nationalizing State should govern compensation matters for enterprises nationalized in the public interest by host states:

Prescriptions and prohibitions for a code of conduct might be general or specific, outright or qualified, mandatory or recommendatory:

The mechanisms for implementation may range from the establishment of permanent institutions entrusted with requisite competence to voluntary procedures; from machinery for periodic review for the instrument for machinery for dispute settlement and for sanctions for non-compliance; several combinations of approach are possible.

Implementation of the legal instrument by national authorities does not exclude the need for external supervision by international institutional organs. This may range from the relatively passive role of an agency responsible receiving information concerning national action on implementing of the instrument to the active monitoring and investigation of pertinent national activity.

Countries vary on whether the code of conduct should be voluntary or binding and whether disputes should be settled by arbitration or exclusive jurisdiction of the courts of the host country.

The African Regional Meeting on a Code of Conduct for Transnational Corporations (E/CN.14/CTNC/3, 11 February 1977) reaffirmed the basic principles proposed above. African countries favour a binding code with mandatory provisions and with disputes settled by the exclusive jurisdiction of the host country. They also believe that TNCs should accept renegotiation of agreements which were not in conformity with the NIEO in a manner consistent with the national development objectives of the host countries;

respect national socio-cultural objectives and values and avoid transplanting undesirable and unacceptable alien customs and practices;

not operate or deal with racist and illegal regimes and those applying policies of apartheid and should not violate sanctions imposed by the United Nations;

abstain from all corrupt practices.

The Report of the Third Committee of High-Level Government Experts (E/CEPAL/1025, 30 March 1977) further confirmed the nature of the work aimed at preparing an International Code of Conduct governing the activities of transnational corporations. The Latin American countries should maintain the position which the developing countries have defended in many forums, to wit, that the code of conduct should be binding.

The report reiterated the need for transnational corporations to comply with laws and regulations of the host country and to refrain from interference in the internal affairs of the States in which they operate. Transnationals should abstain from restrictive commercial practices and comply with national development policies particularly in the development of their scientific and technological capacity.

The Reconvened Tripartite Advisory Meeting on the Relationship of Multinational Enterprises and Social Policy (GB.203/6/2, Geneva 4-7 April 1977) affirmed the positive contribution multinational enterprises could make to economic and social progress. It pointed out at the same time that it is necessary to minimize and resolve the difficulties to which their various operations may give rise, taking into account the United Nations resolutions on the Establishment of a New International Economic Order. Proposals emanating from the Advisory Meeting concerned inter alia the need for multinational enterprises to increase employment opportunities and standards in the host country by means of the following measures:

consultations with national workers and employers organizations;

increase the use of technologies which generate employment;

promote the local processing of raw materials;

participate in programmes which would foster skill formation and vocational guidance among workers;

afford opportunities within the enterprise as a whole in suitable fields such as industrial relations.

The Resumed Second Session and the Third Session of the Commission on Transnational Corporations (E/5986C/C.10/32/Suppl. 5, May 1977) formulated guidelines in regard to the behaviour of transnational enterprises in the less developed countries. It especially elaborated the need for Transnationals to contribute to development objectives, and to forego political interference in the affairs of the host country.

17.3 Contributions of major international bodies, 1974-78

The Manila Declaration (TD/195, February 1976) stressed that agreement should be reached on the following areas:

Measures to be taken at national, regional and international levels in order to ensure that transnational corporations reorient their activities towards more complete manufacturing in developing countries and towards the further processing therein of raw materials for both the domestic and foreign markets. The developed countries should take steps to adjust their policies, particularly in the field of tariff and non-tariff protection, foreign-exchange regulations, foreign investment and fiscal and financial incentives, to facilitate the above-mentioned measures to be adopted by the transnational corporations;

Measures to strengthen the participation of national enterprises of developing countries in the activities undertaken by transnational corporations in their territories, particularly those relating to the export of manufactures and semi-manufactures;

Equitable principles and rules to govern the control of restrictive business practices which include measures for the control of the practices of transnational corporations adversely affecting the developing countries' ability to export manufactures and semi-manufactures;

Measures designed to ensure the regulation and control of the activities of transnational corporations in order that they may be a positive factor in the export efforts of developing countries, so that the latter may acquire greater control over the processing, marketing and distribution of their manufactures and semi-manufactures.

On 21 June 1976 the OECD offered fresh guidelines concerning TNEs in the Declaration on International Investment and Multinational Enterprises. Enterprises should:

> refrain from participating in or otherwise purposely strengthening the restrictive effects of international or domestic cartels or restrictive agreements which adversely affect or eliminate competition and which are not generally or specifically accepted under applicable national or international legislation . . . . allow purchasers, distributors and licensees freedom to resell, export, purchase and develop their operations consistent with law, trade conditions, the need for specialisation and sound commercvial practice;

> Endeavour to ensure that their activities fit satisfactorily into the scientific and technological policies and plans of the countries in which they operate, and contribute to the development of national scientific and technological capacities, including as far as appropriate the establishment and improvement in host countries of their capacity to innovate;

> To the fullest extent practicable, adopt in the course of their business activities practices which permit the rapid diffusion of technologies with due regard to the protection of industrial and intellectual property rights;

> When granting licenses for the use of industrial property rights or when other wise transferring technology, do so on reasonable terms and conditions.

Finally, the Conference on International Co-operation (June 1977) found agreement on the need for legally binding principles for the control of restrictive business practices, particularly by transnational corporations. Developed countries agreed that their investors operating in developing countries should be subject in all their activities to the national jurisdiction of the host country. The Conference reached agreement on a fundamental principle that has been mentioned frequently in the above-mentioned documents, namely, that each country has the right to ask foreign contributors to respect the course it has chosen to follow and to request assistance which fits in, as far as possible, with its development plans.

The proposals contained in the final report of the conference include the following reference:

> Barriers to fair competition between marketing enterprises of developed and developing countries should be eliminated . . . measures should be taken . . . to contain unfair trade practices in advertising.

WORLD ECONOMY ISSUE 18

Improving the Competitiveness of Natural Resources and Ending Their Waste

18.1 The original formulation of the NIEO objective at the United Nations

The problem of natural resources, as that of food, figures prominently in the discussions on the NIEO.   The objectives are particularly defined in respect of protecting natural resources from competition by synthetics, and undertaking conservation measures to end their waste.

The Declaration on the Establishment of the NIEO (May 1974) called for "improving the competitiveness of natural materials facing competition from synthetic substitutes."   To bring about the improved competitiveness of natural materials, the Programme of Action on the Establishment of the NIEO requested that:

> in cases where natural materials can satisfy the requirements of the market, new investment for the expansion of the capacity to produce synthetic materials should not be made.

The Programme of Action further called for measures to expand the markets for natural products in relation to synthetics and to fully utilize the ecological advantages of these products.

Preceding the United Nations Sixth Special Session, the International Development Strategy for the Second United Nations Development Decade (October 1970) called for "appropriate action...to diversify the end uses of natural products facing competition from synthetics and substitutes."   This Resolution also requested that national policies should not give special encouragement "to the creation and utilization of new production,particularly in the developed countries, of directly competing synthetics."

In the Lima Declaration and Plan of Action on Industrial Development and Cooperation (March 1975), the developed countries were asked to "assist the developing countries in raising the competitiveness of their Production from natural raw materials in respect to synthetic substances in order to achieve general progress."

In regard to the conservation and proper use of natural resources, the Declaration on the Establishment of a New International Economic Order called for "full respect of the principle: the need for all States to put an end to the waste of natural resources, including food products."

The Lima Declaration and Plan of Action further recommended that:

> ...In view of the need to conserve non-renewable resources, all countries, particularly developed countries, should avoid wasteful consumption and, in that context, the developing countries possessing such resources should formulate a policy of economic diversification with a view to acquiring other means of financing which are not based on intensive exploitation of those resources.

18.2   Specification and development of the NIEO objective at the
        United Nations, 1974-78

A report by the Executive Director of UNEP (UNEP GC/14/Add.Z, 2
December 1973) proposed working out a more detailed programme for dealing
with the technical and industrial aspects of the ecological-economic
evaluation of the competition between synthetic and natural products. This
programme would:

Identify the products that would need to be studied;

Establish a priority among the studies;

Identify alternative approaches or methodologies for undertaking
such studies and make recommendations as to the most desirable
approach;

Suggest economic and social indicators as well as environmental
components that should be considered, including a methodology for
determining trade-offs.

UNIDO considered the principle regarding the improving of the competitiveness of natural materials facing competition from synthetic substitutes
in a report by its Secretariat (ID/C.3/28, 1 May 1974). This principle,
according to the report, will become an increasingly important feature of the
study programme for, and of the technical assistance provided by UNIDO to
the textile industry in developing countries.
    In September 1974, the UNCTAD Secretariat reviewed the problems of,
and policies for, natural products facing competition from synthetics and
substitutes in a report by its committee on commodities (TD/BC-1/SYN/65).
The general conclusion reached is that the upward tread in synthetic prices
will enable producers of natural products to obtain better prices and will
"offer an opportunity to challenge competition from synthetics in the longer
term." It was felt, however, that the need for concerted measures to improve
the competitiveness of natural products is as great as ever. Such measures
should be directed to:

increase production;

provide stable prices competitive with those of synthetics through
adequate stock holding prices;

improve the efficiency of marketing arrangements including supplies, stocks, availability, and quality.

It was further noted that an associated need is for expanded Research
and Development activities on processing and utilization and efficient sales
promotion techniques including technical services to diffuse the results of
research and development.

The principle of avoiding waste of natural resources has been recognized by the Third United Nations Conference on the Law of the Sea in so far as it is relevant for the exploitation of the resources of the deep sea-bed. Article 150 of the proposed composite negotiating text (A/CONF. 62/WP.10 July 1977) dealing with "Policies relating to activities in the Area," includes inter alia the following:

> orderly and safe development and rational management of the resources of the area, as well as the efficient conduct of activities in the area in accordance with sound principles of conservation and the avoidance of waste.

18.3   Contributions of major international bodies, 1974-78

The Conference of Developing Countries on Raw Materials held at Dakar (E/AC/627/6, February 1975) adopted an Action Programme which set out the main objectives of cooperation among developing countries in the field of raw materials and other commodities.   One such objective was "to improve the competitive position of natural products exported by developing countries versus synthetic products."

This principle was also the subject of discussion by the 1977 Conference on International Economic Cooperation (A/31/478/Add. 1). The report noted that "The participants in the Conference recognized the importance to the economic and social development of certain developing countries of earnings from exports of natural products subject to competition from synthetic products."   Unfortunately, the participants were not able to agree on a common position regarding the production of synthetics.   There was agreement, however, with regard to research and development.   Among the agreed measures were the following:

> Measures to ensure intensified research and encourage the transfer to technology to improve the productivity and quality of natural products to meet market demand and to foster new uses.

> Increased international technical and financial assistance to research centres to promote the competitiveness of natural products subject to substitution from synthetics.

> Measures for research and development by national and international institutions should be considered in the course of discussions and negotiations on individual commodities, subject to substitution from synthetics, within as well as outside the Integrated Programme for Commodities.

The CIEC also discussed the avoidance of the waste of resources.   Its participants held that "it is for each country to frame its development strategy by determining what it regards as the most judicious blend of investment having regard to its own particular situation, general economic policy and development model." The Conference document pointed out that, in this connection, "care must be taken to avoid wasting resources by investment in infrastructure whose construction and operating costs are out of all proportion to the benefits derived."

WORLD ECONOMY ISSUE 19

Providing Equitable Access to the Resources of the Sea-Bed
and the Ocean Floor

19.1   The original formulation of the NIEO objective at the United Nations

Prior to the adoption of the basic documents calling for a New International Economic Order, the subject of sea-bed resource exploitation has received consideration in the General Assembly of the United Nations. In Resolution 2749 (XXV) (17 December 1970), the General Assembly has established certain general principles.   A special committee for sea-bed issues was created to examine further the principles governing the resources of the sea-bed, declared to be "the Common Heritage of Mankind." The deliberations of the sea-bed committee led further to the establishment of the Third United Nations Conference on the Law of the Sea, whose principal task has been to prepare a comprehensive multilateral convention to govern all activities of States in the ocean space.   The conference in its seventh session (Geneva, 1978) had before it a composite single negotiating text whose provisions bear on the here discussed NIEO objective.
Article 29 of the Charter of Economic Rights and Duties of States (December 1974) stated the common responsibilites of the international community with respect to the oceans:

The sea-bed and ocean floor and the subsoil thereof, beyond the limits of national jurisdiction, as well as the resources of the area, are the common heritage of mankind... All States shall ensure that the exploration of the area and exploitation of its resources are carried out exclusively for peaceful purposes and that the benefits derived therefrom are shared equitably by all States, taking into account the particular interests and needs of developing countries; an international regime applying to the area and its resources and including appropriate international machinery to give effect to its provisions shall be established by an international treaty of a universal character, generally agreed upon.

19.2   Specification and Development of the NIEO Objective at the United
       Nations 1974-78

Although the preparation of international treaty mentioned above in
Article 29 of the Charter has been entrusted to the Third United Nations
Conference on the Law of the Sea, other United Nations agencies such as
UNCTAD are also involved in the examination of the impact of sea-bed
mining on the land-based economies of the developing countries.

A report prepared by the UNCTAD Secretariat entitled, "Implications of
the exploitation of the mineral resources of the international areas of the
sea-bed: issues of international commodity policy" (TD/B/C.1/170, January 1975) stated:

> The greater availabilities and presumed lower costs associated with
> production of minerals from the sea-bed - a completely new source
> of supply - would bring benefits to the world economy as a whole.
> However, under a policy of exploitation of such resources that was
> guided by normal commercial criteria rather than social criteria, the
> distribution of the economic benefits concerned would be very
> uneven.   It would bring direct benefits to the consumers of the
> minerals concerned who are, by and large, in the developed
> countries....

> On the other hand, the chief consequence of such production for
> land-based producers of the minerals concerned would be that their
> total export earnings from those minerals would grow less rapidly
> than they would have done otherwise, and might in some circum-
> stances decline from previously achieved levels.   The introduction of
> sea-bed production could be expected to result in lower market
> prices for the minerals concerned...Because output from the sea-bed
> is likely to be relatively low-cost, it would tend to displace marginal
> land-based production...The severity of the impact would vary
> among countries and producing enterprises according to relative
> efficiencies, patterns of trade and market structures.

During 1974-75, UNCTAD had carried out four case studies relating to
cobalt, manganese ore, coffee and nickel, for exploring the possible impact of
sea-bed mining of those metals.   Summarizing its findings,   the UNCTAD
Secretariat pointed out that:

> The earnings of the developing countries from the export of the
> commodities in question would, in each case, be lower than in the
> absence of sea-bed mining...The estimated shortfall in the export
> earnings of the developing countries in a single year, 1980, would
> be... approximately ...   cobalt (50%), manganese ore (42%), copper
> (3%) and nickel (20%).   The implication of the foregoing analysis for
> international policy is that firm and detailed arrangements would be
> required in advance of the production of minerals from the sea-bed
> in order to ensure that such activity would not adversely affect the

interests of developing exporting countries or, better still, would bring to them and to other developing countries positive benefits....

The study outlined three alternative approaches to the problems posed, and the opportunities offered, by the availability of new resources from the sea-bed.

a) The compensatory approach, under which developing exporting countries would receive compensation for the estimated adverse impact upon their export earnings from the net revenues of the sea-bed authority, supplemented by contributions from consuming countries and/or other international financial arangements.

b) The preventive approach, implemented through the centralized marketing by the sea-bed authority of all the output of sea-bed minerals in accordance with internationallly agreed guidelines consistent with the objective of remunerative and equitable prices for commodities of export interest to the developing countries.

c) Another preventive approach, implemented through the mining, associated processing, and marketing of the resources of the sea-bed solely by the international authority, in accordance with internationally agreed guidelines consistent with the fundamental objective of remunerative and equitable prices for commodities of export interest to the developing countries.

UNCTAD has been closely involved in the study of the financial, economic and trade implications of sea-bed mining. Its Trade and Development Board requested theSecretary-General of UNCTAD to prepare "a comprehensive report on the developments reached at the Third United Nations Conference on the Law of the Sea...and to bring up-to-date the studies on the economic consequences, particularly for developing countries." (Report, TDB, A/32/15, 26 October 1977)

The Informal Composite Negotiating Text (A/CONF.62/WP.10, July 1977) contains detailed provisions on the issues raised in connection with this NIEO objective. The articles of the Text deal in great detail with the protection of the special interests and requirements of developing countries, and include the following provisions, of particular interest with respect to the establishment of the NIEO:

Payments and contributions with respect to the exploitation of the continental shelf beyond 200 miles

The coastal state shall make payments or contributions in kind in respect of the exploitation of the non-living resources of the continental shelf beyond 200 nautical miles /.../

A developing country which is a net importer of a mineral resource produced from its continental shelf is exempt from making such payments or contributions in respect of that mineral resource.

The payments or contributions shall be made through the authority which shall distribute them to States party to the present convention on the basis of equitable sharing criteria, taking into account the interests and needs of developing countries, particularly the least developed and the land-locked amongst them.

Benefit of Mankind

Activities in the Area shall be carried out for the benefit of mankind as a whole, irrespective of the geographical location of States, whether coastal or land-locked, and taking into particular consideration the interests and needs of the developing countries as specifically provided for in this part of the present convention...

Following recommendations from the Council on the basis of advice from the Economic Planning Commission, the Assembly shall establish a system of compensation for developing countries which suffer adverse effects on their export earnings or economies resulting from a reduction in the price of an affected mineral or the volume of that mineral exported, to the extent that such reduction is caused by activities in the Area.

19.3 Contributions of major international bodies

While a number of international fora considered the issue of sea-bed resources in the context of the NIEO, they have generally reaffirmed the objectives specified within the framework of the United Nations rather than contributing to their further development directly.

5 Social Issues

WORLD ECONOMY ISSUE 20

Achieving a More Equitable Distribution of Income
and Raising the Level of Employment

20.1 The original formulation of the NIEO objective at the United Nations

The concept of development as it was characterized in the International
Development Strategy for the Second United Nations Development Decade
(October 1970), gave strong emphasis to the problem of social and economic
equality. A more equitable distribution of income and wealth, greater income
security, and a substantial rise in the level of employment would provide the
material basis for a better life for all. According to the IDS of 1970, each
developing country should formulate its national employment objectives so as
to absorb an increasing proportion of its working population in modern
activities and therefore reduce significantly unemployment and underemploy-
ment. Specifically, developing countries should improve their labour force
statistics in order to formulate realistic quantitative targets for employment.
Other policies, such as fiscal, monetary and trade issues, should be promoted
with a view to enhancing the level of employment and economic growth.
Capital-intensive technology should be confined to special uses, and should
not interfere with the rise of the level of employment. Developed countries
are called upon to assist in this process by adopting measures which would
bring about appropriate changes in the structures of international trade.

According to the Lima Declaration (March 1975), social justice should be
a guiding factor in achieving the objectives of raising the living standards and
eliminating extreme social disadvantages and unemployment. The benefits of
industrialization should be distributed equitably among all sectors of the
population.

20.2   Specification and development of the NIEO objective at the United
Nations, 1974-78

A UNIDO report entitled "Industrialization of the Developing Countries,
Basic Problems and Issues for Action" (ID/CONF. 3/5, 21 October 1974) took
up the issues of poverty, economic growth and equal distribution of income.
Growth is a necessary but insufficient condition for the elimination of
poverty. A more equal distribution of income is necessary. The Governments
of most of the developing countries have now come to the conclusion that the
provision of greater employment opportunities is the most important and
direct way of achieving this goal.   The problems of employment, income
distribution and poverty in developing countries cannot be addressed
exclusively to, or be resolved by, one sector such as industry. The entire
social and economic system is involved, and solutions to these problems may
entail a radical redefinition of basic social choices. The report suggested
that market mechanisms which reflect existing income distribution patterns
cannot guide such actions.
The twin problems of employment and income distribution were the
subject of another report, issued by the Secretariats of ILO and UNIDO,
"Industrialization Employment and Social Objective" (ID/CONF.3/9, 14 Nov.
1974).   The International Development Strategy of 1970 is given a critical
assessment for supporting a conventional developmental approach, with
emphasis on the modern sector and making the assumption that the latter will
absorb the labour surplus in the traditional sector. The report emphasizes the
necessity for developing countries to further intensify their efforts to
implement the employment and income distribution objectives in their
development planning.
The themes of income distribution and employment are reiterated once
again in UNIDO's Latin American Conference on Industrialization (ID/CONF.3
/CRP/1/Add.1, 4 December 1974).   The conference stressed that domestic
industrialization policies must take into account the need for an adequate
distribution of income to make possible the rapid expansion of domestic
markets. In that way, industrial growth can be conducive to the attainment
of the objectives of raising the standard of living and eliminating unemployment.
A resolution adopted by the Second General Conference of UNIDO (ID/
CONF.3/RES.3, 16 April 1975) declares that:

The right of human beings to worthy employment is an essential
element to be taken into account in any development process, in
order thus to achieve full employment and guarantee human dignity;

All States have the sovereign right to adopt and accept a variety of
formulae for the organization of enterprises, in accordance with
their own conditions, for the purpose of achieving industrial and
socio-economic development, in order to bring maximum benefit to
the workers and society as a whole;

The participation of workers in industrial enterprises, among other
measures, is essential so that all workers may be integrated with the

industrial development process and thereby enabled to obtain its benefits; in line with this, States should initiate measures in keeping with the particular characteristics of each economic activity and each country, in consultation with the workers and other persons involved;

States should make the greatest possible efforts to ensure, including through legislation provisions, that all undertakings give priority attention to vocational training for all workers, including immigrant workers in the developed countries, with a view to increasing their productivity and ensuring the full development of the human person;

All efforts should be made by States, within the framework of their national legislation, to give immigrant workers conditions similar to those given to their nationals in the economic and social field;

All States should recognize that, in any industrial development process, social justice must the irreplaceable means, in the spiritual, economic and social aspects, to attain the objective of creating a just society pervaded by a spirit of solidarity.

The Declaration of Principles and Programme of Action adopted by the ILO at the Tripartite World Conference on Employment, Income Distribution and Social Progress (Geneva, 4-17, June 1976) noted the firm commitment of the developing countries and of some developed countries to implement the NIEO. The following proposals which relate directly to employment and income distribution were accepted at the conference:

Strategies and national development plans and policies should include explicitly as a priority objective the promotion of employment and the satisfaction of the basic needs of each country's population.

National employment-centered development strategies should include:

An increase in the volume and productivity of work in order to increase the incomes of the lowest income groups;

The introduction of progressive income and wealth taxation policies;

Reform of the fiscal system to provide employment-linked incentives and more socially just patterns of income distribution.

Wage policies should be such that:

they ensure minimum levels of living;

the real wages of workers and the real incomes of self-employed producers are protected and progressively increased;

wage levels are equitable and reflect social productivity.

20.3 Contributions of major international bodies

The issue of employment and industrial relations was treated in the OECD Declaration on International Investment and Multinational Enterprises (21 June 1976). The Declaration stated that, within the framework of law, regulations and prevailing labour relations and employment practices in each of the countries in which they operate, enterprises should, inter alia;

observe standards of employment and industrial relations not less favourable than those observed by comparable employers in the host country;

in their operations, to the greatest extent practicable, utilize, train and prepare for upgrading members of the local labour force in co-operation with representatives of their employees and, where appropriate, the releveant governmental authorities;

in considering changes in their operations which would have major effects upon the livlihood of their employees, in particular in the case of the closure of an entity involving collective lay-offs or dismissals, provide reasonable notice of such changes to represen-tatives of their employees, and where appropriate to the relevant governmental authorities, and co-operate with the employee repres-entative and appropriate governmental authorities so as to mitigate to the maximum extent practicable adverse effects;

implement their employment policies including hiring, discharge, pay, promotion and training without discrimination unless selectivity in respect of employee characteristics is in furtherance of establish-ed governmental policies which specifically promote greater equa-lity of employment opportunity.

WORLD ECONOMY ISSUE 21

Providing Health Services, Education, Higher Cultural Standard and Qualification For the Work Force, and Assuring the Well-Being of Children and the Integration of Women in Development

21.1 The original formulation of the NIEO objective at the United Nations

The resolutions of the Sixth and Seventh Special Sessions of the United Nations (May 1974 and Sept. 1975) touch briefly on social issues. In the Sixth Session, social well-being and social development are part and parcel of a more general framework which focuses on the economic "disequilibriums" which separate the members of the international community. The concept of social development and social well-being appear in conjunction with the solemn proclamation for the establishment of a new international economic order: equity, sovereign equality, interdependence, common interest and co-operation among all States, and peace and justice. The Seventh Special Session is more specific in referring to the need to improve health conditions in developing countries by giving priority to prevention of disease and malnutrition and by providing primary health services to the communities, including maternal and child health and family welfare. The international effort concerning the above cited social issues should be part of the endeavors of the WHO and the United Nations Children's Fund.

The earlier proposals eminating from the International Development Strategy for the Second United Nations Development Decade (Oct. 1970) include social issues in detail. The ultimate objective of development is the sustained improvement in the well-being of the individual through improve-ments in the level of employment, income security, education, health, nutrition, housing, social welfare and safeguarding the environment. These objectives are both determining factors and end-results of development; they should therefore be viewed as integrated parts of the same dynamic process and require a unified approach.

The Lima Declaration (March 1975), proposes that conditions should be created by developing countries which make possible the full integration of women in social and economic activities on the basis of equal rights. The developing countries should also raise the general cultural standard of their peoples, in order to have available a qualified work force not only for the production of goods and services but also for management skills. In addition, social justice should be a guiding factor in achieving the objectives of raising the living standards and eliminating extreme social disadvantages, such as unemployment, particularly among young people.

21.2 Specification and development of the NIEO objective at the United Nations 1974-78

According to a report of the Latin American Conference on Industrialization (ID/CONF.3/CRP/1/Add.1, 4 December 1974), the objective of industrial development must not only be to secure and increase production and productivity, but also to achieve social justice and a reduction of the social costs of production. Industrial development in the developing countries based on this new outlook should lead to an equitable redistribution of the means of achieving the material and spiritual well-being of society, to the improvement or, where appropriate, redefinition of the relationship of production, and to the creation of social models freely determined by each country in the light of its national objectives.

The Declaration of Mexico on the Equality of Women and their Contribution to Development and Peace, adopted by the World Conference of the International Women's Year (E/CONF.66/34) at Mexico City in July 1975, decided to promulgate the following principles:

Equality between women and men means equality in their dignity and worth as human beings as well as equality in their rights, opportunities and responsibilities.

All obstacles that stand in the way of enjoyment by women of equal status with men must be eliminated in order to ensure their full integration into national development and their participation in securing and maintaining international peace.

It is the responsibility of the State to create the necessary facilities so that women may be integrated into society while their children receive adequate care.

National non-governmental organizations should contribute to the advancement of women by assisting women to take advantage of their opportunities, by promoting education and information about women's rights, and by co-operating with their respective Governments....

Women, like men, require opportunities for developing their intellectual potential to the maximum. National policies and programmes should therefore provide them with full and equal access to education and training at all levels, while ensuring that such programmes and policies consciously orient them towards new occupations and new roles consistent with their need for self-fulfillment and the needs of national development.

The right of women to work, to receive equal pay for work of equal value, to be provided with equal conditions and opportunities for advancement in work, and all other women's rights to full and satisfying economic activity are strongly reaffirmed. Review of these principles for their effective implementation is now urgently needed, considering the necessity of restructuring world economic relationships. This restructuring offers greater possibilities for women to be integrated into the stream of national economic, social political and cultural life.

All means of communication and information as well as all cultural media should regard as a high priority their responsibility for helping to remove the attitudinal and cultural factors that still inhibit the development of women and for projecting in positive terms the value to society of the assumption by women of changing and expanding roles.

Necessary resources should be made available in order that women may be able to participate in the political life of their countries and of the international community since their active participation in national and world affairs at decision-making and other levels in the political field is a pre-requisite of women's full exercise of equal rights as well as of their further development and of the national well-being....

The issue of inequality, as it affects the vast majority of the women of the world, is closely linked with the problem of unkerdevelopment, which exists as a result not only of unsuitable internal structures but also of a profoundly unjust world economic system.

The full and complete development of any country requires the maximum participation of women as well as of men in all fields: the under-utilization of the potential of approximatley half of the world's population is a serious obstacle to social and economic development.

The ultimate end of development is to achieve a better quality of life for all, which means not only the development of economic and other material resources but also the physical, moral, intellectual and cultural growth of the human person.

In order to integrate women into development, States should undertake the necessary changes in their economic and social policies because women have the right to participate and contribute to the total development effort.

The present state of international economic relations poses serious obstacles to a more efficient utilization of all human and material potential for accelerated development and for the improvement of living standards in developing countries aimed at the elimination of hunger, child mortality, unemployment, illiteracy, ignorance and backwardness, which concern all of humanity and women in particular. It is therefore essential to establish and implement with urgency the New International Economic Order, of which the Charter of Economic Rights and Duties of States constitutes a basic element, founded on equity, sovereign equality, interdependence, common interest, co-operation among all States irrespective of their social and economic systems, on the principles of peaceful coexistence and on the promotion by the entire international community of economic and social progress of all countries, especially developing countries and on the progress of States comprising the international community....

The attainment of economic and social goals, so basic to the realization of the rights of women, does not, however, of itself bring about the full integration of women in development on a basis of equality with men unless specific measures are undertaken for the elimination of all forms of discrimination against them. It is therefore important to formulate and implement models of development that will promote the participation and advancement of women in all fields of work and provide them with equal educational opportunities and such services as would facilitate housework.

Modernization of the agricultural sector of vast areas of the world is an indispensable element for progress, particularly as it creates opportunities for millions of rural women to participate in development. Governments, the United Nations, its specialized agencies and other competent regional and international organizations should support projects designed to utilize the maximum potential and develop the self-reliance of rural women.

It must be emphasized that, given the required economic, social and legal conditions as well as the appropriate attitutes conducive to the full and equal participation of women in society, efforts and measures aimed at a more intensified integration of women in development can be successfully implemented only if made an integral part of over-all social and economic growth. Full participation of women in the various economic, social, political and cultural sectors is an important indication of the dynamic progress of peoples and their development. Individual human rights can be realized only within the framework of total development....

The solidarity of women in all countries of the world should be supported in their protest against violations of human rights condemned by the United Nations. All forms of repression and inhuman treatment of women, men and children, including imprisonment, torture, massacres, collective punishment, destruction of homes, forced eviction and arbitrary restriction of movement shall be considered crimes against humanity and in violation of the Universal Declaration of Human Rights and other international instruments...

The FAO Council, meeting in Rome 9-20 June 1975, decided that with reference to the integration of women in agriculture and rural development and nutrition policies (FAO document A/AC. 191/8, 21 April 1978)

FAO Council supports the necessary approach to the development of food production, food availability and utilization and the improvement of the quality of rural family life through the full integration of women in rural development.

The Director-General of FAO to ensure that current programmes and projects in nutrition, agriculture (including fisheries and forestry) and rural development be reviewed by all Departments and Divisions concerned with these activities with a view to the incorporation of a suitable component benefiting women.

The Director-General of FAO to assure the integration of women in all FAO programmes and projects by directing all Departments and Divisions concerned with these activities to investigate, design, plan, implement and review, on a regular and systematic basis, all proposed projects and programmes in order to establish a measure of progress in assuring the important participation of women as equal partners with men in the total development process, it being understood that wherever possible women should be directly engaged in the planning, decision-making, implementation, and evaluation of FAO projects and programmes.

21.3 Contributions of major international bodies

The fifth Conference of Heads of State or Government of Non-Aligned Countries (A/31/197 Colombo, 8 September 1976) stressed the need for economic development within the framework of social justice. The focal point of development will be the eradication of poverty. It calls for the formulation and implementation of a policy for satisfying the basic minimum needs of the population of the developing world. It is recognized that structural changes where and when necessary will be required to achieve those objectives. The conference proposed the creation of arrangements and mechanisms for co-operation in the field of health and medicine, particularly the planning of health protection services.

The NAC Conference recommended that the Non-Aligned countries actively promote the implementation of the decisions adopted by the Conference on International Women's Year in Mexico concerning the participation of women in development.

The Conference on International Economic Co-operation (CCEI-CM6, June 1977), advocated that infrastructure should increase the overall productivity of the social-economic system and directly or indirectly serve human advancement through the meeting of basic collective needs, such as nutrition, drinking water, housing, health, education and employment.

A Statement by DAC members on Development and Co-operation Economic Growth and Meeting Basic Needs (Annex II, OECD 1977. Review, October 1977), reported that DAC members are determined to assist developing countries which seek to expand their capabilities for meeting effectively the basic needs of their people within the context of achieving self-sustaining growth. Further, concern with meeting basic human needs is not a substitute for, but an essential component of, more economic growth which involves modernization, provision of infrastructure and industrialization.

Progress towards raising productive income and welfare of the poor requires expanding opportunity for productive employment, rural development, food production, and well-designed, broadly acessible health, family planning, and education.

6 Political and Institutional Issues

WORLD ECONOMY ISSUE 22

Assuring the Economic Sovereignty of States:
Natural Resources, Foreign Property, Choice of Economic System

22.1 The original formulation of the NIEO objective at the United Nations

In view of the dependence of the majority of developing countries on foreign economic interests and trade, safeguarding of their sovereignity in the control and use of their natural resources, the right to nationalize foreign property within their jurisdiction and the right and freedom to adopt the economic system of their choice, constitute issues of major relevance.

The Declaration on the Establishment of the NIEO (May 1974) was "founded on full respect for the following principles":

Full permanent sovereignity of every State over its natural resources. In order to safeguard these resources, each State is entitled to exercise effective control over them and their exploitation with means suitable to its own situation, including the right to nationalization or transfer of ownership to its nationals, this right being an expression of the full permanent sovereignity of the State. No state may be subjected to economic, political or any other type of coercion to prevent the free and full exercise of its inalienable right.

This was reaffirmed in the Program of Action on the establishment of the NIEO.

All efforts should be made:

To defeat attempts to prevent the free and effective exercise of the rights of every State to full and permanent sovereignity over its natural resources;

To insure that competent agencies of the United Nations system meet requests for assistance from developing countries in connection with the operation of nationalized means of production;

Article 2 of the Charter of Economic Rights and Duties (December 1974) stated that:

> Every State has and shall freely exercise full permanent sovereignty, including possession, use, and disposal, over all its wealth, natural resources and economic activities. In the exploitation of natural resources shared by two or more countries, each State must cooperate on the basis of a system of information and prior consultations in order to achieve optimum use of such resources without causing damage to the legitimate interests of others.

The International Development Strategy (October 1970) envisaged that:

> The developing countries will take steps to develop the full potential of their natural resources, including the preparation of them through international assistance of "an inventory of natural resources for their more rational utilization in all productive activities."

The Lima Declaration and Plan of Action (March 1975) provided:

> That every State has the inalienable right to exercise freely its sovereignity and permanent control over its natural resources, both terrestrial and marine, and over all economic activity for the exploitation of these resources in the manner appropriate to its circumstances, including nationalization in accordance with its laws as an expression of this right, and that no State shall be subjected to any forms of economic, political or other coercion which impedes the full and free exercise of that inalienable right;

> No State shall exercise any discriminatory measures or aggression against any other State which decides to exercise its sovereignity over its natural processing and marketing of those resources.

Article 34 of the Lima Declaration states that:

> Effective control over natural resources and the harmonization of policies for their exploitation, conservation, transformation, and marketing consistitute for developing countries an indispensable condition for economic and social progress.

Concerning the control of foreign property, the right of sovereign States to nationalize was historically uncontested. However, the capital-exporting developed countries viewed the exercise of this right as subject to limitations placed by international law. In the context of the NIEO, the developing countries contest this limitation and assert the right to nationalize foreign property within the jurisdiction of sovereign States in accordance with national laws.

The Charter of Economic Rights and Duties of States asserted:

Every State has the right

To nationalize, expropriate or transfer ownership of foreign pro- perty, in which case appropriate compensation should be paid by the State adopting such measures, taking into account its relevant laws and regulations and all circumstances that the State considers pertinent. In any case where the question of compensation gives rise to a controversy, it shall be settled under the domestic law of the nationalizing State and by its tribunals, unless it is freely and mutually agreed by all States concerned that other peaceful means be sought on the basis of the sovereign equality of States and in accordance with the principle of free choice of means.

The freedom of States to choose the economic and political system that is considered best for their internal and external relations is well established, and acknowledged also by the Charter of the United Nations. Its importance for the establishment of a New International Economic Order rests on the general principles relevant for its effective observance and implementation. These general principles are stated sometimes in positive terms - requiring cooperation from States in specific areas, as well as in negative terms - prohibiting states from certain specified types of behavior.

The Declaration on the Establishment of a New International Economic Order proclaimed:

Sovereign equality of States, self-determination of all peoples, inadmissibility of the acquisition of territories by force, territorial integrity and non-interference in the internal affairs of other States; . . . .

The right of every country to adopt the economic and social system that it deems the most appropriate for its own development and not to be subjected to discrimination of any kind as a result.

The Charter of Economic Rights and Duties of States offers the underlying principles in specific terms as they relate to the concept of free choice of States of their economic, social and political system and of their foreign economic relations:

Every State has the sovereign and inalienable right to chose its economic system as well as its political, social and cultural systems in accordance with the will of its people, without outside inter- ference, coercion or threat in any form whatsoever. (Article 1)

In a concrete application of the above principle to the question of foreign investment, Article 2(a) of the Charter states:

> Each State has the right to regulate and exercise authority over foreign investment within its national jurisdiction in accordance with its laws and regulations and in conformity with its national objectives and priorities. No State shall be compelled to grant preferential treatment to foreign investment.

Article 4 further reiterates the freedom of every State to engage in international trade on a non-discriminatory basis with "freedom to choose the forms of organization of its foreign economic relations . . . . consistent with its international obligations and with the needs of international economic cooperation."

In the performance of its primary responsibility to promote the economic, social and cultural development of its people, every State has "the right and the responsibility to choose its means and goals of development, to fully mobilize and use its resources, to implement progressive economic and social reforms and to ensure the full participation of its people in the process and benefits of development." (Article 7)

In order to achieve the above objectives, Article 7 further declares:

> All States have the duty, individually and collectively to cooperate in eliminating obstacles that hinder such mobilization and use.

Finally, in Article 32, the Charter of Economic Rights and Duties of States declares that:

> No State may use or encourage the use of economic, political or any other type of measures to coerce another State in order to obtain from it the subordination of the exercise of its sovereign rights.

In Section VI, paragraph 76 the Lima Declaration and Plan of Action endorses the concepts of the Charter of the Economic Rights and Duties of States, "stressing the need for the international community to comply in full with the precepts contained in the Charter. . . ."

22.2   Specification and development of the NIEO objective at the United Nations, 1974-78

Further discussion of the subject of sovereignty over natural resources in the United Nations brought renewed expressions of support for its exercise. Thus, in discussing the natural resources of developing countries and the relationship of such resources to problems of industrialization, the Secretariat of UNIDO (ID/CONF.3/6 6 November 1974) observed that the principle of permanent sovereignity need not be incompatible with new forms of international cooperation. The UNIDO study referred to the Asuncion Declaration on the exploitation of international rivers, adopted by the countries of the River Plate Basin.

The Latin American Conference on Industrialization (ID/CONF.3/CRP/11 Add.1 1974) reiterated:

That every State has the inalienable right to exercise effective control and permanent sovereignity over its natural resources, both terrestrial and marine, and to exploit them by any means suitable to its situation, including nationalization, in accordance with the legislation of each country, and that no State must be subjected to any form of economic, political or other coercion designed to prevent it from enjoying the full and free exercise of this inalienable right.   (E/CN.14/642, February 1975)

The conference of Ministers of the Economic Commission for Africa (E/CN.14/642, February 1975) declared the following principles in their resolution:

The removal of all forms of constraint to the exercise by African countries of permanent sovereignty over their natural resources;

The promotion of collective self-reliance among African countries in respect of the recovery, exploration, development, marketing and distribution of their natural resources.

Article 194 of the Informal Composite Negotiating Text prepared by the third United Nations Conference on the Law of the Sea likewise recognized "the sovereign right of states to exploit their natural resources."

A further development of the concept of the permanent sovereignty of States over their natural resources may be seen in the proposals made by the International Law Commission on the subject of "State succession." In its report to the General Assembly (A/CONF.62/WP.10 July 1977) the commission commented on the relevant provisions of its proposed draft convention stated in Article 22:

When the successor State is a newly independent State:

No State debt of the predecessor State shall pass to the newly independent State, unless an agreement . . . provides otherwise /.../;

The provisions of the agreement referred to in the preceding paragraph should not infringe the prinicple of the permanent sovereignty of every people over its wealth and natural resources, nor should their implementation endanger equilibria of the newly independent State.

The principle of full permanent sovereignty of States over natural resources has found full expression in the various documents emanating from international conferences held under the auspices of the United Nations. However, during the debates on this subject sharp differences of opinion were expressed on the manner in which the sovereignty right may be exercised in practice. The developing countries interpreted the principle as requiring the State to apply the "National Law Standard" taking into account the social and economic interests of that State. The developed, industrialized countries on the other hand, contend that natural resources must be handled in accordance with international law.

In two reports prepared by the Secretary-General of the United Nations for the committee on Natural Resources (A/9716, 20 September 1974; E/C.7/66, 17 March 1977) the nature of the exercise of the right has been traced, indicating chronologically, the nature of expropriations carried by States, and the quantum and nature of compensation paid for nationalized foreign properties.

The fact that the two sides are claiming fundamentally differing perspectives on the content of the right of permanent sovereignty over natural resources is further evidenced by the debates during the 32nd session of the General Assembly. For example, speaking on the explanation of the vote of the United States in the third committee, the U.S. representative said (5 December 1977):

> The United States believes that the statements in the resolution pertaining to the rights of States to exercise full sovereignty over their natural wealth and resources must be interpreted to include the principle that the exercise of sovereignty over natural wealth and resources has to be conducted in accordance with the principles of international law.

A similar viewpoint was expressed on the proposals contained in the report of the international law commission on the subject of State responsibility. During the debate in the intergovernmental working group of the Commission on Transnational Corporations (EC/OAC2/3 January 1978) a second interpretative issue relating to the concept of permanent sovereignty emerged which was also sharply contested by the developing countries. This related to the scope and meaning of the concept of "full permanent sovereignty." According to the developing countries' formulation, the right in question includes all economic activities related to the exercise of sovereignty over natural resources. The developed countries' representatives contend that the concept of permanent sovereignty must be interpreted in accordance with international law and that in its exercise, the national laws and regulations must conform to standards of international law.

Discussion of the right to nationalize foreign property within national jurisdiction was closely associated with the foregoing debates on sovereignity over natural resources. Already in 1973, Resolution 3171 (XXVIII) of the General Assembly affirmed that:

> The application of the principle of nationalization carried out by States . . . implies that each State is entitled to determine the amount of possible compensation and the mode of payment, and that any disputes which might arise should be settled in accordance with the national legislation of each State carrying out such measures.

UNCTAD's Resolution 1803 (XVII) declared:

> Nationalization, expropriation or requisitioning shall be based on grounds or reasons of public utility, security or the national interest which are recognized as over-riding purely individual or private interests, both domestic and foreign. In such cases the owner shall be paid appropriate compensation in accordance with the rules in force in the State taking such measures in the exercise of its sovereignity and in accordance with international law . . . .

(Following consideration in UNCTAD, the matter of nationalization came up in the 29th session of the General Assembly. Resolution 3281 (XXIX) adopting the Charter of Economic Rights and Duties of States excluded, after considerable debate and exchange of views, the two contentious issues from its formulation: The "public purpose" requirements and the "international law standard.")

Subsequent discussions in the United Nations, although less than conclusive, recognize the rights of States to nationalize foreign property and recommend peaceful resolution of disputes arising from the process. The World Bank has taken the view that:

> Expropriation is the right of any country. The Bank is concerned, however, that the country involved makes serious efforts with the former owners to reach agreement on the payment of fair compensation and it may refuse to lend to members who fail to make reasonable efforts to settle expropriation claims or similar disputes.   Questions and Answers, 1977

In its summary of the "Basic Issues involved in the Formulation of a Code of Conduct" the Report of the Secretariat (E/C.10/17 20 July 1976) prepared by the Centre on Transnational Corporations points out that:

> The issue of nationalization has been one of the most controversial in international economic relations in the past several decades. The principle that States are entitled to nationalize property within their territory . . . has been stated in many instruments adopted by intergovernmental organizations . . . .

> Several important problems would remain to be dealt with even if the Code of conduct set forth the principle of nationalization. The foremost would be to determine the conditions under which the principle could be applied, especially in relation to foreign enterprises. In one view, national law determines the conditions for the lawfulness of nationalization measures and only the national courts of the nationalizing State have jurisdiction over any related claim. In another view, established rules of international law impose constraints on the State's ability to nationalize foreign-owned property. In this view, claims arising out of nationalization are international in character and may approprirately be decided by international tribunals.

The working group responsible for the above document also proposed a principle dealing with the right and freedom of States to adopt the economic, political and social system that is best suited for their interests, and a related principle prohibiting States from the use or threat of coercion in interfering with those rights.

22.3 Contributions of major international bodies, 1974-78

The subject of nationalization of foreign property and compensation for it has come up for discussion at the CIEC in Paris (A/31/478/Add.1, August 1977). The Final Report records agreement and disagreement among the groups of developed and developing countries participating in the Conference as follows:

> The participants of CIEC recognize that in the exercise of their sovereignty the countries concerned determine the role that foreign private investment may be called to play in the development process and define the conditions under which foreign investment would be able to participate in this process.

> In this context it is desirable to establish a suitable framework to encourage and facilitate foreign investment and its harmonious integration and contribution to the development plans and policies of host countries. It is important in this respect to state the conditions which it would be desirable to have implemented by all parties seeking to have productive and satisfactory cooperation in this field, meeting in a fair and equitable way the interests of all parties involved, and thereby contributing to the estblishment of a stable and equitable climate for foreign investments.

In the elaboration of the specific details there was, however, no agreement among the developed and developing countries' representatives who have participated in the conference. For example, according to the group of developing countries:

> Nothing affects the right of a host country to adopt appropriate remedial measures in the event of balance of payment difficulties.

The developing countries, disagreeing with this formulation, advanced the following qualification:

> . . . . except in so far as restrictive measures of limited duration are required by exceptional balance of payments difficulties.

On the question of the standard of treatment to be accorded when foreign properties are nationalized, the developing countries stated:

> Fair and equitable treatment of the investor's property. In case the

host country expropriates or nationalizes the property of a foreign investor appropriate compensation should be paid.

The group of developed countries offered an alternative formulation which reads:

Fair and equitable treatment of the investor's property: In case the host country deprives, directly or indirectly, a foreign investor of its property, prompt, adequate and effective compensation should be paid. Any such deprivation should be exclusively for a public purpose, non-discriminatory and in accordance with due process of law.

On the question of the finality of the national law, there again emerged lack of agreement between the two sides resulting in their separate formulations, and recorded as such in the report of the CIEC. The developing group offered:

Disputes between a host country and a foreign investor shall be resolved in accordance with the national legislation of the host country by its own courts of law except in those cases where the host country government freely choooses to submit the matter to international arbitration. In all cases arbitration proceedings and standards should be transparent and mutually satisfactory to both investors and host government.

The developed countries, disagreeing with this formulation, offered the following as an alternative:

Disputes between a host country and a foreign investor shall be resolved rapidly, in accordance with the above principles and with the procedural standards called for by international law. Access to international arbitration shall be available. Where possible, the procedures to be followed should be agreed upon before any dispute arises. In all cases, arbitration proceedings and standards should be transparent and mutually satisfactory to both investors and host government. . . .

The rights of States to choose the economic system they wish has been reaffirmed in the Final Act of the European Conference on Security and Cooperation (Helsinki 1975) under the heading "Equal Rights and Self-Determination of Peoples.":

By virtue of the principle of equal rights and self-determination of peoples, all peoples always have the right, in full freedom, to determine, when and as they wish, their internal and external political status, without external interference, and to pursue as they wish their political, economic, social and cultural development.

The Helsinki Final Act also has a provision reiterating the participating States' commitment to refrain from any threat or actual use of force or any act of economic coercion:

> The Participating States, <u>Reaffirming</u> that they will respect and give effect to refraining from the threat or use of force and convinced of the necessity to make it an effective norm of international life,
>
> <u>Declare</u> (. . .)
> - to refrain from any manifestation of force for the purpose of inducing another participating State to renounce the full exercise of its sovereign rights;
>
> - to refrain from any act of economic coercion designed to subordinate to their own interest the exercise by another participating State of the rights inherent in its sovereignity and thus to secure advantages of any kind.

The Manila Declaration and Programme of Action of the Third Ministerial Meeting of the Group of 77 (TD/195, 1976) declared:

> that international economic relations should be based on full respect for the principles of equality among States and non-intervention in internal affairs, on respect for different economic and social systems and on the right of each State to exercise full and permanent sovereignity over its natural resources and all its economic activities.

WORLD ECONOMY ISSUE 23

Compensating for Adverse Effects on the Resources of States, Territories and Peoples of Foreign Occupation, Alien and Colonial Domination or <u>Apartheid</u>

23.1 The original formulation of the NIEO objective at the United Nations

In connection with the general concept of "Permanent Sovereignty over Natural Resources," the Declaration on the Establishment of a New International Economic Order (May 1974) declared:

> The right of all states, territories and peoples under foreign occupation, alien and colonial domination or <u>apartheid</u> to restitution and full compensation for the exploitation and depletion of, and damages to, the natural resources and all other resources of those states, territories and peoples.

The Charter of Economic Rights and Duties of States (December 1974) dealt with this question in Article 16. After declaring the right and duty of all States to eliminate colonialism, apartheid, and all forms of occupation and domination, Article 16 provides:

...States which practice such coercive policies are economically responsible to the countries, territories and peoples affected for the restitution and full compensation for the exploitation and depletion of, and damages to, the natural and all other resources of those countries, territories and peoples.

In language identical to that of Article 16 of the Charter, the Lima Declaration and Programme of Action (March 1976), further reiterated the obligation to provide damages to resources depleted or exploited under external occupation.

23.2 Specification and development of the NIEO objective at the United Nations 1974-78

The principle of damages suffered under external domination received concrete application in the series of resolutions adopted by the General Assembly on the subject of "Permanent Sovereignty over National Resources in the Occupied Arab Territories." Commencing with Resolution 3175 (XXVIII) the General Assembly declared:

The right of the Arab States and Peoples whose territories are under foreign occupation to permanent sovereignty over all their national resources....;

the right of the Arab States and Peoples whose territories are under Israeli occupation to the restitution of and full compensation for the exploitation and looting of, and damages to, the natural resources, as well as the exploitation and manipulation of the human resources, of the occupied territories....;

the above principles apply to all States, territories, and peoples under foreign occupation, colonial rule or apartheid.

(During the ensuing debate in the Second Committee of the General Assembly, Israel took the view that "there was no rule of international law which could have the effect of barring Israel from the use of natural resources available in the area." (A/C.2/SR.1579) The vote on the draft resolution as a whole was 91 countries in favour, 5 against, and 27 countries abstaining.)

The principle of restitution and full compensation for the exploitation and depletion of resources under foreign occupation, as enunciated by the General Assembly first during its 28th session was reaffirmed in each successive session without further substantive changes. A resolution bearing on the question of "Palestine and Sovereignty over National Resources in the occupied Arab territories" was also adopted by the Economic Commission for Western Asia, reaffirming the Resolution adopted by the General Assembly during 1975. (E/ECWA/16, 20 March 1975)

During its 32nd session, the General Assembly adopted Resolution 32/161 by a vote of 109-3-26, which took note of "the report of the Secretary-General on the adverse economic effects on the Arab States and peoples resulting from repeated Israeli aggression and continued occupation of their territories," and called upon:

> All States, international organizations, specialized agencies, investment corporations and all other institutions not to recognize, or cooperate with or assist in any manner in, any measures undertaken by Israel to exploit the resources of the occupied territories or to effect any changes in the demographic composition or geographic character or institutional structure of those territories.

The original NIEO principle (that Natural Resources in a State belong only to the indigenous people, and that any exploitation or damages caused by occupying, colonizing or dominating foreign countries is not only illegal but subject to proper restitution and compensation), is also applied to situations in Southern Africa. The Commission on Transnational Corporations (E/5986, May 1977), referring to the "activities of transnational corporations in South Africa and their collaboration with the racist minority regimes in that area,":

> reaffirmed the inalienable right of the peoples of Southern Africa to self-determination and independence and the enjoyment of their natural resources, as well as their right to dispose of those natural resources in their best interest.

The Informal Composite Nogotiating Text prepared by the Third United Nations Conference on the Law of the Sea (A/CONF.62/WP.10 July 1977) has treated the subject under the heading "Transitional Provision.":

> The rights recognized or established by the present Convention to the resources of a territory whose people have not attained either full independence or some other self-governing status recognized by the United Nations, or a territory under foreign occupation or colonial domination, or a United Nations Trust Territory, or a territory administered by the United Nations, shall be vested in the inhabitants of that territory, to be exercised by them for their own benefit and in accordance with their own needs and requirements.

The principle of compensation for damages suffered under external domination finds recognition (although indirectly) in the proposals made by the International Law Commission on the subject of Responsibility of States for Debts Incurred by Predecessor States. In the Report of the International Law Commission on the work of its 29th session, (A/32/10 September 1977), which contains the draft Articles on State Responsibility, Article 22 entitled "Newly Independent States" reads:

When the successor State is a newly independent State:

No State debt of the predecessor State shall pass to the newly independent State, unless an agreement between the newly independent State and the predecessor State provides otherwise in view of the link between the State debt of the predecessor State connected with its activity in the territory to which the succession of States relates and the property rights and interests which pass to the newly independent State:

23.3 Contributions of major international bodies, 1974-78

The Fifth Conference of Heads of State or Government of Non-Aligned Countries (Colombo A/31/186, August 1976), declared that,

The international community is urged to facilitate the effective exercise of the right to restitution and full compensation for the exploitation and depletion of and damages to the natural and all other resources of all States, territories and peoples subjected to foreign aggression and occupation, alien and colonial domination, racial discrimination and apartheid. It is, in addition, the duty of all States to extend assistance to these countries, territories and peoples.

The above principle is further reiterated at the Ministerial Meeting of the Bureau of the Non-Aligned Countries (New Delhi, A/32/74, April 1977).

(The Bureau) reaffirmed the full sovereignty of (these peoples of territories still under colonial domination and occupation) over their natural resources and their right to be compensated for the losses they have suffered in their just struggle against racial discrimination, apartheid and foreign occupation.

WORLD ECONOMY ISSUE 24

Establishing a System of Consultations at Global, Regional and Sectoral Levels with the Aim of Promoting Industrial Development

24.1 The original formulation of the NIEO objective at the United Nations

The need for a system of consultations was already mentioned in the International Development Strategy for the Second United Nations Development Decade (October 1970), in connection with the problem of surplus disposal. The consultations were to avoid or minimize possible adverse effects of disposals of production surpluses or strategic reserves, including those of minerals, on commercial trade, and they were to take account of the interest of both the surplus and of the deficit countries.

Development and International Economic Co-Operation (September 1975), as well as the Lima Declaration and Plan of Action on Industrial Development and Co-Operation (October 1975) call for a system of consultations at the global, regional, interregional and sectoral levels with the aim of facilitating industrial development. The Seventh Special Session resolution states:

> A system of consultations as provided for by the Lima Plan of Action should be established at the global, regional, interregional and sectoral levels within the United Nations Industrial Development Organization and within other appropriate international bodies, between developed and developing countries and among developing countries themselves, in order to facilitate the achievement of the goals set forth in the field of industrialization, including redeployment of certain productive capacities existing in developed countries and the creation of new industrial facilities in developing countries.

Consultations should relate in particular to industries processing raw materials exported by developing countries. Consultations are envisaged in connection with obtaining better terms for developing countries in the areas of acquisition of technology, expertise, licenses and equipment.

24.2 Specification and development ov the NIEO objective at the United Nations, 1974-78

An expert group meeting held under the auspices of UNIDO (ID/132, June 1974), spelled out measures to be taken by developing countries in the area of consultations. It suggested that developing countries should, prior to the consultation meetings, determine their objectives, strategies and policies. The end result would be to strengthen their planning capacity and their institutional set-up for control and decision-making together with developing their information system.

A world industrial programme could not be built in a vacuum, but must start from country industrial programmes which a process of consultations would seek to harmonize. To establish a new international economic structure in industry, the experts were of the opinion that the market mechanism was not sufficient, and that it could not be expected that transational corporations would readily incorporate the development objectives of host or home countries into their decisions. The role of the Governments was therefore indispensable.

It was stressed that across-the-board contracts and agreements, concerning the division of labour among industrial branches on a long-term basis, would be especially important for developing countries. Such contracts and agreements should specifiy the industrial branches and enterprises that produced goods that satisfied the needs of the population. It was further suggested that a system of continuous consultations would be an indispensable instrument for the establishment of the new international economic structure in industry. The experts also drew up a list of the following suggestions:

The consultations should be carefully prepared; they should have specific predetermined purposes to enable them to lead to practical decisions for action;

The first aim of the system of consultations would be to provide the participants with information, as complete and up-to-date as possible, on the industrial development objectives, strategies, policies, criteria and priorities;

The second step would be a comparison among the various partners of their objectives, strategies and criteria, with a view to gaining a better understanding of similarities and differences and to exploring the specific fields where complementarities of interests could be found;

To support the system of consultations, a common technical framework of reference should be built up, comprising industrial information, studies and projections. Sets of quantitative international targets, possibly alternative ones according to various assumptions could be prepared, to provide a basis for discussions and a common language. This quantified picture of the future should not be elaborated through theoretical calculations, but worked out progressively on the basis of national objectives and criteria reconciled progressively through the process of consultations;

Consultations should not only be concerned with the new international economic structure in respect of production, location, supply of the different inputs, and so on; they should also include the distribution of incomes and gains;

The consultations should follow a global approach for the industrialization as a whole to allow for the interdependence and complementaries among industrial sectors and regions. Within this global framework, specific consultations could then be organized at the sectoral and regional level;

Consultations could also take place regarding ways and means of implementing, in practical terms, in the field of industry, the principles of a new international economic order adopted by the General Assembly at its sixth special session. Instruments to be examined could be: codes of conduct, new forms of industrial co-operation, guarantees, long-term bilateral agreements, development contracts and the like;

It could be expected that the system of consultations might facilitate agreements, bilaterally as well as within groups of countries;

Through the system of consultations, Governments might exchange information on the programmes and policies of transnational corporations, prepare joint positions, and countervail the power of transnational corporations, not only through legal instruments, such as codes of conduct, but also by providing them with an economic framework into which the programmes of the companies could be fitted. The consultation process could give priority to strengthening the public sector in the various developing countries;

In the consultation process, special attention should be given to industrial co-operation among developing countries at sub-regional level, such as the Andean Group, within regions and among regions.

The Secretariat of UNIDO proposed, in "Preliminary Notes for the Preparation of A Plan of Action on Industrialization (ID/B/C.3/27, October 1974), that the new international structure should not be designed through the application of technocratic criteria and theoretical studies; agreement on it should be reached through an iterative process of consultations involving both politicians and technicians of the interested countries.

Consultations could be conducted at the regional level and at the world level. Their aim might be:

To study the pattern and trend in world-wide demand for industrial products;

To identify and describe the existing international structure of each branch of industry in respect of location of plants, the capacity and age of plants and sources of important inputs, etc.;

To identify obstacles to moving specific industries to developing countries and recommend ways in which they can be overcome;

To develop information on the industrial development priorities of the developed and developing countries participating in the consultations;

To compare these priorities and identify cases where interests are complementary and new industries can be established in developing countries;

To suggest national and international action that will facilitate more rapid progress in the establishment of new industries in developing countries.

The criteria used to select the type of industry suitable for the consultation approach might include:

Industries which supply the agricultural sector in developing countries;

Industries transforming raw material and commodities produced in the developing countries;

Industries with higher labour content in the manufacturing process;

Industries which can stimulate the development of the engineering industry in developing countries, including their capability to produce machinery and spare parts;

Industries where availability of raw material, space, water and other environmental considerations may favour location in the developing countries.

The Executive Director of UNIDO reaffirmed the need for consultations (A/31/230, 8 October 1976), in view of the global economic interdependence among nations; the role of industrialization in the over-all development process of developing countries; the need for restructuring world industry; the need for closer co-operation among developing countries; the involvement of Governments as well as enterprises and labour in industrial co-operation; and the importance of the participation of foreign enterprises in financing industrialization in developing countries as well as in the process of transfer of technology and possibly technical assistance.

Reports from the Regional Commissions of Latin America and Asia and the Pacific, in particular of June (E/CEPAL/1024/Rev.1) and October (E. ESCAP/IHT/MI/13, 1977) reiterated the importance of the system of consultations. The former report notes the swift rise in bank financing and the relative decline in importance of the International Monetary Fund. Taking this and other events into consideration, it is suggested that consultations would be necessary to start devising the scheme of a new global financial policy.

24.3 Contributions of major international bodies, 1974-78

The Manila Declaration and Programme of Action of the Third Ministerial meeting of the Group of 77 (TD/195, January 1976), re-affirmed that the Secretary General of UNCTAD should enter into appropriate consultation with CMEA member countries and the CMEA secretariat in order to identify trade opportunities for developing countries. The UNCTAD consultative machinery for dealing with problems in trade and economic relations among countries having different economic and social systems should be improved and made more flexible.

The Conference on International Economic Co-operation, (A/31/478/Add. 1, August 1977), re-iterated the need for countries participating in CIEC to actively support and effectively participate in the system of continuing consultations within UNIDO:

Developed countries participating in CIEC, in order to contribute to the objective of the establishment of new industrial capacities in the developing countries, in particular raw materials and commodity processing facilities in those countries..., agree to assist and contribute towards setting up such new industrial capacities with reasonable prospects of viability, by taking the necessary measures and formulating policies for industrial development. In this context the system of continuing consultations should play a useful role.

WORLD ECONOMY ISSUE 25

Restructuring the Economic and Social Sections of the United Nations

25.1 The original formulation of the NIEO objective at the United Nations

The various objectives of the NIEO call for appropriate action by national governments, regional and interregional bodies, multinational enterprises, as well as by the only universal general-purpose organization in existence, the United Nations. Aspects of several issues require planning, coordination and in part, implementation by the relevant economic and social programmes, agencies and organs of the United Nation system.

The Programme of Action on the Establishment of the NIEO (May 1974), noted the need for new commitments, changes, additions and adaptations in the International Development Strategy for the Second United Nations Development Decade in view of the Declaration and Programme of Action on the NIEO. It also called for urgent and effective measures to review the lending policies of international financial institutions, and for more effective participation by developing countries in decision-making. "The competent agencies of the United Nations system must meet requests for assistance from developing countries in connection with the operation of nationalized means of production." The Programme of Action entrusted the task of its own implementation to "all bodies of the United Nations system," and requested that the activities of UNCTAD be strengthened for the development of international trade in raw materials throughout the world.

Development and International Economic Co-Operation (September 1975), the resolution of the Seventh Special Session, called for a whole range of activities in connection with restructuring the economic and social sections of the United Nations. It required the Ad Hoc Committee to take into account:

> the relevant proposals and documentation submitted in preparation for the   Seventh Special Session...pursuant to General Assembly Resolution 3343 (XXIX)...including the report of the Group of Experts...entitled "A New United Nations Structure for Global Economic Cooperation", the records of ECOSOC, TDB, UNDP and UNCTAD IV and UNEP fourth session. All United Nation organs, including the regional commissions,...specialized agencies and IAEA, are invited to participate in the work of the AD Hoc Committee and to respond to requests that the Committee may make to them for information, data or views.

The resources of the development institutions of the United Nations system, in particular UNDP, should be increased. The funds of regional development banks should be augmented. These increases should be without prejudice to bilateral development assistance flows.

UNIDO should be converted into a specialized agency: "It should serve as a forum for consultations and negotiation of agreements in the field of industry."*   Proposals for the establishment of a system of consultations should be examined and "the Industrial Development Board is invited to draw up...the rules of procedure according to which this system would operate."

UNIDO and UNCTAD should jointly undertake study of "methods and mechanisms for diversified financial and technical cooperation which are geared to the special and changing requirements of international industrial cooperation."including guidelines for bilateral industrial cooperation.

UNCTAD should study on a priority basis the options open to the international community to preserve the purchasing power of developing countries, including "direct and indirect indexation schemes and other options," with a view to making concrete proposals on the subject.

UNCTAD should prepare a preliminary study on the proportion between prices of raw materials and commodities exported by developing countries and the final consumer price, particularly in developed countries.

25.2   Specification and development of the NIEO objective at the United
        Nations 1974-78

The Trade and Development Board of UNCTAD in its mid-term review and appraisal concluded that there is a case for initiating institutional change in the trade and development field to accompany that already under way in the international monetary system.   (TD/B/535, "Mid-term Review and Appraisal of the Implementation of the Joint Development Strategy,"   30 December 1974).

Reiterating the General Assembly's decision "to assist in the evolution of a system of world economic relations based on the equality and common interests of all countries" and to "initiate the necessary and appropriate structural changes to make the United Nations system a more effective instrument of world economic cooperation and for the implementation of the International Development Strategy," the Trade and Development Board stated, inter alia:

> ...while   the   case   for   institutional   change   justifies   renewed
> consideration   of   the   question   of   the   establishment   of   a
> comprehensive international trade organization, the question should
> now   be   considered   in   the   context   of   the   broader   process   of
> institutional change...

> ...in response to the need for universality, they should permit the
> participation of all States in the processes of formulating policies
> and taking decisions.

> (The suggested criteria) should be based upon agreed objectives and
> an agreed code of behavior, taking into account the interests of all
> States and recognizing differences in their economic and social
> systems and in levels and patterns of development.

_____

* See Issue 24

...such arrangements should constitute a comprehensive framework for intergovernmental agreement and cooperation on trade and development problems...(with) provision for different forms of international action, e.g., collection, analysis, and dissemination of information; deliberation and recommendation; negotiation of agreements, binding commitments and legal instruments; consultation and settlement of disputes; and technical cooperation...

neither UNCTAD nor the GATT, nor even the two together, satisfy all these criteria and hence new arrangements ought to be made to deal with trade and development problems in a comprehensive manner....

The report of a Group of Experts on the Structure of the United Nations system (E/AC.62/9, "A New United Nations Structure for Global Economic Cooperation" - Report of the Group of Experts, 28 March 1975), recommended the establishment of smaller working groups to negotiate specific issues before finally voting upon them in the concerned organs:

Another important innovation which the Group recommends in the functioning of the Council is the establishment by the Council (ECOSOC) of small negotiating groups to deal with key economic issues identified by it as requiring further negotiations with a view to bringing about agreed solutions.

...It should be understood, of course, that the Assembly and the Council could not be expected to postpone taking decisions if there were an excessively large number of negotiating groups which were all active at the same time...

The consultative procedures here proposed...would normally be initiated at an early stage in the discussion of a given subject and before the stage of the passing of resolutions, but the procedures could also be initiated at the end of a process of debate or even after a decision where this seemed to be appropriate...

In recommending these consultative procedures, the Group... considered the UNCTAD conciliation procedure provided in General Assembly Resolution 1995 (XIX) of 30 December 1964...the UNCTAD procedure would need to be changed in major respects to make it appropriate for use in the Council.   In particular, the provision in the UNCTAD conciliation procedure postponing for a fixed period the voting of disagreed resolutions was not regarded by our Group as acceptable ....

The Group therefore recommends the following arrangements for a system of negotiation...

a) At the request of the General Assembly or the Economic and Social Council, or upon the motion of one-tenth of the members of either body, a small negotiating group would be constituted by the Council to seek agreement on a specific action proposal or related action proposals in the field of development and international economic cooperation...

b) Negotiating groups would normally be created at the beginning of the Council's biennial calendar, although they could be created at other times when the need arises...in deciding upon whether to vote a particular resolution, the General Assembly and the Council would take into account the progress of the negotiation.

c) Each negotiating group would function under the guidance of a full-time chairman with the assistance, as necessary, of a small representative bureau of vice-chairmen, all of whom would be proposed by the Secretary-General and confirmed by the General Assembly or the Council...

d) Each negotiating group would operate on the basis of unanimity...

e) The Council should consider possible arrangements designed to ensure the implementation of policy decisions taken by the General Assembly or the Council after use of the consultative procedures....

During its fourth session, UNCTAD has considered two specific issues directly related to the issues of restructuring (TD/195, 30 May 1976). First, in respect of trade and related matters, measures should be taken to achieve the goals for accelerated industrial development taking into account the present interrelated and mutually supporting measures for expanding and diversifying the export trade of developing countries in manufactures and semi-manufactures and relevant decisions in the context of the NIEO Programme of Action, the Lima Declaration, and General Assembly Resolution 3362 (S-VII).

Secondly, reviewing the institutional arrangements of UNCTAD, it was emphasized that this organization should be strengthened to increase its effectiveness. Member States of the United Nations should cooperate with UNCTAD to make use of its potential for constructive contributions aimed at achieving the NIEO objectives. Toward that end:

UNCTAD's Trade and Development Board should meet at ministerial level every two years between sessions of the conference;

Such meetings should be of short duration and well prepared;

An open-ended committee on Economic Cooperation Among Developing Countries must be established to provide support and assistance to developing countries;

Greater flexibility must be introduced into the operation of the Board and its subsidiary bodies;

The structure of the committees and their subsidiary bodies must be rationalized "on the basis of a redefinition and consolidation... of their current terms of reference";

The existing procedures for intergovernmental consultations and negotiations within the framework of UNCTAD must be improved.

During 1976, the Trade and Development Board decided (TD/B 140 (XVI) 1976), pursuant to earlier resolutions of the Assembly and of the Fourth Session of the Conference, to establish an Ad Hoc Intergovernmental Committee for the Integrated Programme for Commodities:

to coordinate the preparatory work and the negotiations;

to deal with major policy issues including commodity coverage;

to coordinate the implementation of the measures under the Integrated Programme.

In pursuance of earlier decisions seeking to implement the provisions of the NIEO and the recommendations of UNCTAD IV, the Trade and Development Board (TD/B 142 (XVI), decided to establish a Committee on Economic Cooperation among developing countries as an open-ended main Committee of the Board.

During its 32nd session the General Assembly decided (Resolution 32/197)

To invite the Secretary-General to appoint... a Director-General for Development and International Economic Cooperation... who... would effectively assist him in carrying out his responsibilities as Chief Administrative Officer, under the Charter of the United Nations, in the economic and social fields....

Further, as part of the proposed measures for the restructuring of the United Nations system the following recommendations were made in the annex to Resolution 32/197:

The General Assembly

...should function as the principal forum for policy-making and for the harmonization of international action;

the Assembly should...establish over-all strategies, policies and priorities for the system as a whole in respect of international cooperation, including operational activities, in the economic, social and related fields;

The Assembly should review and evaluate developments in other forums... (including)... developments in forums outside the United Nations system and address recommendations to them.

Furthermore, the Assembly should strive to coordinate the functions, by entrusting the appropriate agenda items to the Second and Third Committees. The Chairmen of these Committees should hold consultations for this purpose.

The Economic and Social Council should serve as a central forum for discussion of economic and social issues of a global or interdisciplinary nature and for monitoring and evaluating the implementation of overall strategies and policies.

"The ECOSOC should organize its work on a biennial basis and provide for shorter but more frequent subject-oriented sessions...for the purpose, inter alia of considering action by the United Nations system in particular sectors...;" such special sessions should deal with emerging problems meriting urgent international attention. The council should also "hold periodic meetings at the ministerial or other sufficiently high level, to review major issues..."

The council should give priority to streamlining the various subsidiary expert and advisory bodies or committees and discontinue such bodies unless affirmatively decided to renew and redefine their mandates. Such a task should include:

> The redefinition and regrouping, on the basis of their substantive and methodological interrelationships, of the terms of reference of the functional commissions, or the assumption by the council in appropriate instances of direct responsibility for their work.

> The ECOSOC should examine and improve its consultative relationships with NGO's taking fully into account the principles of the NIEO.

Other United Nations Forums including UNCTAD: All United Nations organs, programmes and specialized agencies should cooperate for the effective discharge of the responsibilities of the Assembly guided by the policy framework of the Assembly and ECOSOC.

Appropriate measures should be taken to assist UNCTAD, within available resources, with negotiation, deliberation, review and implementation in international trade and economic cooperation.

Structures for Regional and Interregional Cooperation: Regional Commissions should be enabled fully to play their role as the main general economic and social development centers within the United Nations system for their respective regions.

Relations between regional commissions and the organizations of the United Nations system should be strengthened...the General Assembly and ECOSOC should take measures to enable them to function expeditiously as executing agencies for intersectoral, subregional, regional and interregional projects.

In order to enable them effectively to discharge the responsibilities indicated in the preceding paragraphs, the necessary authority should be delegated to the regional commissions and, to the same end, adequate budgetary and financial provision should be made for their activities.

Restructuring Measures in Respect of Operational Activities of the United Nations System: Restructuring measures for operational activities should promote:

> real increase in the flow of resources;

> assistance provided should be in conformity with national objectives and priorities;

orientation and allocation of resources must fully reflect the overall strategies, policies and priorities of the Assembly and ECOSOC;

efficiency and economy in administrative costs.

Integration measures should be gradually undertaken under the authority of the Secretary-General for development financed by extra-budgetary resources:

A major premise underlying such integration is that it will stimulate substantially higher levels of voluntary contributions to operational activities for development, and it should accordingly be carried forward with due regard to the current levels of such voluntary contributions. ...There should be held a single United Nations Pledging Conference for all United Nations operational activities for development.

A unified system of administrative, financial,budgetary, personnel, procurement and planning procedures should be achieved.

At the country level there should be improved coherence of action and effective integration of the various sectoral inputs from the United Nations system. For this purpose the UNDP country programming process should be utilized.

The overall responsibility for coordination of operational activities within the United Nations system should be entrusted to a single official to be designated with the consent of the Government concerned who should exercise team leadership and be responsible for evolving, at the country level, a multidisciplinary dimension in sectoral development assistance programmes."

The General Assembly should give consideration to establishing a single governing body responsible for the management and control at the intergovernmental level of United Nations operational activities for development, replacing existing governing bodies.

Planning, Programming, Budgeting and Evaluation

The competent intergovernmental bodies charged with programming and budgeting should develop thematic approaches with a view to ensuring the implementation by the Secretariat units concerned, of the overall priorities established by the General Assembly;

The Committee for Programme and Coordination...should assist the Council and the Assembly in supervising, reviewing and carrying out, as appropriate, evaluation exercises...make recommendations regarding the establishment and harmonization of medium-term plans and programmes;

The Committee...should formulate...relative priorities of United Nations Programmes; in this context subsidiary intergovernmental and expert bodies should accordingly refrain from making recommendations on the relative priorities...and...instead propose, through the committee (such) priorities to be accorded to the various sub-programmes;

The CPC should make such further improvements in its programme and methods of work and the General Assembly and ECOSOC should keep under continuous review the terms of reference of the Committee;

Measures should be taken to improve the effectiveness of internal evaluation and to assist the Joint Inspection Unit in their external evaluation;

The United Nations system should develop harmonized budget presentations and a common methodology of programme classification;

Improve procedures for prior consultation of proposed work programmes;

Strengthen the procedures for elaborating the medium-term work planning;

Continue existing representation by States' members of the CPC by meeting the travel and per diem expenses of one representative of each Member State member of the committee;

The ACABQ should be guided by the priorities of the General Assembly and ECOSOC. To ensure more equitable representation, membership of the ACABQ should be increased to at least 16;

The Secretary-General should make the necessary adjustments to facilitate CPC and ACABQ to work jointly and maintain continuous contact;

Intergovernmental bodies should enforce existing rules concerning the submission of Programme-budget implications of proposals submitted to them.

Inter-Agency Coordination at the intergovernmental levels should be governed by Assembly and ECOSOC guidelines. At the inter-secretariat level it should integrate into a coherent whole the relevant expertise and inputs of the organizations of the United Nations system. It should also be a built-in element of the substantive support to be provided to the intergovernmental bodies concerned for the discharge of their policy-making functions and also for policy and programme execution. Their specific tasks include:

Preparing concise and action-oriented recommendations for consideration by intergovernmental bodies;

Concerting implementation of programmes and agencies concerned of policy guidelines, directives and priorities;

Developing cooperative and joint programme planning as well as the coordinated execution of programmes decided upon at the intergovernmental level.

Inter-agency coordination should be pursued with full respect for the competence, where relevant, of the regional commissions. Machinery for inter-agency coordination at the inter-secretariat level should center on the ACC and should be streamlined to make the most use of flexible, ad hoc arrangements where possible. Steps should be taken to merge the Environment Coordination Board, the Inter-Agency Consultative Board and the UNIDO Advisory Committee with the ACC. The ACC Agenda, functioning and reporting systems should be adjusted to respond fully and promptly to priority concerns. Reporting schedules should conform to the calendar of meetings of the intergovernmental bodies concerned and the executive secretaries of the regional commissions should fully participate in the work of the ACC. Further agreements are needed to improve communication between the ACC and the intergovernmental bodies. The review by ECOSOC of these relationship agreements between the United Nations and the Specialized Agencies should be guided by the need to ensure that the agencies give full and prompt effect to the recommendations made by the General Assembly and by the ECOSOC.

Secretariat-Support-Services. The following guidelines are recommended to the Secretary-General, who would carry them out in exercise of his powers under the Charter:

In the economic and social sectors the United Nations Secretariat should be restructured so as effectively to meet the requirements and the policy directives of the General Assembly and ECOSOC and in the context of the provisions of the Charter, to take fully into account the development requirements of the developing countries.

In extending support to the relevant intergovernmental bodies, the Secretariat should concentrate on:

Interdisciplinary research and analysis, preparing on a regular basis global economic and social surveys and projections and undertaking in-depth intersectoral analyses and synthesis of development issues with action-oriented recommendations on emerging issues;

Identifying and bringing to the attention of Governments emerging economic and social issues of international concern;

Substantive support for technical cooperation activities in economic and social sectors which are not covered by other United Nations organs, programmes or Specialized Agencies. These functions include, inter alia, the provision of technical expertise in the formulation, implementation and evaluation of country and intercountry programmes and of specific projects;

the provision of direct advisory assistance to governments; the development of training materials and support of training institutions;

Management of technical cooperation programmes including projects under technical assistance programmes, UNDP projects under United Nations executing direction and projects financed by voluntary contributions and trust funds;

Provision of technical secretariat services, substantive support services in order to ensure that the substantive units and bodies concerned are informed of relevant developments, including resolutions and decisions adopted by them;

Research, including the collection of relevant data and analysis in those economic and social sectors that do not fall within the purview of other United Nations organs, programmes and Speccialized Agencies.

The new Director-General for Development and International Economic Cooperation should be in charge of:

Providing effective leadership to the various components of the United Nations system and in exercising over-all coordination within the system in order to ensure a multi-disciplinary approach to the problems of development on a system-wide basis;

Ensuring within the United Nations the coherence, coordination and efficient management of all activities in the economic and social fields.

(On March 14, 1978, the Secretary-General announced his intention to appoint Mr. K.K.S. Dadzie to the post of Director-General for Development and International Economic Cooperation with effect from 24 April 1978 (E/1978/28, 21 April 1978).

As part of the restructuring process recommended in the report of the Ad Hoc Committee (A/C.5/32/86), the Secretary-General announced the establishment of three new organizational units, in place of the existing Department of Economic and Social Affairs and the Office for Inter-Agency Affairs and Coordination. These are:

Department of International Economic and Social Affairs;
Department of Technical Cooperation for Development;
Office of Secretariat Services for Economic and Social Matters.
(ST/SGB/161-163 of 23 March 1978)

25.3 Contributions of major international bodies, 1974-78

The Member States of the Conference of Non-Aligned Countries on Raw Materials (E/AC.62/6, 15 April 1975), recommended the creation of an International Trade Organization.

The Manila Declaration and Programme of Action adopted by the Third Ministerial Meeting of the Group of 77 (TD/195, 7 February 1976), emphasized:

> the need for appropriate institutional arrangements...to provide a framework that would impart further impetus to the promotion of economic cooperation among developing countries...Among the possibilities that could be considered would be a strengthening of the role of UNCTAD, including the establishment of a Committee on Economic Cooperation among Developing Countries.

In their third and Final Report entitled "Towards a New International Economic Order" (14 March 1977) the Commonwealth Group of Experts made Inter alia the following recommendations:

In the monetary field, the ultimate goal should be the evolution of the IMF into an institution performing functions in the international sphere similar to those of a Central Bank in a national economy. More balanced participation in the decision-making process of the IMF by all countries, including developing countries, will necessitate making changes in the voting rights in the IMF and in IBRD.* The developing countries should also have more participation in the management of these institutions.

Referring to international trade, the Report states:

> we also believe that there should be serious examination of the possibility of a comprehensive international trade organization in place of the multiplicity of existing organizations.. .

> ...Apart from the formal constitutional changes, we consider that UNIDO needs to sharpen its own priorities...There could also be a vital role for UNIDO as a catalyst for the establishment of centres for industrial education and training (including management and production engineering)...

> ...But we suggest that the ECOSOC should give attention to establishing a more manageable and effective machinery for comprehensive negotiations.

---

* See Issue 13 for details

Part II
The Positon of Some States and
Groups of States on the Issues

7 Aid and Assistance Issues

WORLD ECONOMY ISSUES 1 AND 2

Attaining United Nations Official Development Assistance Targets;
Providing Technical Assistance for Development and
Eliminating the Brain Drain

The Position of Denmark*

At an early stage, Denmark accepted the 0.7 target. In 1970, Danish official development assistance equalled 0.38 percent of our GNP. Next year 1970 we shall reach the target within the time frame set at the 7th Special Session of the General Assembly.

We are aware that developed countries pursue various ways to increase their ODA. We agree that the most important thing is a fast increase in real terms. Predictability is very important, however, for developing countries as well as for our own planning. This is the reason why Denmark is basing its contributions to international cooperation on

---

* This and the following excerpts from position papers and statements of Member States and Groups of States (produced at the first session of the Committee of the Whole established to deal with the NIEO issues, at the United Nations, 3-12 May 1978), are chosen to illuminate the respective national and group positions on the particular issues of direct relevance to the NIEO, and do not necessarily mirror everything contained in the original papers and statements. Materials which (i) provide information rather than indicate a position, and those which (ii) discuss matters not immediately associated with the here identified 25 world economy issues, have been omitted.

rolling five year plans.

According to the present plan, Danish ODA is being increased yearly by almost 8 per cent in constant prices.

Our commitment to contribute to the global development process is strongly supported by the Danish public. This is why we have been able to increase our aid programmes according to the plans even in the present situation, where our national economy suffers from serious difficulties, including an intolerably high rate of unemployment. On this background... I would like to appeal to all developed countries - irrespective of their economic system - to strengthen their efforts towards increasing their transfer of resources to developing countries. This does not least apply to countries with sizable balance-of-payments surpluses. The volume of ODA made available to the developing countries depends on the political will of the developed countries; the efficient utilization of the means, on the other hand, depends on the developing countries and will in turn have an impact on the public opinion in the developed countries.

(Statement by Minister Lise Ostergaard, Denmark, pp. 1-2)

The Position of the European Economic Community

The dependence of the developing countries on external financial flows calls for a greater international effort on the part of all those countries able to do so to provide official development assistance, particularly for the poorest countries. To begin with, there must be an effective and substantial increase in official development assistance so that the target of 0.7 per cent of GNP can be attained as soon as possible.

Given the great diversity of development situations, the terms of aid should be tailored to the particular circumstances of the recipient countries. In this connection, mention should be made of the consensus reached at the ninth session of the UNCTAD Trade and Development Board, which was held at the ministerial level in March 1978. These terms should also be improved in order to maintain the over-all grant element at a minimum of 86 per cent of financial commitments, or increase it to that level as soon as possible, and give the least developed and most needy countries as large a grant element as possible.

(Position Statement submitted by Denmark on behalf of the European Economic Community, paras. 34-35)

About the volume of ODA, may I recall that most of our Member States have already made provision for an immediate increase of 10 to 30% for the current calendar year over 1977, and of 40 to 60% for the whole period 1977-81.

About the quality of ODA, may I recall that all our Member States are now well above the new DAC terms Recommendation which was revised last March in pursuance to the CIEC. In addition, several Member States have now adopted standard soft terms applying automatically to the ODA directed to poorest developing countries.   We have also committed ourselves, in Geneva last March, on the question of adjustment of the terms of past bilateral ODA.

...we must take seriously into account the legal and political framework in which aid decisions have to be taken, and that donor countries should be given a fair degree of flexibility as to the choice of the ways and means they want to use in improving the volume and the quality of their assistance.   We are committed to substantial progress vis-a-vis the developing countries and we have given the proof of our willingness to achieve this progress.   Since CIEC, we have managed considerable increases in assistance budgets by convincing our Parliamentary and public opinion. Moreover, a system that attempted to fix the long-term level of aid flows in advance would not necessarily - or at least not in every case - result in a greater flow of aid.

> (Statement of the Minister Lise Ostergaard on behalf of the EEC, pp. 5-6)

As for Official Development Assistance (ODA), the Member States of the European Community have undertaken to increase the volume of their ODA effectively and substantially in accordance with the agreement concluded at the Seventh Special Session of the United Nations General Assembly envisaging attainment of the 0.7% target by the end of the decade, having in mind the form in which it was concluded. The lower their relative performance, the greater the effort they will make to achieve this target. In this respect, the Member States of the European Community have recently reaffirmed the usefulness and the need for an increase in aid flows: "a general increase in the flow of aid to developing countries would better enable these countries to play a more important part in the general recovery of the world economy."

The Member States of the European Community are also considering adopting or continuing to apply specific measures to facilitate such an increase and have agreed that the volume of ODA should, as far as possible, not be affected in the future by budgetary difficulties, balance of payment problems or other related factors.

...on a qualitative level, at the CIEC, the Member States of the European Community expressed one of the basic principles of their development policies, namely adaptation of ODA terms to the particular curcumstances of the recipient countries, in the form of concrete commitments. The improvements which they agreed to put into effect consist of: increasing the overall grant element of ODA to 86%, supplying ODA to the least developed countries essentially in the form of grants, increasing the flows of untied ODA or seeking alternative arrangements to the untying of aid, seeking a rational and equitable distribution of ODA among developing countries and looking for forms of aid which are most appropriate to their developmental needs and priorities. In addition, they have agreed to explore further the possibilities of adopting changes in the definition of ODA.

> (Position Statement of the European Economic Community on the Transfer of Real Resources, pp. 9, 10, 11)

The Position of the Group of 77

The present total transfer of ODA is inadequate to meet the most pressing problems of developing countries and can only contribute marginal support to the structural transformation required for the New International Economic Order. Over the period 1970 to 1976, ODA has averaged only 0.33 per cent of the GNP of Development Assistance Committee (DAC) countries. As stated in the report of the Commonwealth Experts' Group on the New International Economic Order: "The reasons developed countries have advanced in an attempt to explain why annual aid appropriations have failed to allow them to reach the 0.7 per cent target already, and in some cases have resulted in backsliding, have little economic substance or validity. Ultimately, it comes down to a question of priorities which governments themselves attach to the needs of the developing countries as compared with domestic demands. It is a question of political will."

> (Position Statement submitted by Jamaica on behalf of the Group of 77, p. 2)

Bilateral flows

(a) -The target of 0.7 per cent of GNP for ODA should be attained as early as possible by all the developed countries who have not done so, and not later than 1980. To achieve this end and to ensure that ODA flows are predictable, continuous and assured, developed countries should adopt, inter alia, the following measures, either single or in any appropriate combination:

- include quantitative ODA targets in their economic planning;
- increase their aid budgets in real terms by an appropriate percentage each year, in order to meet the target;
- set aside at least 1 per cent of the increase in their annual GNP;
- establish interest subsidy mechanisms as a means of generating a large expansion of concessional flows;
- introduce a development tax.

(b) ODA should be distributed rationally and equitably among all developing countries, and the continuity of such financial flows should be ensured on more favourable terms and conditions. In this context, the relevant resolutions and decisions of the United Nations and other bodies in favour of the least developed, the most seriously affected, land-locked and island developing countries, should be urgently implemented without prejudice to existing bilateral or multilateral agreements between developing and developed countries.

Quality of flows

The following changes in the conventional concept of ODA should be adopted:

(a) ODA should be calculated as net of both amortization and of interest payments.

(b) All ODA should be in the form of grants or loans on IDA terms, and for the least developed countries it should be entirely in the form of grants. Special attention should be paid to the needs of the other special categories of developing countries in the proportionate distribution between loans and grants in disbursements of ODA to them.

(c) The minimum grant element for qualifying for inclusion in ODA should be raised from the present 25 per cent to 50 per cent.

(d) ODA loans should be untied and grants should be untied as far as possible.

(e) Assistance to countries/territories not regarded by donor countries themselves as sovereign political entities should be excluded in measuring a country's performance in fulfilling its ODA target.

(f) ODA should be given increasingly and substantially in the form of non-project and programme assistance, including local currency financing.

> (Position Paper submitted by Jamaica on behalf of the Group of 77, paras. 13-14)

...the principal lesson from the workings of the existing arrangements for transfer of resources must be that ways and means should be found to complement the present voluntary arrangements, by the establishment of more mechanisms for the transfer of resources on a more predictable, continuous and assured basis. Official development assistance should be distributed rationally and equitably among all developing countries, with special regard for the problems of the least developed countries.

Again, a major weakness of the existing arrangements under which resource transfers take place is that the distribution of ODA, and the conditions under which it is provided are not sufficiently tailored to the development objectives of developing countries.

(Statement by Ambassador Mills of Jamaica on behalf of the Group of 77, pp. 9-10)

The Position of Japan

The Official Development Assistance (ODA) given by Japan amounted to $1,105 million in 1976. Its ODA increased tenfold in the recent 15 years and its share in the total ODA of the DAC countries had increased from 2.1 per cent in 1961 to 8.1 per cent in 1976. With a view to further strengthening these efforts, the Government announced at the Conference on International Economic Cooperation in May 1977 its intention to more than double its ODA within five years.

It had also recently decided to make its best efforts, to improve its ODA both in quantity and in quality by promoting general untying, increasing the volume of grants, softening the terms of loans, and other similar measures with the aim of attaining the 86 per cent target for the grant element.

(Position Statement submitted by Japan, paras. 11,12)

The Position of India

The role of international cooperation through adequate transfer of real resources from the rich developed to the poor developing countries as a step in the establishment of the New International Economic Order can scarcely be over-emphasized. In this context, we are disappointed at the fact that the Official Development Assistance (ODA) transfers have been substantially smaller than the 0.7 per cent target accepted by the international community in the Second United Nations Development Decade. We would, therefore, like to urge the imperative need for the developed countries to adopt a time-bound agreed target of 0.7 per cent for ODA transfers.

(Position Statement submitted by India, para. 11)

The Position of New Zealand

...We remain fully committed to the target of 0.7 per cent of GNP for ODA transfers though the serious balance-of-payments position which New Zealand has experienced since 1973 has inevitably constrained our ability currently to sustain an expanding assistance programme vis-a-vis our developing partners. It is hoped that we shall be able to make more rapid progress towards the target as soon as our economic circumstances permit. New Zealand is not a significant creditor country in relation to developing countries and despite constraints in the quantity of assistance we are able to give at the present time, the Official Development Assistance New Zealand provides is almost entirely in grant form.

(Position Statement submitted by New Zealand para. 10)

The Position of Sweden

Sustained and increased ODA flows will continue to be of central importance for the developing countries also in the future.

The general trend regarding ODA flows from the industrialized countries during this decade, is not encouraging. In real terms, net ODA flows increased from close to 12 billion dollars in 1970 to 14 billion in 1976 (1976 prices: ODA deflator). Expressed as a percentage of GNP ODA flows decreased from 0.34 per cent in 1970 to 0.33 per cent in 1976.

It is clear that the 0.7 per cent target set for this decade will not be met in time. The Conference on International Economic Cooperation agreement on ODA was hoped to become a turning point towards improved volume performance. So far, however, it has not proved to be instrumental and there are few signs of substantial increases in the near future. In this context it should be recalled that the following suggestions, contained in the Conference agreement, regarding specific measures to be applied by donor Governments, are still relevant as means of increasing ODA flows:

(a) Increase annually their ODA budgets by a specific percentage on a multiyear basis;

(b) Set aside at least 1 per cent of their annual GNP increase expected to accrue to be devoted to augment ODA flows;

(c) Include aid volume targets in their economic planning;

(d) Undertake long-range planning of aid budgets.

In the present economic situation, Governments and politicians are faced with a heavy political responsibility to maintain and further develop public support for increased ODA flows. The volume of ODA should, as far as possible, not be affected by budgetary difficulties, balance-of-payment problems or other relevant factors, so as to assist in rendering ODA flows predictable, continuous and increasingly assured. Renewed efforts must be made within a framework of an equitable sharing of efforts where the ODA increases should be the greater the lower the relative performance. The larger donor countries with strong economies have a special responsibility to increase their aid efforts in response to the 0.7 per cent target and the Conference commitment.

Also, the contributions of the centrally planned economy countries of Eastern Europe must be of a totally different magnitude if the statements of global solidarity with the developing countries are to be reality in the 1980's.

Participants in the Conference agreed that developed donor countries should explore further the possibilities of adopting changes in the de-inition of ODA. To this end, the Swedish Government is in favour of the following measures:

(a) ODA should be calculated as net of both amortization and of interest payments;

(b) The minimum grant element for qualifying as ODA should be raised from 25 per cent to 50 per cent;

(c) The flows to dependent territories should not be considered as ODA flows.

The final terms of ODA flows should be further improved. In addition to extending assistance to the least developed countries essentially in the form of grants, each donor should endeavour to maintain an average grant element of at least 95 per cent in its aid commitments to the poorer developing countries. Sweden favours an early resumption of international discussions aiming at a multilateral agreement on recipro-cal untying of ODA flows.

On a per capita basis more assistance is still extended to middle-income or richer developing countries than to the poorest developing countries. There is thus a need for a reallocation and concentration of ODA flows to the poorest countries.

All donor countries should be prepared to provide additional assistance to developing countries launching new basic needs-oriented approaches to development.

...The present system of annual voluntary contributions to other United Nations organizations for technical assistance (i.e. the United Nations Development Programme, the United Nations Children's Fund, the United Nations Fund for Population Activities, the World Food Programme, and the United Nations High Commissioner for Refugees), has a number of drawbacks.

Contributions are provided on an annual basis although the programmes are long-term. Individual donor countries perceive differently their responsibilities versus the financing of the Programme. Financing efforts are not equitably shared. The programmes are far from their optimal size. It is also possible that the present system of short-term pledges has contributed to the proliferation of funds.

...about 85 per cent of the total technical assistance from the United Nations system derives from voluntary contributions to UNDP and the specialized agencies. A considerable shift has, however, taken place from UNDP to the specialized agencies, reducing the UNDP share of voluntary contributions from about 90 per cent in 1972 to 60 per cent in 1976. This is in itself a matter which should be further studied and commented upon.

> (Position Statement submitted by Sweden, paras. 1-9,15,16,18)

The Position of Switzerland

For the developing countries, official assistance is an essential component of these transfers, especially for funding infrastructures. A number of countries find themselves in a particularly difficult situation in this respect. Since their productive and export capacities are limited, they should be able to obtain loans on favourable terms. Efforts should therefore be directed to expanding official development assistance (ODA) and to adapting the terms on which it is provided to the specific situation of each developing country, while ensuring that it is more effective and more responsive to the priorities of the individual developing country and to the specific needs of the poorest populations.

> (Position Statement submitted by Switzerland, para. 8)

The Position of the Union of Soviet Socialist Republics and Socialist Countries

The socialist countries recognize the importance to the developing countries of external economic assistance, which, if it is used effectively and properly, can successfully supplement the internal resources that they are directing towards economic development goals. These additional resources should come mainly from those imperialist Powers - and their monopolies - which are seeking to continue and intensify the exploitation of the developing countries. In our opinion, the volume of these resources should be substantially greater, in both absolute and relative terms, than what the developing countries are quite rightly demanding, for even then it will only make good in a relative sense a tiny part of what the imperialist Powers are stealing from these countries by maintaining the system of colonial and neo-colonial exploitation.

...we reaffirm our position of principle concerning the generally recognized unacceptability of the application by certain Western countries to the socialist countries of the very same requirements that are applied by the developing countries to the developed capitalist States, including the requirement concerning the mandatory transfer to the developing countries, in the form of economic assistance, of a fixed portion of the gross national product.

The strategy of the socialist States in their economic cooperation with the developing countries remains unchanged. Its main goal is to help those countries in their efforts to solve the problems of economic development and in the strengthening of their economic independence. In view of that consideration, the socialist countries intend to continue, in the future, to adhere to the policy of expanding mutually advantageous commercial ties based both on traditional bilateral and long-term multilateral forms of commercial and economic cooperation, in the spirit of the recommendations contained in the Charter of Economic Duties and Rights of States and the progressive proposals adopted at the sixth and seventh special sessions of the United Nations General Assembly. For that purpose, the socialist countries would be prepared:

- to extend the practice of concluding long-term trade agreements and also agreements on economic and technical co-operation which could also, where possible and appropriate, extend over two to three five-year planning periods;

- to continue to concentrate their efforts in the field of economic and technical assistance to the developing countries on the development of production forces, and particularly industry, within the framework of the State enterprise.

> (Position Statement submitted by the USSR also on behalf of Bulgaria, Byelorussian SSR, Czechoslovakia, German Democratic Republic, Hungary, Mongolia, Poland, and the Ukranian SSR, paras. 3,4,5)

The Position of the United States of America

We will endeavor to continue to increase official development assistance substantially and progressively, both bilaterally and through multilateral institutions. We applaud the increased assistance from a number of OPEC countries and from other developed countries. Recognition by this Committee of the importance of increased bilateral and multilateral aid, and of a common effort by donors and recipients to insure its most effective use, can provide an impetus to the kind of cooperation and to the improved international economy which this Committee was established to promote.

> (Remarks of Mr. Robert Hormats, Delegation of the USA, p.10)

WORLD ECONOMY ISSUES 3 and 4

Renegotiating the Debts of Developing Countries;
Undertaking Special Measures to Assist Land-Locked, Least-Developed and
Island Developing Countries

The Position of Austria

While it has not yet been possible to find global solutions for the problems of indebtedness of developing countries, new impulses have been provided by the recent Ministerial Meeting of the Trade and Development Board which will lead to further progress in this highly complex domain. In this context, the ideas put forward by the Federal Chancellor of Austria, Dr. Bruno Kreisky, concerning a programme of massive transfers of resources for the development of the infrastructure of developing countries, especially in Africa, could also bring about considerable relief with respect to the debt situation.

(Position Statement submitted by Austria, par. 12)

The Position of Denmark

The fact that it proved possible at the ministerial session of the UNCTAD Trade and Development Board in March to reach agreement on a compromise resolution of substance is an important and positive new step in the dialogue. So is the willingness of donor countries expressed in the resolution of the UNCTAD meeting to seek to adopt measures for an adjustment of terms of past bilateral ODA or equivalent measures. I have made it clear that Denmark is prepared to go into individual negotiations with developing countries concerning adjustment of the conditions of past ODA with a view to finding the most appropriate solution in each case. Action taken in pursuance of this declaration will be reviewed in Manila in 1979. It is our hope that on that occasion we shall be able to record a considerable improvement of the net flows to developing countries and in particular to the poorest among them.

(Position Statement made by Minister Lise Ostergaard, Denmark, pp. 4-5)

The Position of the European Economic Community

The geographical allocation of aid should take account of the situation of the developing countries which are experienceing the greatest difficulties, without, however, neglecting existing relations. All donor countries must recognize the need to distribute official development assistance in such a way that the main beneficiaries of any redirection of the increase in aid are those developing countries which are experiencing the greatest difficulties and whose situation has been assessed according to a variety of criteria, objectively reflecting their needs.

> (Position Statement submitted by Denmark on behalf of the European Economic Community, par. 56)

The Position of the Group of 77

The rise in the burden of debt servicing has adversely affected their development process in a number of ways. Debt servicing is a prior charge on the meagre foreign exchange earnings of developing countries and in their efforts to discharge fully this obligation, they have had to disrupt the implementation of their development plans by curtailing investment. Moreover, this servicing has to be effected in foreign exchange and constitutes a serious restraint on the most readily useable form of external resources. In the absence of effective remedial measures, developing countries as a whole will continue to be faced with rising debt service charges and will be forced to impose further restrictions on their imports and investment programmes. This will have disastrous effects not only on their efforts to improve the conditions of life of their poeple, but it would also seriously compromise their contribution to the maintenance of aggregate demand which could facilitate stable growth in the global economy including that of developed countries. Therefore, immediate measures should be undertaken to alleviate the debt burden of developing countries.

A system of debt reorganization should be established which would take into account the development needs of developing countries and principles of international cooperation.

> (Position Statement submitted by Jamaica on behalf of the Group of 77, p. 3)

ODA should be distributed rationally and equitably among all developing countries, and the continuity of such financial flows should be ensured on more favourable terms and conditions. In this context, the relevant resolutions and decisions of the United Nations and other bodies in favour of the least developed, the most seriously affected, land-locked and island developing countries, should be urgently implemented without prejudice to existing bilateral or multilateral agreements between developing and developed countries.

> (Position Paper submitted by Jamaica on behalf of the Group of 77, para. 13 (b))

The Position of India

At the recent meeting of the Trade and Development Board at Geneva in March 1978, there was a recognition by the developed countries that the debt problem has a developmental connotation. However, in spite of this development, the problem itself remains unsolved. The developed countries should, therefore, now take urgent steps so that the debt burden of the least developed countries and the most seriously affected countries is alleviated and they are assisted in implementing their development plans in an orderly and flexible manner.

(Position Statement submitted by India, para. 10)

The Position of Japan

Concerning the distribution of ODA, Japan has attached a greater importance to the aid to poorer countries. In fact, in 1976, 61 per cent of Japan's bilateral ODA was extended to the poorer countries with per capita GNP of less than $265. This is above the average performance of DAC countries.

...Regarding the debt problem on which world attention has been focused in various fora for the past several years, consensus has been reached at the Ministerial Meeting of the ninth special session of the Trade and Development Board in March 1978. Japan, as one of the active participants in this issue, highly values the result as a substantial achievement in the context of the North-South dialogue. Japan will make its utmost efforts in line with the agreement.

(Position Statement submitted by Japan, paras. 13,17)

The Position of New Zealand

The debt of developing countries, a large proportion of whose deficits have been financed at commercial rates, has now become very burdensome. A good deal of the aid received by developing countries is now effectively offset by their debt servicing liabilities. The UNCTAD secretariat has forecast that the ratio of debt service payments to export earnings will increase from 18 per cent in 1976 to 25 per cent this year.

New Zealand is regrettably well placed to understand these difficulties. Among developed countries, New Zealand's situation is distinguished by a relatively high degree of instability in export earnings, akin to that experienced by many developing countries. Our terms of trade with the rest of the world are currently at historically low levels, some 25 per cent below the average for the decade 1962-1972. The balance-of-payments deficit was of the order of 15 per cent of GNP in 1974/75 and has continued at lower but serious levels since then. The rate of domestic economic activity has been severely depressed. Recourse to substantial overseas borrowing has been required to offset the effects of the external sector on domestic production and employment. And strenuous efforts have been made internally to effect the adjustments that have been necessary in the short and medium term. Against this background, New Zealand can fully appreciate how much more difficult to sustain and accelerate their economic development it is for developing countries. For this reason, New Zealand remains committed to maintenance of an open interdependent world economy.

(Position Statement submitted by New Zealand, paras. 8,9)

The Position of Sweden

There is general recognition that debt issues cannot be dealt with in isolation. Indebtedness forms part of a much broader economic picture where established systems of resource transfers play an essential role. Consequently, debt problems should be related to the general developmental situation of the countries concerned. Some of these problems can be seen as a reflection of insufficiencies in present resource transfer systems.

With regard to the poorest developing countries, most ODA is now being provided in the form of grants. This development has raised the issue of adjustment of terms of past bilateral ODA credits. At the third ministerial part of the ninth special session of the Trade and Development Board, a general commitment was made by developed donor countries to seek to adopt measures for such terms adjustment, or other equivalent measures as a means of improving net ODA flows (TD/B/L.501). Implementing action will be reviewed at the fifth session of the United Nations Conference on Trade and Development.

This commitment should be noted as an important step forward. In view of the fact that the poorest countries will continue to find even low levels of indebtedness burdensome, action in the field of terms adjustment - combined with ODA increases essentially in the form of grants- will no doubt be crucial responding means on the part of the donor community. It should be noted in this context that the non-ODA part of these outstanding debts of the poorest countries is rapidly increasing. Given their pressing resource needs - and the inadequacy of export earnings and ODA - they have often no other choice than resorting to the expensive and volatile market of short-term private loans, commercial credits, etc.

With regard to richer, middle-income countries - mainly relying on resource transfers on non-concessional terms - renewed efforts should be made to establish a proper and equitable framework with a view to avoiding and managing general debt problems. This area is no doubt an important element in the precarious international interdependence. A firm basis for these efforts have been laid in the Trade and Development Board resolution, referred to above, including agreement on certain basic concepts. In the view of Sweden, the proposals made by developing countries and by the United States of America and the European Economic Community on this issue contain common elements, which warrant a further search for agreed solutions.

(Position Statement submitted by Sweden, paras. 33-36)

WORLD ECONOMY ISSUE 5

Using Funds from Disarmament for Development

The Position of Romania

Romania has stressed for a number of years and on various occasions, including in the document relating to disarmament questions which it submitted to the thirieth session of the General Assembly and in its proposals in the Preparatory Committee for the Special Session of the General Assembly Devoted to Disarmament, that the arms race and the spiralling of military expenditure constitute a heavy burden on all the peoples of the world. They hinder economic and social progress, cause inflation, upset the balance of payments, create artificial barriers to the development of cooperation among States and the transfer of technology and equipment, result in the irrational management of human resources and raw materials, contribute to pollution and upset the ecological balance, and constitute an obstacle to efforts to eliminate under-development and solve the other problems on which the future of mankind depends. The adverse effects of the arms race and military expenditure have been illustrated in detail in the Secretary-General's recent report to the General Assembly at its thirty second session on the economic and social consequences of the armaments race (document A/32/88 of 12 (August 1977).

Romania has advocated a series of measures relating to disarmament, including a halt to the arms race, the freezing and reduction of military budgets, and the allocation of a substantial part of the resources thus freed to the financing of the development of the developing countries, and is working resolutely to translate those measures into reality.

(Position Statement submitted by Romania, paras. 14,15)

8 International Trade Issues

WORLD ECONOMY ISSUE 6

Improving the Terms and Conditions of Trade of Developing
Countries: Tariff and Non-Tariff Barriers, GSP, Duties and
Taxes on Imports, Invisible Trade

The Position of Australia

In Australia's view there is the need, in the first instance, for continued
rigorous management of national economies. Such management should be
directed particularly to the maintenance of effective anti-inflation
policies.

Those policies should be accompanied by a thorough-going attempt to
review and expland multilateral cooperation. There is a need to increase
understanding of the dangers of the transmission of economic problems in
an interdependent world. The main features of such an approach should
be:

(a) An attempt to reduce barriers to international trade, to expand that
trade and make its terms fairer and more open;

(b) Action to increase greatly the over-all participation of developing
countries in the world economy and in the taking of decisions of mutual
economic interest.

The Australian Government believes that the full participation of developing countries in global economic activity should assist in maintaining the
momentum of economic growth in the short term and contribute to
accelerated over-all growth in the long term. In doing so, it would
contribute to the maintenance of international political stability.

In the field of trade liberalization, Australia is concerned that little progress has been achieved in the Multilateral Trade Negotiations, especially in respect to agricultural products and special and differential treatment for developing countries. Disturbing protectionist trends are apparent internationally and these must be countered if the world is not to revert to the sort of narrow nationalism that was so damaging in the 1930's. The Tokyo Round could well be the last such trade negotiating forum of its type for some time. It must not be allowed to peter out at a time when world trade problems are so paramount for the recovering of the world economy.

(Position Statement submitted by Australia, para. 6-9)

The Position of Austria

Recently, we have been witnessing a mounting tendency towards protectionism in international trade. Such measures tend to hit smaller countries most of all. In the longer run, they will be detrimental to all other countries as well. No efforts should therefore be spared in order to avoid the repetition of an escalation of protectionism which, already once during this century, has led to a long-lasting and serious world economic depression.

(Position Statement submitted by Austria, par. 4)

The Position of Ecuador

...it is imperative now, for the equitable stabilization of the world in which we live and for the well-being of the developing countries, to reach agreement on suitable terms of international cooperation, which could well be negotiated multilaterally, in the forum of the United Nations, and bilaterally, on a Government-to-Government basis. The aim should be to achieve sustained growth in the purchasing power of the export earnings of the developing countries, to give their manufactured and semi-manufactured goods a greater share in world trade, to make currencies more stable, to reduce balance-of-payments deficits, and to provide access on favourable terms to international financial institutions and to the technology market, together with an acceleration of transfers, so that they will be tailored to the real needs of individual countries.

(Position Statement submitted by Ecuador, p. 3)

The Position of the European Economic Community

The expansion of world trade brought about by the progressive liberalization of international trade has been one of the essential features of the sustained economic growth of the past 20 years. In addition, it has enabled the developing countries to increase their export earnings and speed up their development process.

Efforts must therefore be made to improve and strengthen the present framework of international trade in order to keep economies as open as they have become and to bring about a progressive liberalization of trade that would take account of the economic situation of each country.

The Community considers that a conscious and responsible process of liberalization will be required in order to overcome the present economic difficulties by permitting a renewal of economic activity, which is bound to benefit all countries in the context of the growing interdependence of economies. This renewal of economic activity should, in particular, enable the developing countries to become fully involved in the world economy more rapidly.

International action should be concentrated primarily on the nomenclatures for the classification ofgoods and the application of the Generalized System of Preferences.

In this context, multilateral trade negotiations should soon lead to the achievement of the objectives set for them by the Tokyo Declaration, in particular the application of differentiated and more favourable treatment for the developing countries in those areas where this is possible and appropriate. The Community has already moved in that direction by implementing its offer on tropical products beginning in 1977. In addition, the Generalized System of Preferences must continue to serve as the main instrument of development cooperation in the field of trade. The Community is prepared to make improvements to its system in the light of the economic situation of the recipient countries and the need to coordinate the efforts of the donor countries in order to adjust their projects with a view to simplification and better utilization of the preferential advantages which should be of benefit to the least developed countries, in particular. The developing countries which are able to do so should take part in the progressive liberalization of international trade and thus support the industrialized countries in the efforts they are making in that area. Such participating should, in particular, bring about an increase in trade flows between the developing countries themselves.

(Position Statement submitted by Denmark on behalf of the European Economic Community, paras. 22-26)

... I would like to add some remarks concerning the importance of trade expansion as a vehicle of economic growth and as an important means of ensuring external revenues for the developing countries, thus facilitating their industrialization and economic diversification. The Committee consensus about the importance of trade is no surprise, but I would like to add here, taking up the valuable remark of Minister Perez-Guerrero: trade on an equitable basis. As you are well aware, the European Community has already in many ways taken care of the special situation of the LDC's and its imports from these countries have rapidly increased in the past. I may assure you that the intention of the European Community is to go on in that way.

In this connection, the utmost importance must be attached to the universally expressed determination to resist protectionist tendencies. This determination is in line with one of the main conclusions arrived at at the last meeting of the Heads of Government of the European Communities in Copenhagen. In this respect, we cannot stress enough the importance of a success for the on-going MTN negotiations under GATT, one of the main elements of which is special and differential treatment in favor of the LDC's.

The Community has already initiated contacts and talks with developing countries to this effect and is ready to continue in the mutual interest of all, in the context of the improvement and reinforcement of the actual framework.

(Position Statement made by Minister Lise Ostergaard, Denmark, pp. 9-10)

The Position of Finland

The structural adjustments to changing patterns of trade and global economics will require time and planning. But the inevitable process has begun, and, notwithstanding the economic difficulties of today, it must continue. Still, however efficiently developed countries plan the transition there will undoubtedly be occasions on which they have to take actions against sudden surges of imports. There must, however, be internationally agreed rules on and multilateral surveillance of these safeguard actions. If there are no restraints, the developed countries would be tempted to abuse these means in support of protectionism rather than of the process of adjustment. On the other hand, if the industrialized countries are not allowed to take any safeguard action at all, there will be in these countries a danger of economic and social disturbances which in turn affect negatively the political will to respond favourable to calls for liberalization in international economic relations. In order not to hamper the structural adjustment process towards the goals of the new international economic order, the safeguard actions taken must be temporary and their harmful effects on international trade and development should be limited to a minimum, taking particularly into account the interests of developing producers in the early stage of building up their initial production capacity. Thus it should be possible to apply these measures selectively, in other words, exclusively against the imports causing or threatening to cause serious injury.

(Position Statement submitted by Finland, para. 7)

The Position of the Group of 77

Regrettably, one of the reactions by developed countries to the present circumstances has been the growth of protectionism. Whereas in the past such a policy was designed to provide protection against other developed countries, it now seems to be directed mainly against the developing countries and especially against their more dynamic export sectors. In this way, the quantitative restrictions applied by most developed countries to imports of manufacturers from the developing countries are three times heavier than those applied to the imports from other developed countries. Moreover, the recent tendency to ask for voluntary restrictions of exports (under the threat of permanent legislative action) is also equivalent to an extension of the prevailing system of quantitative regulation on the imports of manufactures from developing countries.

This entire situation is of real concern since, according to the 1976/77 GATT report, protectionist pressures are particularly acute on some of the export industries upon which those developing countries carrying large amounts of foreign debt are dependent for export earnings.

The cyclical fluctuating nature of commodity prices also has long-term consequences. Moreover, even when commodity prices decline, prices of consumer goods continue to increase. In the case of agricultural products the developed countries, with a few rare exceptions, practice a policy of subsidies as an incentive to production and export, while discouraging imports from developing countries. Certain tropical products also suffer from this policy because of measures taken to protect the production of substitutes.

Another serious problem for developing countries is the discouragement by developed countries, through the use of tariff and non-tariff barriers, of the processing of primary products in producing developing countries.

> (Position Statement submitted by Jamaica on behalf of the Group of 77, pp. 3-4)

The developed countries should take immediate measures to enhance the access of developing countries to their money and capital markets so as to increase substantially the volume, improve the terms and conditions and secure the continuity of the resources available to the developing countries. In addition, access of the least developed countries to capital markets should be facilitated by the developed countries.

There is need for action by developed countries to provide incentives designed to stimulate the flow, and improve the terms and conditions of private capital flows to developing countries through fiscal measures and encouragement from the appropriate monetary and fiscal authorities.

...The foregoing requires action by the developed countries to relax restrictions and remove obstacles hindering the access of developing countries to their capital markets for financing development projects and programmes. Such action should include in particular the following measures to improve the terms and conditions governing the granting of bank loans to nonresidents from developing countries:

(i) giving more favourable fiscal treatment to income derived from loans by the private sector to developing countries.

(ii) exclusion of credits to developing countries from ceilings on domestic credit expansion.

(iii) provision of rules for preferential treatment in favour of developing countries.

(iv) relaxation of regulations and practices which restrict participation of developing countries in secondary market operations.

(v) facilitating the issuing of securities by non-resident foreign borrowers from developing countries in the capital market of developed countries; measures to facilitate developing countries' access to Euro-markets.

...Developed countries should not impose any restrictions including fiscal and financial measures for balance of payments or other reasons on the freedom of their companies to engage in foreign investment operations in developing countries. They should provide significant additional tax or other incentives to their investors operating in developing countries.

> (Position paper submitted by Jamaica on behalf of the Group of 77, paras. 27-29, 34)

The Position of India

Of the problems facing the international economy and, in India's view, one of the major concerns at the present moment, is the adoption of protectionist policies by the developed countries vis-a-vis the products exported by the developing countries, especially those in which the comparative advantage has shifted decisively in favour of the developing countries, with serious repercussions within the developing countries and with the possibility of the impact on their development plans being far-reaching.

...It is imperative that the ongoing multilateral trade negotiations culminate within a short period of time in an agreement that would lead to more open trade and greater access for the products of the developing countries to the markets of the developed countries. In this connection, the objective of the Tokyo Declaration of securing additional benefits for the trade of developing countries should be recalled and concrete steps should be taken for the achievement of this objective. It would be unrealistic to expect developing countries to take continued and keen interest in the multilateral trade negotiations if the outcome is not to have a significant impact on international trade as a whole and on developing countries' trade in particular.

It is also necessary that the multilateral trade negotiations provide enduring and progressive solutions to the problems of international trade in commodities of special interest to developing countries, such as textiles, notwithstanding the short time and expedient solutions that the developing countries had to agree to in the course of the negotiations on the Multi-Fibre Agreement.

(Position Statement submitted by India, paras. 2,5,6)

The Position of New Zealand

To increase trade in these products (agricultural commodities, raw materials or manufactured products), requires concerted efforts by both developing and developed countries. A major barrier - and one to which New Zealand is itself exposed - is that of access to markets. There can be little question today that the structural adjustment of the international economy can only occur if the world community, and in particular the developed industrial nations, address themselves to the question of improving access to their markets. For this reason the current multilateral trade negotiations hold a special importance and it is hoped that a spirit of cooperation will emerge to bring the negotiations to a successful conclusion with mutual benefits to all.

(Position Statement submitted by New Zealand, par. 11)

The Position of Romania

The development of international trade, particularly in manufactured goods, is greatly hindered by the existence of discriminatory practices and tariff and non-tariff restrictions and barriers. Despite the adoption of a number of international measures to reduce and eliminate such barriers, such as the multilateral trade negotiations under the auspices of GATT, in a number of developed countries protectionism continues to worsen and grow apace. Romania, for its part, favours the elimination of all discriminatory practices, restrictions and other obstacles that severely hamper the free conduct of world trade and the development of international economic cooperation. Highly useful steps towards that end would be the successful completion of multilateral trade negotiations, the adoption of an international convention on the control of restrictive trade practices and the conclusion of agreements and long-term sales contracts to ensure trade stability.

Romania considers that in order to accelerate the development of backward countries, the preferential trade treatment accorded all developing countries must be expanded to cover all products exported by those countries.

(Position Statement submitted by Romania, paras. 11, 12)

The Position of Switzerland

The increasing share of developing countries in international trade in manufactures, a reflection of their gradual industrialization, makes these countries increasingly vulnerable to any fluctuation in developed country demand, whether caused by temporary economic factors or by the application of measures to restrict imports. Economic policy measures, whether taken individually or collectively, should therefore take account of the process of the development of productive capacities in the third world. This means that the fight against protectionist pressure should be waged jointly, as should the development of an open world market.

(Position Statement submitted by Switzerland, par. 10)

The Position of Turkey

To enable the industrial world to increase exports towards the developing countries, the latter should also increase exports through stable and gradually liberalized access to the markets of the former. It is understandable that the current unemployment in the industrial countries renders lowering the barriers against the developing country exports a politically sensitive question. None the less, scientific research in this field confirms that increases in imports will equally give rise to additional exports which in turn ensures the redeployment, not displacement, of labour to industries where the factors of production have higher competitive advantages in the industrial world. On the one hand, such a shift will have small economy-wide employment effects and on the other, the adjustments involved will be equally small as compared to those occurring as a result of technical change. Increased security to the effect that new protectionist practices will not proliferate and their scope and duration will be reduced in time, will enhance the investment atmosphere in the developing country export industries. It is important that new quantitative restrictions should only be justified by real rather than potential damage to naional industries. Need for such a protectionist practice should be decided by a more effective process. The removal of protection should be applied within a clear time-table and future recourse to such practices rendered impossible. Newly elaborated international rules should cover all types of restrictions including "voluntary" ones. In addition, a compensation scheme should be considered for those whose interests are undermined by the safeguard measures. In line with their level of development, the developing countries which for various reasons implement trade liberalization for imports from the industrial countries, should enjoy, on priority basis, privileged treatment on the markets of the industrial countries.

Elimination of tariff and non-tariff barriers against developing country exports will gradually bring about better industrial division of labour. This will enable developing countries to sell more value added goods on better prices in real terms and in return buy more investment and intermediary goods essential for development. The indirect beneficial effect of this trend on the industrial countries will be of disciplinary character, restricting private consumption and encouraging fixed capital investment.

(Position Statement submitted by Turkey, pp. 7-8)

The Position of the Union of Soviet Socialist Republics and Socialist Countries

The socialist countries consider that the successful development of international trade relations depends on the efforts of all parties. They believe that the prospects for the development of commercial and economic cooperation with the developing countries will also depend largely on the response of the latter. They are counting on the developing countries to implement the provisions of the Charter of Economic Rights and Duties of States concerning the granting to socialist States of conditions no less favourable than those granted to the developed capitalist countries. They expect that the developing countries will increase their efforts to study markets in the socialist countries and to adapt their export goods to the specific needs of the latter and that they will also actively seek means of increasing their purchases from socialist countries.

In view of the close links between all channels of international trade, the socialist countries consider it essential to eliminate the commercial, political and other barriers which, having been created by certain Western countries, continue to exist and obstruct the development of international trade.

(Position Statement submitted by the USSR on behalf of Bulgaria, the Byelorussian Soviet Socialist Republic, Czechoslovakia, the German Democratic Republic, Hungary, Mongolia, Poland and the Ukrainian Soviet Socialist Republic, paras. 5-6)

The Position of the United States of America

The developed countries have been largely successful in resisting restrictive trade measures. They have, in the OECD, pledged to avoid trade restrictions and largely adhered to this shared political commitment through the recession. Seven world leaders rejected protectionism at the London Summit one year ago because "it would foster unemployment, increase inflation, and undermine the welfare of our peoples."

Appropriate government policies to facilitate trade and domestic adjustment can help to stem protecionism. Effective adjustment assistance programs can more equitably distribute the benefits of an open trading system and avoid the imposition of undue costs on any one group. Those developing countries which have been most successful in raising levels of income have relied on outward-looking trade strategies. Many have managed to increase exports significantly even during the recent period of recession and slow recovery in the industrial countries. These countries can make an important contribution to the containment of protectionist pressures by reducing their own barriers. As developing countries compete more actively, they can benefit from and can accomodate more competition in their own markets from developed and other developing nations. The Multilateral Trade Negotiations (MTN) are an important opportunity for all countries to maintain and expand an open trading system and thus contribute to economic development. A successful MTN outcome, including contribution by the developing countries, will help considerably to restrain protectionist pressures.

The World Bank estimates that a feasible combination of lower tariffs and non-tariff barriers in industrial markets and policy improvements by the developing countries would increase developing country earnings from manufactured goods by an additional $20 billion by 1985. Developed countries would also benefit from more open markets in LDC's. Both groups are important for the prosperity not only of developed but also of developing countries, since trade among developing countries can be expected to increase substantially in the next decade.

Developing countries have benefited from the various systems of generalized tariff preferences (GSP) which developed countries have implemented. U.S. imports of products eligible for GSP from all source were approximately 20 per cent higher in 1977 than in 1976. Preference-receiving LDC's accounted for about one-quarter of the total; and total GSP duty-free imports rose almost 24 per cent to $3.9 billion. While these preference systems are being extended, GSP is only a temporary substitute for the significant benefits which comprehensive liberalization on a most favored nation basis will bring.

...The gains for the LDC's, particularly those high-income LDC's already actively involved in international trade, from the MTN can be widespread and long-term, but they will depend importantly on what LDC's are willing to contribute. Special and differential treatment for developing countries will be included in a number of agreements under negotiation. But far more important for LDC's will be the broader agreements -- in such areas as tariff cuts, use of safeguard measures, and subsidies/ countervailing duties -- to be worked out. The extent of the benefits the LDC's obtain will depend, however, on the contribution they can make.

(Paper presented by the USA, pp. 10, 11, 21, 22)

WORLD ECONOMY ISSUE 7

Adopting An Intregated Approach To Commodities:
The Integrated Programme, Buffer Stocks,
Producers' Associations, Indexation

The Position of Australia

The importance of commodity trade is well appreciated by the Australian Government. This is reflected in the further development of Australia's attitude towards the Common Fund. The Prime Minister announced at a regional meeting of Commonwealth Heads of Government in February 1978 support for the idea that part of the financial resources of the Fund should be made up by direct government subscriptions, and agreement in principle that the Fund have a role in financing measures other than buffer stocking. Australia would like to see such other measures directly related to the stabilization of commodity prices, which could include a variety of commodity related assistance schemes, and a system of nationally held stocks of certain commodities internationally coordinated by producer/consumer arrangements. Details of such matters would have to be worked out during the course of further negotiations on the Fund, which should be resumed soon.

(Position Statement submitted by Australia, para. 10)

The Position of Austria

Austria shares the concern voiced recently by the Secretary-General of the United Nations Conference on Trade and Development as to the slow progress of negotiations within the framework of the Integrated Programme of Commodities. Negotiations for the establishment of a Common Fund have come to a halt already five months ago. Austria is convinced that common efforts, implying also the readiness to mutual and reasonable concessions, could and should provide the necessary impetus for a successful conclusion of these negotiations. In view of the political and economic significance of the Common Fund and the rapidly approaching date of the fifth session of the United Nations Conference on Trade and Development, Austria values the efforts undertaken by the Secretary-General of the United Nations Conference on Trade and Development aimed at an early resumption of the negotiations.

(Position Statement submitted by Austria, para. 13)

The Position of the European Economic Community

The instability of raw material prices and the uncertainties as regards investment and conditions of supply are detrimental for both producer and consumer countries. It is therefore necessary to continue, inter alia, to improve raw material market structures, particularly in the context of the UNCTAD integrated programme, including the possibility of establishing a common fund, while bearing in mind the need to create at the same time conditions conducive to the financing of the development of raw material production in keeping with the trend of foreseeable requirements. In this connexion, market stabilization measures should also provide greater security as regards access to resources and markets and should be accompanied by measures designed to ensure the necessary investment flows.

(Position Statement submitted by Denmark on behalf of the European Economic Community, para. 40)

...It is our firm wish that the negotiations concerning the Common Fund as well as in the field of individual commodities should progress and succeed.

It is indeed in our mutual interest to improve market structures, by vigorously avoiding excessive erratic fluctuations in prices and revenues. Such fluctuations are neither in the interest of producers nor consumers.

(Position Statement of the Danish Minister Lise Ostergaard on behalf of the European Economic Community, p. 10)

The Position of the Group of 77

With respect to trade in primary commodities, the Integrated Programme for Commodities proposed by the United Nations Conference on Trade and Development is designed to respond to the current unbalanced situation. The mechanisms proposed would stabilize markets and protect at an adequate level and in real terms the export earnings of developing countries in the field of commodities. Such a regulation of markets through commodity agreements, in the framework of the Integrated Programme within which the Common Fund would play an important role, would facilitate an efficient planning of production and investment in the producing countries.

(Position Statement submitted by Jamaica on behalf of the Group of 77, p. 4)

The Position of India

Developing countries have shown sufficient flexibility in their attitude. They have also provided confrontation on this issue. Prospect for resumption of fruitful negotiations will therefore depend on the accommodation that States, which have taken a hard line, show in forging a compromise.

As regards commodity agreements, progress has been disappointingly slow. India views with concern the strong objectives being raised by the developed countries to the concept of buffer stocking of jute and jute products within the context of negotiations for a Jute Agreement.

(Position Statement submitted by India, para 8, 9)

The proposal regarding the creation of a Common Fund for Commodities, in our belief, is a key element in regard to an integrated programme for commodities. However, in our anxiety to make an early start to provide a mechanism for the stabilization of prices we should not forget that it is essential, indeed fundamental, to provide a part of the Common Fund resources for optimizing the export earnings from commodities through diversification, processing, research and development and other measures.

(Position Statement by Mr. Romesh Bhandari, India, para 15)

The Position of New Zealand

The New Zealand Government has welcomed the decision to establish a Common Fund and is participating actively in the negotiating of detailed arrangements. New Zealand has a common interest with developing countries in achieving improved conditions for comodity trade, and hopes to see the UNCTAD negotiations resumed at the earliest opportunity.

It should be acknowledged that the Common Fund by itself will not necessarily bring about long-run improvements in developing country or primary producers' terms of trade. Some rationalization is essential. The time has come to question old trading patterns and to work towards an interdependent world economy in which countries . seek to produce, and are encouraged to produce, goods and services in which they are efficient.

(Position Statement submitted by New Zealand, paras. 14, 15)

The Position of Romania

An effective and lasting solution to the problem of raw materials and energy requires a guarantee of a fair relationship between the prices of raw materials and industrial goods and a suitable relationship between the prices of industrial goods and those of agricultural products. Obviously, countries which produce raw materials must be paid prices which will enable them to achieve as rapid economic and social development as possible. At the same time, industrial goods must be priced in such a way as to stimulate the sustained development of industrial activity. It is also highly important to ensure greater price stability. To that end, it would be necessary to adopt principles and specific measures with the aim of eliminating speculative fluctuations which disrupt the normal conduct of international economic relations, putting a stop to the artificial raising or lowering of prices, and ensuring price stability over a period of several years.

(Postion Statement submitted by Romania, para. 10)

The Position of Switzerland

The bulk of the foreign exchange revenue of most developing countries is still derived from their commodity exports. Fluctuations, often excessive, in the prices of those commodities endanger the implementation of various components of development plans. It is therefore desirable that, without jeopardizing the market mechanism, progress should be made towards stabilizing the markets for the principal raw materials exported by these countries, thereby also ensuring that supplies to importers are not interrupted. While negotiations on stabilization machinery - commodity agreements, common fund - are still in progress, the consideration of methods of stabilizing export earnings should also continue. The fight against inflation, together with adjustments of the price ranges under the relevant provisions of commodity agreements, could likewise help to alleviate terms-of-trade problems.

(Position Statement submitted by Switzerland, para. 9)

The Position of the Union of Soviet Socialist Republics and Socialist Countries

At the present time a number of international discussions are being held in the United Nations on various key problems. The socialist countries are taking an active and constructive part in these talks. In the Negotiating Conference on a Common Fund under the Integrated Programme for Commodities the socialist countries have submitted concrete proposals on basic and specific questions relating to the Fund which are elements of the integrated approach of our countries to all aspects of the functioning of the Fund. Those proposals should be viewed in the general context of the approach of the socialist countries to that problem. We share the view that there must be an integrated approach to the solution of the problems of raw materials, i.e., the adoption of a whole range of interrelated measures which would cover the production, processing and sale of primary commodities and would effectively limit the operation of market forces. The socialist countries are in favour of the formulation and adoption of effective measures for the regulation of the trade in primary commodities on a just basis, taking into account the interests of all countries, both exporters and importers. Our countries support the proposals of the developing countries on trade in raw materials with the developed capitalist countries which would guarantee them genuine economic independence and would be directed against the practices, followed by the transnational corporations in exploiting the natural resources of the developing countries.

> (Position Statement submitted by the USSR also on behalf of Bulgaria, the Byelorussian SSR, Czechoslovakia, the German Democratic Republic, Hungary, Mongolia, Poland and the Ukranian SSR, para.6)

The Position of the United Kingdom

...I will here mention in particular our firm commitment to the Integrated Programme for Commodities and to the establishment of a Common Fund, and our intention to work with all those involved to bring about a successful conclusion to the various negotiations.

> (Position Statement by Minister Frank Judd, United Kingdom, p. 2)

WORLD ECONOMY ISSUE 8

Developing An International Food Programme

The Position of the European Economic Community

The improvement of food security is a priority task in the context of interdependence. Although it is primarily the responsibility of the developing countries to develop their rural areas and increase agricultural production and productivity, the industrialized countries and the relevant multilateral agencies have their part to play in supporting such efforts.

Such action would include, for example, the mobilization of aid to enable the developing countries gradually to utilize their production potential and equip themselves with storage capacities that could improve their food security.   Greater attention must, however, also be paid to the organization of the world market, particularly the cereals market, in order to promote greater stability in marketing, on which the stability of production ultimately depends. Food aid, which is complementary to the main means of promoting food security, will continue to play an important role for a long time to come.

(Position Statement submitted by Denmark on behalf of the European Economic Community, para. 42)

The Position of the United States of America

Maintenance of the supply of food grains at reasonable prices is a major short-term issue. Agriculture is a world industry. In the United States, for example, one hectare in three is being harvested for the world market. International cooperation to remedy national shortfalls, build up reserves, and maintain steady prices can add stability in many nations. This would be of particular importance to food-deficit LDCs, whose number is likely to increase. Of course, supply management efforts and food aid programs need to be linked with long-term domestic and world efforts to increase food production in food-deficit areas.

...Devising solutions to world food problems -- the reduction of malnutrition and the improvement of agriculture in developing countries --is a concern of all countries.   Unless steps are taken to increase production and limit population growth, the number of food deficit countries will increase, and per capita food levels will fall.   While the prime responsibility for agricultural development rests with the developing countries themselves, such efforts require bilateral and multilateral assistance.   Added incentives to increase food production, rural development, and greater attention to the health, education and productivity of people living in rural areas are complementary objectives of a sound development strategy.

(Position paper presented by the United States, pp. 13, 27-28)

WORLD ECONOMY ISSUE 9

Adjusting The Economic Policies Of Developed
Countries To Facilitate The Expansion And
Diversification Of The Exports Of Developing Countries

The Position of Austria

A programme of massive transfer of resources to developing countries would not only help those countries to maintain or increase their rate of economic expansion, but would also be beneficial to industrial countries by creating additional demand for their products thus leading to a better utilization of their productive capacities and the stimulation of their economic growth in a non-inflationary manner. In view of the magnitude of the resources required and so as to ensure a maximum range of options to developing countries the programme would have to be designed on a multilateral basis.   Thus, it could be expected to represent a major contribution to world economic recovery and a more open international trading system.   It would furthermore help to alleviate balance-of-payments problems as well as the debt burden of developing countries and enhance the transfer of technology.

It is with this broad objective in mind that the Federal Chancellor of Austria, Dr. Bruno Kreisky, has repeatedly; called for a large-scale economic solidarity programme aimed, in particular, at an accelerated infrastructure development in developing countries. The Government of Austria is at present studying ways and means by which such massive transfers of resources could be initiated in a manner compatible with the interests and capabilities of industrial as well as developing countries. The Government of Austria intends in due course to pronounce itself in greater detail on the technical issues involved in the formulation and implementation of such a multilateral programme.

(Position Statement submitted by Austria, paras. 11, 12)

The Position of the European Economic Community

At the national level, action should be taken to:

...Initiate action aimed at reducing uncertainties and promoting the necessary structural adjustments. Any policy involving the opening up of markets in industrialized countries to manufactures and semi-manufactures from the developing countries necessarily has consequences in the field of industrial structures. Because of this situation, and given its concern to maintain liberal trade arrangements, the Community has set about adjusting the structure of its industries to present and foreseeable trends in world production.   Obviously, it is difficult to conceive of significant progress being made in this area unless there is an expansion of world production, and internal economic and social constraints must clearly also be taken into account. In particular, the present employment situation in the Community and the way it is expected to develop preclude switching production to capital-intensive sectors alone. Restructuring should be carried out primarily for the benefit of industries which employ highly skilled labour, and this implies the introduction of appropriate back-up policies.

> (Position Statement submitted by Denmark on behalf of the European Economic Community, par. 20 (e))

The Position of the Group of 77

There has been a growing tendency in the developed countries to cite their own internal problems and stresses in the face of continuing economic difficulties as reasons for not meeting their international obligations and commitments. However, what is required is the acceptance by the industrialized countries of the discipline of the limitation of consumption and decreasing material benefit which the present circumstances dictate and to see and accept that the future may require of them a greater realism and restraint in these matters, as well as necessary adjustments of their economic systems to meet, not only their own requirements, but the pressing requirements of the global community.

> (Position Statement submitted by Jamaica on behalf of the Group of 77, p.3)

The Position of India

There is an urgent need for the developed countries to vigorously and systematically implement appropriate internal adjustment policies. In this context, it is worth while noting that the expansion of the trade of the developing countries is a major factor contributing to the increased demand potential within the developing countries much of which can be met only by the products of the developed countries. The alternative to an expanding world economy would entail economic costs to all and avoidable confrontation.

> (Position Statement submitted by India, para. 3)

The Position of the United States of America

The growing ability of LDCs to sell exports of manufactures requires developed and socialist countries to make adjustments which are neither frictionless nor costless, but which are necessary if producers and consumers are to benefit from international specialization. These adjustments are undertaken more easily in a milieu of expansion and low levels of unemployment and in situations where the benefits of open access to export markets can be demonstrated to exceed the temporary losses associated with adjustment.

Rapid technological change and resultant adjustment in the developed countries have created concerns about the equitabale distribution of costs and benefits of an open trading system. Some national groups believe that their jobs suffer in the cause of improved comparative advantage, especially when imports increase at a pace which injures domestic firms and workers. These concerns are reinforced by the perception that LDC exporting countries often continue to maintain trade barriers to protect inefficient domestic producers from the competition of developed and other developing countries. The responsibilities for adjustment, therefore, cannot be viewed in isolation; they must be part of a mutual effort on the part of all trading nations to open their markets and thus to facilitate the flows of competitive products to consumers.

Where a product can be most efficiently produced changes over time, depending on market conditions, relative factor costs, technological innovations, and the availability of alternative manufacturing opportunities. As products become more standardized and technologies more widely known certain industries will tend to develop in LDCs which compete with established industries in DCs. At the same time, new industries, requiring new technologies and skills will emerge in the developed countries. These industries will expect markets in LDCs to be open to these new as well as to the more traditional DC exports. Only if the world trading system can accommodate these shifts in dynamic comparative advantage will it increase the long-term economic gains from trade.

(Position Statement submitted by the United States of America, pp.19-20)

...certain sectors in developed countries have had to adjust dramatically to particular types of exports from developing countries. In fact, however, adjustment within developed countries to technological changes and shifts within their economies is generally far greater than adjustment to imports -- although it is less visible and probably less rapid. Also, of course, over time developing countries will spend the revenues they earn through increased exports on increased imports, in many cases high technology goods, from developed countries thereby creating new jobs in high productivity industries. But internal adjustment in developed countries to this changing structure of trade take time and are especially difficult when unemployment is high and displaced workers cannot find jobs. Although successful adjustment will depend primarily on policies of the developed countries, developing countries can help in this process by increasing access to their markets as they grow.

(Remarks by Mr. Robert Hormats, United States of America, p.8)

WORLD ECONOMY ISSUES 10 AND 11

Improving and Intensifying Trade Relations
Between Countries Having Different Social And
Economic Systems

Strengthening Economic And Technical
Cooperation Among Developing Countries

The Position of Romania

However, the efforts of the individual developing countries, no matter how great, are not and will not be sufficient to overcome underdevelopment. Thus, in addition to the intensification of those efforts, an important role must be played by cooperation on a new basis among developing countries, as well as between developing countries and other States in the world. By cooperating among themselves, developing countries can meet a number of each other's needs in raw materials, industrial goods, technology and financing, which will help to strengthen their solidarity and unit of action, which are so necessary for the establishment of the new international economic order. /.../

(Position Statement submitted by Romania, para.7)

The Position of the Union of Soviet Socialist Republics and Socialist Countries

The strategy of the socialist States in their economic cooperation with the developing countries remains unchanged. Its main goal is to help those countries in their efforts to solve the problems of economic development and in the strengthening of their economic independence. In view of that consideration, the socialist countries intend to continue, in the future,to adhere to the policy of expanding mutually advantageous commercial ties based both on traditional bilateral and long-term multilateral forms of commercial and economic cooperation, in the spirit of the recommendations contained in the Charter of Economic Rights and Duties of States and the progressive proposals adopted at the sixth and seventh special sessions of the United Nations General Assembly. For that purpose, the socialist countries would be prepared:

- to extend the practice of concluding long-term trade agreements and also agreements on economic and technical cooperation which could also, where possible and appropriate, extend over to three five-year planning periods;

- to continue to concentrate their efforts in the field of economic and technical assistance to the developing countries on the development of production forces, and particularly industry, within the framework of the State enterprise;

- to continue to concentrate efforts on providing economic and technical assistance to the developing countries for the development of their productive forces, especially their industries within the framework of State enterprise;

- to make a maximum contribution to the promotion of imports of finished goods from national industries on the basis of unilateral tariff preferences to the developing countries and other measures of a basically preferential nature;

- to provide where appropriate, in agreements and contracts, for deliveries in repayment of credits and for the purchase under commercial conditions of the products of enterprises set up with the assistance of the socialist countries;

- to unite efforts with interested developing countries for the overall solution of the major economic problems of those countries; particularly through the creation of territorial production complexes;

- to provide in their economic development plans for a constant expansion and strengthening of trade and economic ties with the developing states;

- to improve, together with their partners, the machinery for cooperation, particularly:

By broadening the functions of the bilateral intergovernmental commissions on economic, scientific and technological cooperation, by broadening the scope and improving the quality of economic and pertinent administrative information, and by broadening contacts between the planning organs of the socialist and the developing countries, taking account of the cooperation between them on questions of mutual interest;

- to expand the practice of drawing up long-term programmes for cooperation in such fields as foreign trade, industry, science and technology;

- to make wider use of the practice of concluding compensatory agreements in order to develop export sectors in the developing countries;

- to assist interested developing countries in formulating plans and programmes for economic development, including foreign trade;

- to provide assistance to developing countries in respect of the processing of their raw material resources;

- to help to find ways of putting clearing operations with developing countries on a multilateral footing;

- to promote cooperation between the International Investment Bank and developing countries through the provision to developing countries of funds from the special fund to provide credit for economic and technical assistance;

- to strengthen the multilateral aspects of commercial and economic relations, in particular by:

Extending the use of multilateral accounting based on the transferable rouble;

Promoting multilateral cooperation between CMEA and individual developing countries and their organizations;

Studying the possibility and desirability of organizing multilateral industrial cooperation with the participation of socialist, developing and developed capitalist countries, taking into account the specific problems of the developing countries involved.

The socialist countries consider that the successful development of international trade relations depends on the efforts of all parties. They believe that the prospects for the development of commercial and economic cooperation with the developing countries will also depend largely on the response of the latter. They are counting on the developing countries to implement the provisions of the Charter of Economic Rights and Duties of States concerning the granting to socialist States of conditions no less favourable than those granted to the developed capitalist countries. They expect that the developing countries will increase their efforts to study markets in the socialist countries and to adapt their export goods to the specific needs of the latter and that they will also actively seek means of increasing their purchases from socialist countries./.../

(Position Statement of the USSR also on behalf of Bulgaria, Byelorussian SSR, Czechoslovakia, the German Democratic Republic, Hungary, Mongolia, Poland and the Ukranian SSR, paras. 5, 6)

9 International Financial Issues

WORLD ECONOMY ISSUES 12 and 13

Reforming the International Monetary System:
Using Special Drawing Rights for Development Assistance and as the
Central Reserve Asset of the International Monetary System, Promoting
Stable Rates of Exchange and Protection from the Effects of Inflation

Assuring Adequate Participation by Developing Countries
In World Bank and IMF Decision Making

The position of the European Economic Community

In order to improve the process of international adjustment, an attempt
must be made to diminish the uncertainty and avoid the risks of imbalance
connected with erratic fluctuations in exchange rates. For its part, the
Community is currently examining the possibilities of reducing the
fluctuations occurring within the Community through closer coordination
of economic, monetary and foreign exchange policies. It also believes
that it would be advisable, by means of more active international
cooperation, to avoid movements in the main currencies which are not
justified by trends in prices and underlying costs.

In this connection, the ratification of the amendments to the Articles of
Agreement of IMF should enable that body to monitor exchange rate
movements so as to reduce distortions of competition at the world level.
Some developing countries suffer more than other countries, directly and
indirectly, from the effects of the present monetary situation and would
be the first to benefit from an improvement in that situation.

The problem of adjustment cannot, however, be separated from the
problem of financing... If international organizations were to play a

greater role in the recycling process it would be possible simultaneously to encourage, facilitate and coordinate the adjustment efforts being made by various countries. Improved control of international liquidity would reduce the risks of inflation and of perpetuating imbalances evident at the national level. With this in mind, the Community feels that it is necessary to strengthen the role of Special Drawing Rights in order to make them the principal reserve instrument of the international monetary system.

> (Position Statement submitted by the European Economic Community, paras. 27-29)

The Position of the Group of 77

With respect to international monetary problems, a new monetary system should be created since the current situation continues to reflect the interests of only a small number of the most developed countries. The continued instability of exchange rates shows no signs of abating and the situation is even deteriorating further. This exposes developing countries to substantial losses in the value of their holdings of foreign reserves.

The world's monetary gold has been held by the developed countries, while the developing countries have held most of their reserves in the form of dollar and sterling deposits.

The situation has therefore been aggravated by the sharp fall in the value of the United States dollar against the value of the currencies of some major industrialized countries. Furthermore, a large portion of the domestic purchasing power of the dollar has also been eroded by inflationary pressures, thus creating and exacerbating problems for dollar-holding countries.

Developing countries must be compensated for the deterioration in purchasing power which they have suffered by having to hold their monetary reserves in the form of depreciating United States dollars.

The principle of building up SDR's as the principal reserve asset which has been reaffirmed in the Jamaica Agreement should be implemented on the basis of internationally agreed criteria, taking into account the special needs of developing countries.

The developed countries should distribute to developing countries at least part of their capital gains from the revaluation of gold which has occurred since1971, in the form of turning over an equivalent value of special drawing rights (SDR's).

> (Position Statement submitted by Jamaica on behalf of the Group of 77, p. 5)

In order to make the international monetary system more responsive to the needs of the developing countries, concrete measures should be taken by the IMF in order to achieve the following aims and objectives:

(1) Greater participation of the developing countries in the decision-making process.

(2) A substantial increase in the quotas of developing countries.

(3) Reorientation of the IMF to strengthen its capacity to provide resources to developing countries consistent with their developmental needs;

    (a) the conditionality attached to drawings from the IMF by developing countries should take fully into account the structural problems of the economies of the developing countries.

    (b) a long-term financing mechanism should be established in the IMF for the developing countries to meet their balance-of-payment needs.

(4) The establishment of SDR's as the principal reserve asset of the international monetary system increase in the role of SDR's in the creation, control and the equitable distribution of international liquidities between developing and developed countries. Establishment of the link between the creation of SDR's and development financing.

(5) Expansion of the capacity of the IMF to alleviate the impact of fluctuations in exchange rates particularly of major currencies on the purchasing power of earnings from commodity exports of developing countries.

The following measures should be taken in order to improve the Compensatory Financing Facility:

    (a) calculation of export shortfalls in terms of purchasing power of exports by deflating flows by import prices and around a growing trend which should be assured to be not less than the rate of growth of the volume of world trade over the previous years;

    (b) provision to developing countries of a right to base claims in shortfalls in commodities export earnings or on other categories of current account receipts as they may choose;

    (c) provision for full compensation of shortfalls without quota limitations;

    (d) repayment should be triggered only by "overages" just as drawings are triggered by shortfalls;

    (e) expansion of the grant element in Compensatory Financing particularly for the least developed countries; in appropriate cases drawings under the Facility should take the form of grants.

(Position Paper submitted by Jamaica on behalf of the Group of 77, paras. 24, 25)

...the process of decision-making in international financial and monetary institutions must reflect the realities of the present perceptions and provide adequate scope for the involvement of developing countries.

> (Statement by Ambassador Mills of Jamaica on behalf of the Group of 77, p. 10)

The Position of India

...we believe that concrete steps need to be taken to bring SDR's into the centre of the International Monetary System. We also believe that there should be greater participation and involvement by developing countries in the decision making process determining the international financial and monetary systems and mechanisms...

> (Statement by Mr. Romesh Bhandari, India, par. 12)

The Position of Romania

A prerequisite for the development of the world economy and international trade is the establishment of a new international monetary system that is sound, equitable and capable of providing a stable basis for currency transactions. The current crisis of the international monetary system is one of the causes of the disorganization in international pricing mechanisms, stimulates inflation, creates inequities in international settlements and hampers the long-term development of international economic cooperation. The measures adopted so far under the auspices of the International Monetary Fund are of a partial nature and constitute only the first step in a reform of the monetary system. They must be followed up by additional measures for the establishment of a new international monetary system which can truly serve as a factor for promoting monetary stability and equity at the international level, free from fluctuations, distortions, disproportions and crises, and which can ensure the necessary conditions for the full and effective participation of all States in the discussion and solution of monetary problems.

> (Position Statement submitted by Romania, par. 13)

The Position of Switzerland

Generally speaking, monetary conditions cause one of the fundamental problems. The sharp fluctuations in rates of exchange have a disruptive effect on economic growth, on monetary relations and on trade flows. It should be one of the primary objectives of international cooperation to take effective coordinated measures to re-establish conditions of stability and confidence and, in particular, to obviate erratic movements in rates of exchange. A suitable extension of balance-of-payment support facilities would also contribute to this end by enabling developing countries in this kind of difficulty to reduce their current account deficits and so prevent those deficits from impeding their economic expansion.

> (Position Statement submitted by Switzerland, par. 14)

WORLD ECONOMY ISSUE 14

Increasing the Transfer of Resources
Through the World Bank and IMF

The Position of Denmark

The Danish Government intends to continue to distribute our official development assistance about equally between multilateral and bilateral activities. This policy we have pursued for many years, and we are convinced that the multilateral institutions continue to deserve our strong support.

By far the largest share of our multilateral assistance is channeled through the United Nations' system. We do so because we strongly want to support the role of the United Nations, also in the field of international development cooperation. We also do it because the developing countries themselves wish to see a high share of the international development assistance channeled through the United Nations, and last but not least, because we find that the United Nations development organizations are working efficiently.

(Statement by Minister Lise Ostergaard, Denmark, pp. 2-3)

The Position of the European Economic Community

...Since the deficits of the developing countries cannot be financed entirely by bilateral official development assistance or injections of private capital for quite a long time, further consideration will have to be given by both IMF and IBRD to possible ways of increasing the resources of the two agencies and thus widening the scope for granting credit on terms which take account of the purpose of each of these two agencies and the specific nature of the problems of each country.

(Position Statement submitted by Denmark on behalf of the European Economic Community, par. 31)

...with regard to ODA contributions to multilateral institutions, the Member States of the European Community have recognized the need to increase the resources of bodies such as the World Bank, regional development banks and the UNDP.

(Position Statement submitted by the European Community on the transfer of real resources, p. 10)

The Position of the Group of 77

(a) The allocation of development resources from multilateral financial institutions should be fully consistent with the development objectives and priorities of developing countries.

(b) International financial institutions should make their policies more favourable to developing countries by such measures as softening the terms of their assistance, interest subsidies, increasing local currency financing, adjusting the amount of their loans for the effect of inflation on the cost of projects and by facilitating access of developing countries to capital markets through appropriate measures including guarantees.

(c) Adoption and implementation of necessary measures should be expedited to ensure that the developing countries obtain the largest possible share in the procurement of equipment, consultants and consultancy services.

(d) Donor countries are urged to expedite outstanding disbursements for the fourth replenishment and to implement their commitments for their fifth IDA replenishing. An institutional mechanism may be immediately set up within the existing framework to increase the resources of IDA, by borrowing in the capital markets and/or from interested countries through multilateral guarantees or other suitable arrangements; the differential between the borrowing and lending interest rates being met through budgetary appropriations by part I members of the IDA.

(e) The resources of the Third Window of the World Bank should be expanded to meet the target of $1 billion and should be placed on a continuing basis.

(f) All members of the World Bank should immediately implement the selective increase in the Bank's capital which has been approved; this should be followed not later than 1980 by a general increase both being in real terms. There should be a periodical review of the adequacy of the capital base of the Bank in relation to the evolving capital requirements of developing countries. Special attention should also be given to increasing the capital base of regional development banks, bearing in mind the need to enable them to continue and expand their concessional lending.

> (Position paper submitted by Jamaica on behalf of the Group of 77, par. 15(a)-(f))

A closer relationship must be achieved between the operations of the international monetary and financial systems and global developmental activities and discussions. The resources available to the International Monetary Fund, including those related to compensatory financing, need to be significantly increased.

> (Statement by Ambassador Donald Mills of Jamaica on behalf of the Group of 77, p. 6)

The Position of Norway

...good reasons can be put behind the view that injection of additional liquidity of purchasing power into developing countries would not only be a most effective way of meeting their pressing needs for faster economic development. In the actual situation it could also be the most effective way of giving the world economy the stimulus and impetus which is needed to the benefit of unemployed and wanting people in all parts of the world. Well managed, such a stimulation of demand in developing countries would probably also be of little inflationary effect.

Some efforts in this direction have already been made. It is here worth mentioning the increase in the capital of the IBRD and of the resources of the IMF. Of special importance in connection with the IMF is the new supplementary financing facility of $10 billion, the so-called Wittereen facility. However, these and other steps, important as they are, are still small compared with the magnitude of the tasks and the unfulfilled needs. Thus, the Wittereen facility of $10 billion becomes small when compared with the increases in debt of some $30 to $40 billion which non-oil exporting developing countries have accumulated during each of the last couple of years. More bold and diversified actions therefore seem to be called for, including, if possible, some link between liquidity creation and development assistance. With the necessary degree of international management and supervision such further steps would be likely to benefit developing and developed countries alike.

> (Position Statement submitted by Norway, p. 3)

The Position of Sweden

In line with the general aim to increase the transfer of resources to developing countries, we should work out a system of voluntary agreements to cover the needs of the central sources within the United Nations family for financing development assistance. The financing of IDA and the development funds of the regional banks demonstrate that constitutional and technical problems can be overcome. Such negotiations as those pursued before the replenishments of these agencies would favour stability and predictability in funding, which is as desirable for technical assistance.

A possible agreement on contributions along these lines must contain clear commitments on steady and long-term increases in the funds available to the programmes concerned.   An equitable sharing among donors of the responsibility for the adequate financing of these programmes must be indicated.

(Position Statement submitted by Sweden, paras. 19, 20)

The Position of the United Kingdom

...We in Britain are playing a vigorous part in the replenishment of the Asian Development Fund and similar institutions and want particularly to see a large increase in the capital of the World Bank...

(Statement by Minister Frank Judd, United Kingdom, p.3)

The Position of the United States of America

-The multilateral development banks play a vital role in promoting growth and development in the developing countries, and their concessional facilities are particularly important to the efforts of the poorer LDC's. The U.S. supports real growth in lending commitments of the World Bank.

...While several replenishments of multilateral development bank facilities have been agreed, we strongly support expeditious progress toward completion of negotiations for replenishment of the Inter-American Development Bank's regular capital and soft funds, and the general capital increase for the World Bank.

(Remarks of Mr. Robert Hormats, United States of America, p. 4)

10 Issues of Industrialization, Technology Transfer and Business Practices

WORLD ECONOMY ISSUES 15, 16, 17, 18 and 19

Negotiating the Redeployment of Industrial Productive
Capacities to Developing Countries;

Establishing Mechanisms for the Transfer of Technology
To Developing Countries;

Regulating and Supervising the Activities of Transnational
Enterprises and Eliminating Restrictive Business Practices;

Improving the Competitiveness of Natural Resources
and Ending Their Waste;

Providing Equitable Access to the Resources of the
Sea Bed and the Ocean Floor

The Position of Austria

Industrialization has come to be recognized as a cornerstone of the
development process. If the target set by the Lima Declaration and Plan
of Action is to be attained, a massive financial, technological and
management input will be required in expanding the industrial capacity of
the developing countries. The mechanism designed to bring about these
results are mainly focused in the United Nations Industrial Development
Organization and should be fully utilized.

...Austria is deeply convinced that international cooperation in the field of
science and technology has to be further strengthened. The United
Nations Conference on Science and Technology for Development will
provide an excellent opportunity to achieve this objective. In drawing up
a programme of action particular attention will have to be paid to
devising ways and means of applying science and technology to the
specific needs of developing countries and to build up their scientific and

technological capacity.   In doing so, the programme of action could become one of the foundations of the new framework for international development cooperation in the 1980's.

(Position Statement submitted by Austria paras. 14, 16)

The Position of Ecuador

With respect to the qualitative aspects of the factors that affect the economies and the development of the developing countries, the Ecuadorian   Government has identified inter alia, the following:

...Scarcity of technical know-how at the disposal of the developing countries owing to insufficient cooperation from the industrialized countries which develop technology.   At present, the transfer of technology is very limited in volume and scope.   The developing countries have to pay dearly for the transfer of technology, the cost of which must be borne in financing industrial development and all kinds of investment. As a result, Ecuador attaches special importance to the choice of appropriate technology, tailored to the actual situation in individual developing countries.

Uncertainty about the consumption of commodities, owing to the speculative practices of transnational corporations, which manipulate the transport, financing, marketing, storage and distribution of those commodities and unrestrainedly engage in restrictive practices, which have a particularly adverse effect on small countries and small producers within those countries.

(Position Statement submitted by Ecuador, pp. 2,3)

The Position of the Group of 77

The priority status of industrialization in developing countries was stated at the Second General Conference of the United Nations Industrial Development Organization, Lima, 1975.   The Conference concluded that the share of the developing countries in world industrial production should be 25 per cent at the end of the century, compared with the present 7 per cent.   So far there is no indication that measures which are required of developing countries to achieve this goal will be forthcoming.

These measures should include, inter alia, the expansion of access to markets for manufactured products of developing countries and specific measures in order to promote acquisition, development and application of appropriate and modern technology.   Unless the industrial structures of developed countries themselves evolve in a complementary manner, thus allowing more imports in a more diversified manner of manufactured products from developing countries, the obstacles to access to market would   remain   and   be   even   reinforced.   This   requires   industrial reconversion and structural changes within developed countries.   It should become fully operational.

The code of conduct on technology transfer, and the principles and rules for the regulation of restrictive business practices, the revision of the patent system, as well as the code of conduct for transnational corporations under negotiation will constitute a new and favourable institutional framework for ensuring, inter alia, that the activities of transnational corporations, do not hinder but support and promote the industrialization objectives of host developing countries.

> (Position Statement submitted by Jamaica on behalf of the Group of 77, pp. 4-5)

Private direct investment should make a substantial contribution to the development of developing countries in terms of transfer of technology, managerial and other associated skills; increasing output, employment, and strengthening the balance of payments. In order to facilitate this contribution, the elaboration of a Code of Conduct for Transnational Corporations should be accelerated.

...Developed countries should urgently adopt necessary measures to safeguard the interest of developing countries against the restrictive business practices of their enterprises. Negotiations within UNCTAD for the formulation of a set of multilaterally agreed equitable principles and rules for the control of restrictive business practices having adverse effects on international trade, particularly that of developing countries and on the economic development of these countries, should be completed as soon as possible. Negotiations on a model law or laws on restrictive business practices should be brought to a successful conclusion within the United Nations Conference on Trade and Development.

> (Position Paper submitted by Jamaica on behalf of the Group of 77, paras. 32, 35)

The Position of Romania

Given the conditions of the contemporary revolution in science and technology, which have become an essential factor in development, it is imperative that all States and especially developing States should be able to share in the advances of modern science and technology in order to accelerate their economic and social development. Accordingly, work should be speeded up on the preparation of an international code of conduct on the transfer of technology that will ensure the free and unrestricted access of all States to the advances of modern science and technology, the elimination of discrimination and restrictive trade practices and the granting of preferential treatment to developing countries.

> (Position Statement submitted by Romania, para. 8)

The Position of the Union of Soviet Socialist Republics and Socialist Countries

The socialist countries are actively participating in the discussions on questions relating to the transfer of technology on the premise that the development of the materials and equipment bases, the creation in the developing countries of their own scientific and technical potential, the training of national cadres, the optimum selection of technology, action to put a stop to the "brain drain" and so forth should serve the purposes of the economic development of the developing countries. Our countries share the view that the transfer of technology should not lead to technological or other dependence, which in certain circumstances could be a serious obstacle to sovereign economic development. The socialist countries consider that the real result of the establishment of equitable and just relations with respect to the transfer of technology should be, inter alia, the creation and broadening of scientific and technical potential in the developing countries, the development of equitable and mutually beneficial relations on a stable, planned, long-term basis free from any form of dependence or exploitation, the establishment of close links between science and production and the effective training of national cadres in the developing countries. In connection with the elaboration of a code of conduct concerning the transfer of technology, the socialist countries have made specific proposals to regulate the transfer of technology among all countries without dividing them into separate groups and the creation of conditions in which that transfer would be based on democratic principles and would not serve to maintain discriminatory situations with respect to individual countries or groups of countries.

(Position Statement submitted by the USSR also on behalf of Bulgaria, the Byelorussian SSR, Czechoslovakia, the German Democratic Republic, Hungary, Mongolia, Poland and the Ukranian SSR, par. 7)

The Position of the United States of America

The United States supports the work toward a Code of Conduct relating to Transnational Corporations (TNC's). To this end it would be desirable for nations to participate actively at senior policy levels in the next meeting of the intergovernmental working group (IGWG) of the United Nations Commission on TNC's and work toward a consensus on key issues.

(Remarks of Mr. Robert Hormats, Delegation of the USA, p.13)

(Positions on World Economy Issues 18 and 19, concerning the competitiveness of natural resources, and the resources of the sea respectively, were not stated at the May 1978 session of the Committee of the Whole).

11 Social Issues

WORLD ECONOMY ISSUES 20 and 21

Achieving a More Equitable Distribution of Income
and Raising the Level of Employment;

Providing Health Services, Education, Higher Cultural Standards
and Qualification for the Work Force, and Assuring the Well-Being
of Children and the Integration of Women in Development

The Position of Austria

The concept of development has to centre on the improvement of welfare
and well-being of all segments of the population. A strategy to meet
basic human needs constitutes indeed the human dimension of a New
International Economic Order. It should be defined by each country with
due regard to the different conditions and factors determining its path of
development.

(Position Statement submitted by Austria, par. 9)

The Position of Denmark

As regards the nature of Denmark's ODA, I wish to underline that we aim
increasingly at directing our assistance towards covering the basic needs
of the poorest sections of the populaions of the poorest developing
countries. This is true of our bilateral assistance, and we also pursue this
aim in the multilateral development institutions of which we are a
member. This policy reflects our opinion that the alleviation of absolute
poverty is the most urgent need in the world today. In the global context
of development policy, high priority must be given to the fight against the
terrible agony, tremendous waste of human resources caused by

malnutrition and lack of shelter and of access to even the most basic training and education.

(Position Statement submitted by Denmark, p.4)

The Position of the European Economic Community

The primary responsibility for the economic development of the developing countries rests with these countries themselves and they must make all necessary efforts to solve their problems, to carry out the necessary improvements in their economic and social structures, to mobilize fully their basic resources and to increase the participation of their peoples, particularly the poor majority, in the process and benefits of development, in accordance with their development plans and objectives.

This responsibility is based on three main requirements:

- an increased mobilization of national savings and the pursuit of sound economic, financial and social policies that can promote the development and in particular the welfare of their populations;

- a rational and efficient use of flows of external resources;

- the creation of a welcoming climate to encourage the flow of direct investment to those developing countries that wish to have recourse to this type of flow.

The responsibility of the developed countries, whether of market of centrally-planned economy, and of the oil-producing developing countries, is essentially to supply, under appropriate conditions, the external resources needed to supplement the developing countries' own efforts.

...Whatever the circumstances, the ultimate objective of development cooperation, which must also be reflected in the sectoral orientation of the transfer of resources, is the promotion of man. It is therefore fitting to stress the importance of basic needs such as nutrition, housing, health, education and employment.

...the development of economic and social infrastructure is crucial for development of the least equipped developing countries, in particular in the fields of communications (transport infrastructure, especially in Africa) and urban infrastructure (satisfaction of basic needs in housing, health and hygiene, drinking water). These are sectors which are of particular importance for employment and the level of economic activity in the developing countries and in which the industrialized countries can make a positive contribution.

(Position Statement submitted by the European Community on the Transfer of Real Resources, pp.5,6,23,24,25)

The Position of India

...the strategy for the Third Development Decade must aim at the establishment of a new international economic order, that is, a restructuring of international economic relations. We are, therefore, strongly against any attempt to divert the attention of the international community to alternative approaches to development cooperation such as the basic needs approach. The meeting of basic needs is a part and parcel of the over-all objectives of the plans of the national governments whose sovereign right it_is to identify and determine their development needs. It is, therefore, for the national governments to identify such gaps which need to be filled   from external resources either through finance or through technological transfers or through the application of appropriate commercial policies.

India is fully committed to the principle elaborated in the International Development Strategy for the Second United Nations Development Decade that the "primary responsibility for the development of developing countries rests upon themselves, but however great their own efforts, these will not be sufficient to enable them to achieve the desired development goals as expeditiously as they must unless they are assisted through increased financial resources and more favourable economic and commercial policies on the part of developed countries." India believes that the relationship between developed and developing countries should be based on equity, sovereign equality, interdependence, common interest and cooperation among all States, irrespective of their economic and social systems for the establishment of the New International Economic Order.

(Position Statement submitted by India, paras. 14, 15)

The Position of Japan

...the development of those areas which will meet basic human needs should be ragarded as a matter of great importance. Needless to say, it should be left to each nation to formulate its own development plans, and to determine what are the basic human needs and in which fields of social development national priorities should be set.   Such development plans should be formulated so as to bring about the increase and a more equitable distribution of income for all the prople and the improvement of their welfare. This could be attained by dispersing to the rural areas the benefits of development, which have so far tended to be concentrated in the agricultural and local industrial sectors, which forms a part of the integrated industrialization of non-metropolitan areas.   In this regard, reference should be made to the Integrated Rural Development Programme of the Economic and Social Commission for Asia and the Pacific and its Integrated Industrialization Programme of Non-Metropolitan Areas.

(Position Statement submitted by Japan, par. 9)

The Position of Turkey

...The developing countries have every reason to view the conjunctural trends in the light of their impact on the new international economic order. In our efforts, we should never lose sight of the fact that development ultimately aims at the well-being of masses. Economic rights of people are the integral part of human rights. This is not an essentially socio-political issue but in every sense an economic one. More active participation of people in the rural traditional sector in the production process and consequently in the distribution of national income will increase the production and enlarge the domestic market. At the same time, economically organized and politically active manpower will internationally enhance the bargaining power of the developing countries with regard to real prices of their exports. Given the level of their development, most of the middle or upper income developing countries may find it politically increasingly difficult and economically unfeasible to keep artificially low some of their factors of production in order to ensure international competitiveness. In this context, whether there is trade-off between basic needs and sophisticated development strategies depends on the way in which this international policy will be implemented. The developing countries as fully sovereign actors of the international system, should collectively participate in the shaping of this policy.

(Position Statement submitted by Turkey, p.8)

The Position of the United Kingdom

But it is not enough simply to channel the main thrust of our aid efforts to the poorer countries. We also need to concentrate development more specifically on helping the poor in each country. We cannot just rely on the benefits of economic growth trickling down to them. This principle underlies our own policy on development aid. Redistribution within any society is naturally a matter for that country alone. But aid can be used to contribute towards redistribution and to the satisfaction of people's basic needs through the generation of economic growth. For this, an old-fashioned welfare approach to aid will not work. It is only through an increase in the output and incomes of the poor that they can achieve a permanent and continuing increase in their living standards. This therefore is the basis of British aid strategy. It implies a need for the direct improvement of, for instance, rural health services and urban water supplies, which are essential to people's welfare: and we therefore continue to support projects of this kind. But it also implies a need for indirect support through large infrastructure schemes - all with the aim of improving basic needs through self-sustaining growth directed for the benefit of the poor....

(Statement by Minister Frank Judd, United Kingdom, pp. 4,5)

The Position of the United States of America

...the United States has supported a basic needs approach to development assistance, and indeed has concentrated an increasing proportion of its assistance on the least developed countries and on sectors most directly affecting the poor. This effort stresses the distributional impact of economic policies. It requires an emphasis on rural employment and development, on employment-generating industries and on government policies to supplement domestic incomes with public services necessary to upgrade the lives of people through access to health care, clean water, and family planning.

(Position Statement submitted by the USA, pp. 33-31)

...resources available for development, however much they are increased, are not unlimited. It is therefore of greatest importance that they make the maximum contribution to development by promoting growth with equity -- that they improve the ability of the poor to meet their basic needs on a sustainable basis. I join our Chairman in calling attention to the view that the basic needs approach is not a matter of charity but of enabling the poor to fully contribute their productive capabilities to the economy in a self-reliant way. Hence this strategy emphasizes increasing employment opportunities and improving the skills of the poor, with the twin objectives of raising incomes and increasing production of goods and services.

(Remarks of Mr. Robert Hormats, USA, p. 6)

12 Political and Institutional Issues

WORLD ECONOMY ISSUES 22 and 23

Assuring the Economic Sovereignty of States: Natural
Resources, Foreign Property, Choice of Economic System;

Compensating for Adverse Effects on the Resources of States,
Territories and Peoples of Foreign Occupation, Alien and
Colonial Domination or Apartheid

The Position of the Group of 77

More vigorous and concrete steps and actions still remain to be taken,
collectively and individually, by all the members of the international
community to end without delay colonialism, imperialism, neo-colonial-
ism, interference in internal affairs, apartheid, racial discrimination and
all forms of foreign aggression and occupation, which constitute major
obstacles to the economic emancipation of the developing countries. It is
the duty of all States effectively to support and extend these practices so
as to restore their national sovereignty, territorial integrity and all other
inalienable and fundamental rights, including the right to self-determination, in order to enable them to achieve independence, and to promote
development and international cooperation, peace and security. All
countries should therefore restrain from participating in, encouraging or
promoting, in any way, any investment or economic activities aimed at
trade, or exploitation of any resources, or investments in economic
activities in the territories subjected to the aforementioned practices.

> (Position Statement submitted by Jamaica on behalf of the
> Group of 77, p. 5)

The Position of Roumania

Romania considers that the adverse phenomena of crisis in the world economy and international economic relations are the direct result of the imperialist, colonialist and neo-colonialist policy of domination and oppression of peoples, of the plundering of their national wealth, of the development and enrichment of certain States at the expense of others, and the unjust economic relations which exist between States. For these reasons the harmonious and balanced development of each country's national economy and the world economy as a whole requires as a primary and essential condition the establishment of new relations based on full equality of rights of all nations and respect for the right of each people to control fully its resources, to choose its own path of social and economic development free from outside interference, and to have free and unrestricted access to the advances of contemporary science and technology...

(Position Statement submitted by Romania, par. 3)

WORLD ECONOMY ISSUES 24 and 25

Establishing a System of Consultations at Global, Regional
and Sectoral Levels with the Aim of Promoting Industrial Development;

Restructuring the Economic and Social Sections of the United Nations

The Position of Austria

Intensifying and enhancing economic cooperation on a global scale call for improved institutional structures. The ongoing reform of the economic and social sectors of the United Nations system constitutes a timely and necessary exercise in order to enable the world organization to respond more forcefully to the need for closer and more effective international economic and social cooperation.

...If the target set by the Lima Declaration and Plan of Action is to be attained, a massive financial, technological and managment input will be required in expanding the industrial capacity of the developing countries. The mechanism designed to bring about these results are mainly focused in the United Nations Industrial Development Organization and should be fully utilized. The system of consultations has already resulted in a deeper awareness of major factors influencing the scope of production capacities in such areas as fertilizers, iron and steel, leather, vegetable oils and fats with other sectors to be decided upon. Features common to all these areas have emerged which, in turn, might constitute subject matters for global consultations.

(Position Statement submitted by Austria, paras. 8, 14)

13 List of Document Sources

PART I

Document Sources for "The Original Formulations of the NIEO Objectives at the United Nations."

Declaration on the Establishment of a New International Economic Order. 3201 (S-VI) 1 May 1974.

Programme of Action on the Establishment of a New International Order 3202 (S-VI) 1 May 1974.

Charter of Economic Rights and Duties of States. 3281 (XXIX) 12 December 1974.

Development and International Economic Co-Operation. 3362 (S-VII) 16 September 1975.

International Development Strategy for the Second United Nations Development Decade. 2626 (XXV) 24 October 1970.

Lima Declaration and Plan of Action on Industrial Development and Co-Operation. United Nations, 1975: PI/38. 26 March 1975.

Document Sources for "Specification and Development of the NIEO Objectives at the United Nations, 1974-78"

GENERAL ASSEMBLY OFFICIAL DOCUMENTS

General Assembly Resolutions and Decisions (1974-1978)
Reports and Notes of the Secretary-General
Board of Governors of the United Nations Special Fund - Annual Reports
Resolutions of the Second Committee

Reports of the UNCITRAL (Commission on International Trade Law)

Reports of the United Nations Conference on the Law of the SEA, UNCLOS III

Reports of the International Law Commission

ECOSOC

Resolutions and Decisions Adopted by the Council

Reports by the Committee for Development Planning

Reports of the Advisory Committee on the Application of Science and Technology to Development

Reports of the Committee on Natural Resources

Reports of Committees on Review and Appraisal

Reports of the Committee on Transnational Corporations

Reports of Intergovernmental Working Groups on Problems of Transnational Corporations

Documents of the Centre on Transnational Corporations

Report of the World Conference of the International Women's Year

UNCTAD

Reports and Notes by the Secretary-General

Reports, Notes and Studies by the Secretariat

Reports by Groups of Experts

Reports of Intergovernmental Working Groups

Reports of the Main Committees of UNCTAD

Reports and Resolutions of the Trade and Development Board

Resolutions and Recommendations Adopted by UNCTAD Conference IV.

UNIDO

Notes and Reports by the Secretariat

Notes and Reports by the Executive Director

Reports of the Permanent Committee

Reports of the Industrial Development Board

Reports of High-Level Experts

Annual Reports

Reports of the Second General Conference

General Conference Reports

Joint Reports with other United Nations agencies, e.g., ILO, FAO, UNCTAD

Reports of Preparatory Meetings to General Conference

IMF

Annual Reports

Documents of the Committee of Twenty

WORLD BANK

Annual Reports
Report of the Joint Ministerial Committee of the Board of
    Governors of the Bank and the Fund on the Transfer of Real
    Resources to Developing Countries (July 1976-June 1977)

GATT

GATT Activities in 1973
International Trade 1976/77

ILO

Draft Declaration on Multinational Enterprises
Report of the Tripartite Advisory Meeting
Expert Meetings
World Symposium on the Social Implications of a NIEO
World Employment Conference
Reports of the General Director
ILO African Regional Conference

UNESCO

Reports of the Executive Board
Reports and Records of General Conferences, 18th and 19th Sessions

WORLD FOOD COUNCIL

Report of the World Food Conference, Rome, 1974
Reports of the World Food Programme
Annual Reports
Reports of the Executive Director
Notes by the Secretariat

ECE

Committee on the Development of Trade
Annual Reports of Economic Developments

ESCAP

Reports of Committee on Natural Resources
Reports of Preparatory Committees to General Conferences
Reports of Committee on Trade
Reports of Committee on Shipping and Transport and
    Communications
Reports on Meeting of Directors of National Trade Development
    and Promotion Agencies
Reports of Trade Negotiations Group
Reports of Meeting of Ministers of Industry
Reports of Committee on Social Development

Notes and Reports by the Secretariat
Reports of Committee on Agricultural Development
Reports of Committee on Industry, Housing and Technology
Reports of Regional Meetings
Progress Reports on Regional Projects
Resolutions and Decisions
Annual Reports
Reports of Special Conferences
Reports of Committee on Development Planning
Special Body on Land-Locked Countries
Expert Group Meetings
Intergovernmental Meetings
Annual Economic and Social Surveys

ECA

Reports Commissioned by GA
Executive Committee Reports
Meetings of Conference of Ministers
African Regional Meetings
Meetings of Panels of Experts (e.g., Trade and Development)
Reports on Assessment of UNCTAD Meetings
Report of Association of African Central Banks
Reports Commissioned by ECOSCO
Resolutions and Decisions
Annual Reports

ECWA

Reports Commissioned by GA
Notes and Reports of Secretariat
Resolutions and Decisions
Annual Reports
Reports of Governmental Seminar Committees
Reports of Arab Centre for the Transfer and Development of
    Technology
Mid- term Appraisals of International Development Strategy
    for the Second Development Decade
Annual Reports on Development Problems

ECLA

Notes and Reports of the Secretariat
Reports of High-Level Government Experts
Annual Reports
Resolutions and Decisions
GA Commissioned Reports
ECOSOC Commissioned Reports
Secretariat Research Projects (e.g. development and external
    relations)

Reports of Expert Meetings
Reports of Jointly Sponsored Commissions (IBRD, UNDP)

UNITED NATIONS CENTRE FOR DISARMAMENT
 Preparatory Committee for the Special Session of the General
  Assembly Devoted to Disarmament
 Report of the Secretary-General on Disarmament

Document Sources for "Contributions of Major International
Bodies, 1974-78"

Commonwealth:

1. Final Communique of the Heads of Government Meetings 1975,
   1977.
2. Reports of the Group of Experts on the NIEO, 1975, 1976, 1977.

Non-Aligned Summit Conferences:
1. Reports and Resolutions of the NAC held at Dakar
2. Reports and Resolutions of the NAC held at Lima
3. Reports and Resolutions of the NAC held at Colombo
4. Reports and Decisions of the Bureau of NAC held at New Delhi
   (1977)

Conference of Developing Countries on Raw Materials, Dakar, 1975

Manila Declaration and Programme of Action of the Third Ministerial
 Meeting of the Group of 77 (1976)

Reports of the Conference on International Economic Cooperation (Paris)
 1975-1977

Final Act of the European Conference on Security and Cooperation
 (Helsinki Accord) 1975.

PART II

Document Sources for "The Positions of Some States and Groups of States
on the Issues"

Position statements submitted by States and Groups of States at the First
Session of the Committee of the Whole Established Under General

Assembly Resolution 32/174, 3-13 May 1978. A.AC. 191/3 through A.AC. 191/26

Texts of Statements of Delegates to the Committee of the Whole Established Under General Assembly Resolution 32/174, 3-13 May 1978.

Position paper submitted by Jamaica on behalf of the States Members of the United Nations which are members of the Group of 77. Conference Room Paper No. 1 (I), 2 May 1978

Index

About The Authors

ERVIN LASZLO is a Special Fellow of the United Nations Project on the Future and is Director of the NIEO Project, both at UNITAR. He is also a Professor of Philosophy at the State University of New York at Geneseo. He has taught and conducted research at Yale, Princeton, and Portland State University, among other institutions, and has written and lectured extensively on philosophy and world affairs. Prior to his current activities he was director of a study for the Club of Rome and was an internationally renowned concert pianist.

ROBERT M. BAKER, JR. was educated at Cornell University and the New School for Social Research where he is presently a Ph.D. candidate in economics. He has been a staff economist with economic consulting firms and the New York City Planning Commission, and has taught at the University of Zambia and St. John's University in New York.

ELLIOTT EISENBERG has graduate degrees in history and sociology from the University of Wisconsin and Boston University and has studied political science and economic planning at The Freie Universitat in Berlin, Germany. He is currently coordinator for the research project on Obstacles to the New International Economic Order at UNITAR.

K. VENKATA RAMAN is Professor of Law at Queen's University, Kingston, Ontario, Canada and has been a Fellow in the Department of Research, UNITAR. He is the author of a forthcoming study titled "Management of Ocean Resources" which will be published by UNITAR in 1978. His "Toward a General Theory of International Customary Law" which appeared in Toward World Order and Human Dignity (1976) outlines the prize-winning doctoral work he did at Yale University Law School.